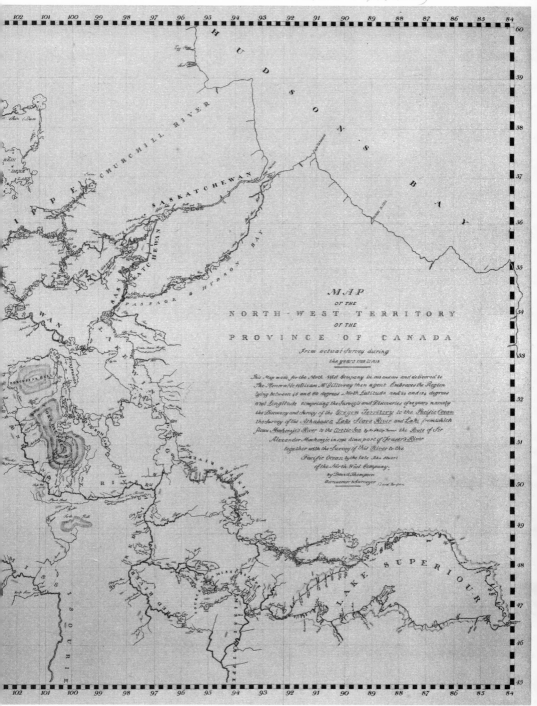

MAP
OF THE
NORTH-WEST TERRITORY
OF THE
PROVINCE OF CANADA
From actual survey during
the years 1792 to 1812

This Map made for the North West Company in 1813 and 1814 and delivered to
The Honorable William McGillivray then agent. Embraces the Region
lying between 45 and 60 degrees North Latitude and 84 and 125 degrees
West Longitude comprising the Surveys and Discoveries of 20 years namely
the Discovery and Survey of the Oregon Territory to the Pacific Ocean
the Survey of the Athabasca, Lake Slave River and Lake from which
flows Mackenzie's River to the Arctic Sea by the Author the Route of Sir
Alexander Mackenzie in 1792 down part of Fraser's River
together with the Survey of this River to the
Pacific Ocean by the late John Stuart
of the North-West Company,
by David Thompson
Astronomer & Surveyor

EPIC WANDERER

EPIC WANDERER

DAVID THOMPSON AND THE
MAPPING OF THE CANADIAN WEST

D'Arcy Jenish

UNIVERSITY OF NEBRASKA PRESS
LINCOLN

Library of Congress Cataloging-in-Publication Data
Jenish, D'Arcy, 1952–
Epic wanderer: David Thompson and the mapping of the
Canadian West / D'Arcy Jenish.
p.   cm.
Includes bibliographical references and index.
ISBN 0-8032-2600-4 (cloth: alk. paper)
1. Thompson, David, 1770–1857
2. Cartographers—Canada—Biography.
3. Cartography—Canada—History—18th century.
4. Cartography—Canada—History—19th century.
5. Canada, Western—Geography.
6. Hudson's Bay Company.
7. North West Company.   I. Title.
GA473.7.T48J46   2004
526'.092—dc22
2003025655

Endsheet map from Old Fort William

"*I was placed at table, between one of the Miss M----'s and a singular-looking person of about fifty. He was plainly dressed, quiet, and observant. His figure was short and compact, and his black hair worn long all round, and cut square, as if by one stroke of the shears, just above the eyebrows. His complexion was of the gardener's ruddy brown, while the expression of his deeply-furrowed features was friendly and intelligent, but his cut-short nose gave him an odd look. His speech betrayed the Welshman, although he left his native hills when very young . . .*

"*. . . I afterwards travelled much with him, and have now only to speak of him with great respect, or, I ought to say, with admiration . . .*

"*. . . Never mind his Bunyan-like face and cropped hair; he has a very powerful mind, and a singular faculty of picture-making. He can create a wilderness and people it with warring savages, or climb the Rocky Mountains with you in a snow-storm, so clearly and palpably, that only shut your eyes and you hear the crack of the rifle, or feel the snow-flakes melt on your cheeks as he talks.*"

— JOHN BIGSBY, PHYSICIAN AND AUTHOR,
DESCRIBING DAVID THOMPSON IN 1820.

CONTENTS

ACKNOWLEDGEMENTS

Most of this book is based on contemporary sources, but it could not have been written without the generous assistance of many individuals. I would like to thank David Anderson of Bethune-Thompson House in Williamstown, Ont., Bill Moreau, Hugh P. MacMillan, Jack Nisbet, Jean Murray Cole, Conrad Heidenreich, James Laxer, John Warkentin, Victor Hopwood, Richard Ruggles, Ken Brown, Thomas Thompson, Sandra Ferguson, Steve Hopkins, Jack Hanna, the staff of the Windermere Valley Museum in Windermere, B.C., and three very fine editors, Martha Kanya-Forstner, Meg Taylor and Shaun Oakey.

As always I am indebted to my wife, Helene, and children, Jesse, Isabel and Patrick.

PREFACE

DAVID THOMPSON IS ONE OF THE MOST REMARKABLE FIGURES IN Canadian history. His origins were humble, his career varied. He was a fur trader, an explorer, a surveyor, a mapmaker and an entrepreneur. He experienced triumph and failure, affluence and poverty, comfort and hardship. He died penniless and obscure in 1857 and remained unknown to the Canadian public until the publication, in 1916, of *David Thompson's Narrative*, his account of the twenty-eight years (1784–1812) he spent roaming the Canadian West.

Thompson's story has been told before, usually in abbreviated biographies that conveyed the basic facts but missed most of the drama. Or the focus was exclusively on his western travels. My aim here is a more complete telling, providing a more thorough account of Thompson's early years with the Hudson's Bay Co. and an examination of Thompson's career after his fur-trading days, from 1812 till his death in 1857.

In endeavouring to produce a clear and vivid portrait of the man and the times, my first source was *David Thompson's Narrative*, a roughly chronological work supplemented by the author's observations on the flora and fauna, the seasons and the climate, the geography and the peoples of the lands he visited. I have drawn heavily upon his largely unpublished daily journals, which are rich in facts and details hitherto unused. In the journals and the *Narrative,* Thompson describes several encounters with aboriginals, including conversations, and reveals an uncanny ability to capture the rhythm and vocabulary of native speech. In all his writing, Thompson was preoccupied with his work and the world around him. He rarely said anything about his wife, Charlotte, or their children, and I have avoided trying to fill this gap in the story through speculation or supposition. I also relied on the daily journals of the Hudson's Bay Co. posts where he served, which shed invaluable light on the youthful Thompson. For the sake of authenticity, I have retained the spelling and punctuation found in the Hudson's Bay Co. journals, as well as those of Thompson. Finally, I consulted the published works of his contemporaries and, of course, secondary analyses of major historical events that occurred during his lifetime.

Thompson's life, fascinating in its own right, provides us with an unparalleled view of a tumultuous and pivotal era in Canadian history. He served on both sides of the desperate, cutthroat battle for supremacy between the Hudson's Bay Co. and its Montreal-based rival, the North West Co. This was more than just an average commercial rivalry. It was a fight between an imperial and a colonial enterprise, between an old and a new way of organizing a business.

The Hudson's Bay Co. was controlled by distant shareholders and run by men who were essentially branch managers. The North West Co. was controlled by Montreal merchants and run by ordinary traders who had become partners, or shareholders. Thompson flourished among the dynamic and entrepreneurial Nor'Westers. He and a handful of others made the company North America's first transcontinental enterprise. They also provided an inspiring example of what English, French and aboriginals could accomplish when they worked together.

Thompson also takes us into a time when the dynamics between whites and aboriginals were very different than they have been for most of the past two centuries. When Thompson worked in the West, natives were the majority. White men operated at the margins of a world dominated by First Nations. As such, many traders—and Thompson was certainly one of them—were free of the bigotry and prejudice that arrived with the settler and so poisoned relations between the races.

Finally, Thompson can offer contemporary Canadians a rare and jolting view of life without a social safety net. Many elderly people in his time ended their days in poverty. Few recorded the experience in a daily journal. Thompson did, and the story that emerges is one of remarkable strength and courage in the face of adversity.

The Old Man

THE OLD MAN WAS WRITING AGAIN, HUNCHED OVER THE TABLE, shoulders stooped, the pen slender and reedlike in his thick, callused hand. He had been at it for months now, seated amid his leather-bound journals, dozens of them, each crammed with the notes and minutiae, the observations and tales of nearly three decades spent roaming the great Northwest. He had seen more of that country—the interior of British North America—and come to know it better than any man of his time.

Then, he had been a fur trader, an explorer and a surveyor; he was young and robust and certain of himself. Now, nearing eighty, he was poor. His sight was failing and he struggled to decipher the words he had written decades earlier. Misfortune had befallen him in the years since he left the Northwest. He had quarrelled with his eldest son. His investments had gone bad. He had lost money. He had no savings, no pension, no prospect of employment. Who would hire a surveyor with poor eyesight?

Several years earlier, lawyers had seized the family home in Williamstown and his extensive landholdings in the surrounding

County of Glengarry, Upper Canada, after he had defaulted on the mortgages. He and his wife, Charlotte, and seven of their ten surviving children had departed for Montreal, getting by for several years on whatever work he could find and then, when he could find no employment of any kind, living in painful and humiliating poverty until saved from complete ruin by their daughter Elizabeth and her husband, William Scott, who took them in and gave them a room in their home.

Yes, they were poor, too poor to contribute to the cost of running the household or to put food on the table or even to buy the pens, ink and paper he needed for his writing. Elizabeth, born in 1817 at Williamstown on the Raisin River, five miles north of the St. Lawrence, provided for them now, and on occasion she would read his manuscript too.

His yarns still made her chuckle, or shake her head in amazement, even though she had heard them many times before, as a child, on long winter nights in their spacious and comfortable Williamstown home. They would sit around the stove, she and her siblings and their mother and sometimes neighbours—strong, ruddy-faced farmers or former fur traders who had settled in Glengarry—and he would be on his feet, fully immersed in recounting some adventure among the Indians or on one of the country's wild rivers.

He still had a way with a story—despite the poverty and hardship, which had so wounded his pride, and despite the infirmities of old age that sometimes made it difficult to pick up the pen. He rose early each day and, health permitting, wrote a few pages, spinning his notes into a narrative, telling the tale of his travels. How in May 1784, as a youth of fourteen, a waif educated for seven years at a school for poor and parentless boys, he had sailed from London aboard the *Prince Rupert,* a vessel of the Hudson's Bay Co., crossed the Atlantic and landed in September of that year at Churchill Factory, at the mouth of a river on the west coast of the bay, an apprentice with the "Company of Adventurers" come to learn the intricacies of the fur trade: haggling with Indians; keeping ledgers; turning a profit.

How he had spent thirteen years in the employ of the company and had been sent inland to help recapture the trade lost to the dynamic interlopers from Montreal, the Canadians of the North West Co. How he had developed a passion for exploring and surveying, had become adept with a compass, a sextant and a telescope, had learned to read the stars better than most people could read a book and to calculate, based on celestial observations, his precise position on the face of the earth.

And how the Salish Indians, a nation of the forested valleys beyond the Rocky Mountains, had come to call him Koo Koo Sint, the Man Who Looks at Stars. He would stand on clear, dry nights, wind blowing and wolves howling, and gaze at magnificent western skies peppered with glittering stars, and his Indian friends would sometimes stand with him. They saw the homes of illustrious ancestors—warriors, shamans and hunters—gone to their rightful places in the heavens, but he saw Arcturus, Aldebaran and Capella and other distant beacons that could be used to determine degrees of latitude and longitude.

The Company of Adventurers had had no need for his skills as an astronomer and surveyor so he had quit, and joined the Nor'Westers, an unpardonable transgression in the eyes of his former employers, who were, at that moment, losing an epic struggle for control of a vast commercial empire based on the beaver pelt. He had flourished among the entrepreneurial Canadians, working as an ordinary trader, trudging across the Northwest, travelling among the Indians of the eastern forests, the great plains and the west coast, and embarking on voyages of discovery.

He had spent twenty-eight years in the fur trade, travelled fifty thousand miles, paddled up and down prairie rivers, crossed and recrossed the Rocky Mountains and followed the long, serpentine Columbia River from its headwaters on the western side of the Rockies all the way to the Pacific. He had played a lead role, along with Alexander Mackenzie, Simon Fraser, Meriwether Lewis and William Clark, in the frantic, headlong rush to explore the northern half of the continent and claim as much as they could for distant political masters.

Through his travels and thousands of celestial observations for latitude and longitude he had filled a void in the maps of his time. His "Map of the North-West Territory of the Province of Canada," two years in the making, measured six feet, nine inches by ten feet, four inches and laid out with astonishing accuracy the major river systems and mountain ranges from Hudson Bay to Lake Superior to the shores of the Pacific and from the upper Missouri River to the sixtieth parallel. It hung in the Great Hall at Fort William, the North West Co.'s wilderness headquarters at the head of Superior, and provided the hired hands of the fur trade with a snapshot of the rivers, lakes and landmarks of the immense country in which they worked.

His map proved even more valuable to the British government and the mapmakers of Europe and America. He had surveyed 1,200,000 square miles of Indian country and legitimized British claims to the Northwest. But what had come of all his service to the Crown, service performed on his own initiative and for the good of his country? And what of the work that was so useful to the cartographers? He had earned next to nothing from it, never lived to see the map published.

Others did put the work to use, however. Britain's leading cartographer, Aaron Arrowsmith, obtained a copy from the Hudson's Bay Co. after its 1821 merger with the North West Co. With Thompson's map in hand, the Arrowsmith firm revised its own map of North America to include the first complete and accurate image of the northwestern interior. But the London mapmaker did not credit or compensate the author.

The British government treated him no better. In 1826, he sent the Foreign Office a copy of the map, but it was returned with a note politely explaining that the government was well served by maps obtained from the Hudson's Bay Co. In the early 1840s, he sent a copy to Lord Aberdeen, the foreign secretary, who agreed after many requests to pay him a hundred and fifty pounds, a tidy sum but barely enough to cover his debts. On this occasion, the map was of substantial value to Her Majesty's government. The Foreign Office was then preparing for negotiations with the United States to draw the border between American and British possessions west of the Rockies. The two powers were trying to carve up the Oregon Territory, which embraced lands drained by the twelve-hundred-mile-long Columbia River, lands rich in fish and lumber and minerals.

The negotiations took place in Washington. The British representative, Richard Pakenham, and American Secretary of State James Buchanan huddled over old maps and musty documents while far to the north, in Montreal, the old man fretted and stewed. He knew what usually happened at such gatherings. The Americans were assertive and demanding, the British easy and accommodating. He had seen America's presence on the continent grow and Britain's shrink every time the two countries drafted a treaty. This time, they were talking about priceless, beautiful Oregon, the country he had explored, opened and surveyed. Thanks to him, the Union Jack had flown over these lands at the same time as the Stars and Stripes. He had established Britain's presence there and, in his mind, Britain's claim.

He had written letters to Lord Aberdeen and the British prime minister, Robert Peel, arguing that the Columbia River rather than the forty-ninth parallel should form the border. But they paid no attention. And in the Buchanan-Pakenham Treaty of 1846, the forty-ninth parallel was enshrined as the border and most of the Oregon country lost to the United States.

All this was more than Thompson could abide. He was a proud man. He was principled. He had never courted the wealthy or the powerful. He knew nothing of self-aggrandizement, abhorred the thought of profiting from the work of others. But others had profited from his work, and some had ignored it. He had been wronged. And so the old man rose each morning and went to his table and wrote to set the record straight about his life and his accomplishments.

PART ONE

Grey Coat School: Leaving there for Hudson Bay, Thompson felt he was being exiled from family, friends and his beloved London.

To the New World

(1784)

THE BOY, JUST FOURTEEN BUT STOCKY AND SQUARE SHOULDERED
and bright eyed, spent many idle hours alone that fall at the edge
of cold, windy marshes listening to the strangely melodious
prattle of countless waterfowl. He'd steal through tall, dense
rushes—measuring each step, treading as lightly as possible,
hoping for a shot—but invariably startling the wild creatures he
would watch spellbound as those nearest lifted off and raised the
alarm and others followed, all the way across the water, until he
could see nothing but the blur of thrashing wings. The young
hunter would watch the birds retreat, and when they looked like
specks of pepper against the big northern sky, he would emerge
muddy and disconsolate and begin the long walk back, wonder-
ing as he trudged along why he, David Thompson, had been
yanked from a comfortable life at Grey Coat School, in London,
his home for the previous seven years, and sent to Churchill Factory, a flimsy and forlorn fur-trade post on the western shore of
Hudson Bay.

David had been happy at the school, a royally endowed
charitable institute that endeavoured to educate poor boys and

instill the virtues required to lead a sober Christian life. There, a short distance from Westminster Abbey in the heart of London, he had learned to read and write, had studied mathematics and navigation, read ancient tales from Persia and Arabia and the modern works *Robinson Crusoe* and *Gulliver's Travels*. He had exulted in school vacations, eighteen days, even twenty to roam the city: exploring the magnificent abbey, reading the inscriptions on the tombs of the poets and monarchs buried there, walking to London Bridge or strolling through St. James's Park and other places that were, as he put it, all beauty to the eye and verdure to the feet.

What a different place Churchill was: a miserable cluster of wooden buildings, unpainted, barely a year old yet already weathered and weary looking, a factory standing on the barren shore of the broad, rumbling Churchill River, five miles from where it drained into the bay. It was surrounded by timber stockades 170 feet long, 164 deep and 12 high—walls that would withstand an Indian attack but provided no protection against the real foes he would encounter here: the cold, the darkness and the isolation that could corrode the spirit.

The climate was beyond anything he had imagined. By late September the waterfowl and shorebirds began to depart, flock after noisy flock rising from the vast marshes above the fort and disappearing over the distant southern horizon just ahead of winter. The first snow fell in early October and the swamps and marshes froze up shortly afterward. The river, a mile and a half wide, was icebound by mid-November. Polar bears appeared in great numbers and remained in the neighbourhood until ice had formed along the shore of the bay and they could hunt seals. As the cold became deep and prolonged, rocks shattered with a sharp crack that sounded like gunfire.

David had not chosen to come here. His path had been set in December 1783, when the secretary of the Hudson's Bay Co. visited Grey Coat looking for boys to apprentice as clerks. The school's board of governors, always eager to move out older boys and make room for younger waifs, had offered two pupils: himself and Samuel John McPherson. Upon hearing the news, McPherson had run away and never returned.

But David had stayed, and the following May packed his paltry possessions and said farewell to all those who were close to him; his teachers, his classmates and what little family he had—a brother, John, who was two years younger, and his widowed mother, Ann, who had emigrated to London from Wales with her husband, David, given birth to two sons and then lost her spouse when her boys were babies. He had no idea whether he would see any of them again as he boarded the *Prince Rupert,* one of three vessels sailing to the bay that summer, and began a seven-year apprenticeship with the Company of Adventurers.

The ship arrived in early September and stayed for about a week while supplies were unloaded and bales of fur taken aboard. David would remember those first days in the new world for the rest of his life and many years later would write: "While the ship remained at anchor, from my parent and friends it appeared only a few weeks' distance, but when the ship sailed and from the top of the rocks I lost sight of her, the distance became immeasurable and I bid a long and sad farewell to my . . . country, an exile for ever."

David had been sent to learn the fur trade, though he would not be paid for his labour until he had completed his apprenticeship. He served his first winter under Samuel Hearne, the governor at Churchill, who was six feet tall, well built and robust, and had a high forehead, large eyes and a penetrating glare. Hearne's superiors in London had instructed him to keep the young apprentice busy with clerical duties and the business of the fur trade, which would allow him to manage a post one day. He was also to keep the boy away from the factory's servants, most of them clannish, illiterate Orkneymen who hunted geese and cut firewood and performed manual labour without any expectation that they would rise in the company and become traders. But there was almost no work for him that first fall. Two years earlier, smallpox had ravaged the Indians to the west and southwest, the Chipewyans and the Cree. Nine out of ten had died in some communities and most of the trade went with them.

Hearne had no time to keep his new apprentice either occupied or amused. He was too busy running the factory, so his officers—Mr. Jefferson, the deputy governor; Mr. Hodges, the physician; and Mr. Prince, who sailed a sloop up the west coast of Hudson Bay each summer to trade with Eskimos—looked after him. When there was no work, they would give him a gun to shoot waterfowl or, once winter arrived, they would send him out to hunt ptarmigan. Fortunately, there was a Sunday service almost each week. It was held in the governor's chamber and led by one of the officers. David was grateful for even this much worship since he had taken seriously the Christian teachings at Grey Coat and come away from the school with a deep and abiding faith.

Toward the end of December, a storm out of the northeast lashed the coast for three days and nearly buried the little factory. Snow drifted to the top of the stockades and to a depth of six to ten feet in the yard. Afterward, the servants dug walkways four feet wide, but snowshoes were required anywhere else. David ventured out aboard these ungainly devices whenever the weather permitted. Too often, though, the cold was prohibitive.

On those occasions, Jefferson or one of the other men lent him books, and he sat at a table in the cramped, two-storey officers' residence, shivering in his heavy coat of dressed beaver, hands and feet and the tip of his nose numb. Fuel was scarce at Churchill, and Hearne allowed only two fires a day, one in the morning and another in the evening, although the governor kept his upstairs room tolerably comfortable most of the time. David watched frost creep into the dwelling, first at the joints and around the windows. Then it spread across the thin, uninsulated wooden walls and accumulated to a depth of four inches in places, at which point the servants applied water to the interior to form a barrier of ice that would keep out the frost, the wind and the worst of the cold.

As they worked, the men grumbled about the inadequacies of Churchill, and David listened. Most disliked the factory, especially those who had served under Hearne at its predecessor, Prince of Wales's Fort, which had stood on low, barren Eskimo Point at the mouth of the Churchill River. Stone Fort, the servants called it, an imposing structure with ramparts twenty-five feet thick at the base, had been started in 1733 and completed in 1771.

But the old post had fallen in August 1782 to a French naval commander, Admiral de La Pérouse, who arrived in the waters off Churchill with a fleet of three-masted vessels, the *Sceptre,* a warship armed with seventy-five guns, and two frigates, the *Astrée* and the *Engageant,* each equipped with thirty-six guns. The admiral sent ashore a force of four hundred soldiers. Seeing the enemy advance, Hearne had his men hoist a white towel up the flagpole and surrendered without firing a shot from the forty-two cannons mounted on the ramparts. The French took the governor and his men captive, burned the buildings and shelled the walls until they were rubble, then sailed off to capture York Factory, a hundred and fifty miles to the south at the mouth of the Hayes River.

David Thompson had seen the ruins of the stone fort when he arrived in August aboard the *Prince Rupert.* He learned of the assault from the men, some of whom accused Hearne of cowardice for surrendering meekly. But others defended him. The governor had only thirty-nine men under him, and many were off goose hunting when the French arrived. Besides, they said, the company had sent Hearne back with a crew of thirty-three in the summer of 1783 to re-establish a post on the Churchill River.

The men told David how they had arrived in late August. They had hauled several tons of sand and gravel to level the site and hastily assembled the two-storey residence shipped in pieces from England. The walls were only half an inch thick and uninsulated, and the men complained that they had hardly known a moment's comfort that first winter. And now he was there, numb and shivering in the same compact structure, which also served as shop, store and warehouse.

Reading took his mind off the cold and the tedium, but he often wondered: what would happen if he did not practise writing? He was an apprentice clerk after all, and clerks were supposed to write. One day he asked Hearne for paper, but the governor hadn't enough to indulge such adolescent yearnings. Instead, he gave the boy a couple of invoices to copy and later put him to work transcribing parts of a manuscript he had been working on for twelve years. "A Journey to the North" it was called, although there were actually three voyages. The first two had failed dismally, but the third, which began in December 1770 and ended nineteen months later, in July 1771, was successful.

David copied only a few pages of the manuscript, but read many more. At age twenty-four, Hearne had been sent west from Churchill to cross the Barren Grounds, an Arctic wasteland as vast as a sea, to look for copper deposits located near the mouth of a distant river—the Coppermine—that flowed into the northern sea. For seventy years Chipewyan Indians from that country had been bringing tantalizing samples of ore with them on trading missions and plying the traders with reports that rich veins had thrust the metal to the surface. At least four other adventurous Englishmen, all sea captains, had gone forth in search of the mine before Hearne. They failed, and one had died with his men in a shipwreck.

David found the governor's stories as strange as any he had read in the works of Dafoe or Swift. There were accounts of snowstorms in July and the summer sun that did not set; tales of men eating raw fish or uncooked venison, or not eating at all for days on end, and Hearne's encounter with a band of Copper Indians who had never met a white man.

"It was curious to see how they flocked about me," he wrote, "and expressed as much desire to examine me from top to toe, as an European Naturalist would a non-descript animal. They, however, found and pronounced me to be a perfect human being, except in the colour of my hair and eyes: the former, they said, was like the stained hair of a buffaloe's tail, and the latter, being light, were like those of a gull. The whiteness of my skin also was, in their opinion, no ornament, as they said it resembled meat which had been sodden in water till all the blood was extracted."

The stories about the customs of the Indians and the practices of their medicine men were curious and amusing. "For some inward complaints, such as, griping in the intestines, difficulty of making water, etc., it is very common to see those jugglers blowing into the anus, or into parts adjacent, till their eyes are almost staring out of their heads: and this operation is performed indifferently on all, without regard either to age or sex. The accumulation of so large a quantity of wind is at times apt to occasion some extraordinary emotions, which are not easily suppressed by a sick person; and as there is no vent for it but by the channel through which it was conveyed thither, it sometimes occasions an odd scene between the doctor and his patient."

But there was one story—Hearne's account of a Chipewyan massacre of Eskimos in July 1771—that sent a shiver through David even as he sat in a cold dwelling amid a frozen land. The governor's Indian companions had guided him to the Coppermine, a journey of many months and hundreds of miles, largely to make war on their ancient enemies, the Eskimos. Upon reaching the river, spies went ahead to seek out a camp and found a tiny cluster of five tents on the west bank a few miles from where it met the sea. The whole party waited until the sun was at its lowest and their victims asleep. They painted their faces and removed most of their clothing. Then they struck.

"Men, women and children, in all upward of twenty, ran out of their tents stark naked, and endeavoured to make their escape;

but the Indians having possesion of all the landside, to no one place could they fly for shelter. One alternative only remained, that of jumping into the river; but as none attempted it they all fell a sacrifice to Indian barbarity!

"The shrieks and groans of the poor expiring wretches were truly dreadful; and my horror was much increased at seeing a young girl, seemingly about eighteen years of age, killed so near me, that when the first spear was stuck into her side she fell down at my feet, and twisted round my legs, so that it was with difficulty that I could disengage myself from her dying gasps. As two Indian men pursued this unfortunate victim, I solicited very hard for her life; but the murderers made no reply till they had stuck both their spears through her body, and transfixed her to the ground. Then they looked me sternly in the face, and began to ridicule me, by asking if I wanted an Esquimaux wife; and paid not the smallest regard to the shrieks and agony of the poor wretch, who was twining round their spears like an eel!"

There were other shocking details; the Chipewyan men murdered a solitary woman, aged and blind, who was fishing at the foot of a waterfall. They plundered another camp of seven lodges on the far shore of the Coppermine. They threw the dwellings in the river, smashed stone kettles and destroyed a winter's supply of dried fish and muskoxen, while the inhabitants, standing on a shoal in midstream, were, as the governor wrote, "obliged to be woeful spectators of their great, perhaps irreparable loss."

Afterward, Hearne surveyed the river to its mouth, eight miles away, and then the party began its return. They came to the copper deposits after travelling south-southeast thirty miles. "This mine, if it deserves that appellation, is no more than an entire jumble of rocks and gravel," the governor later wrote, "which has been rent many ways by an earthquake."

Hearne had spent two decades in the service of the company. The elements had ruddied his complexion; the country had hardened his character. The boy did not like the governor, but reading the manuscript awakened his curiosity. He began to think less of boarding a ship that would take him back to London and Grey Coat, and felt the first stirrings of a desire to see the country and meet its peoples.

David Thompson left Churchill in early September 1785 in the company of two Indians, packet carriers entrusted with transporting mail from one post to another, lean, sinuous men who could run swiftly and possessed enormous endurance. Each had a gun and a blanket, but they brought no provisions. The land and the waters would provide for them until they reached their destination: York Factory.

Hearne sent the boy and his companions off in the factory sloop and ordered the servants to drop them at Cape Churchill, thirty-six miles southeast of the mouth of the river, where they were to start walking. Someone gave the Indians a gallon of liquor and they began drinking as soon as they were on their own. Before long, they were staggering, their speech became loud and incoherent and, a short time later, they lay down and went to sleep, leaving David to pass the day alone, contemplating the latest turn in his life.

He had learned a few days earlier that he was being reassigned. Hearne had summoned him to his office and read a memo from London, which had been among the letters and documents sent with the annual supply ship. David was grateful that he would no longer serve under Hearne. The governor was a non-believer, and had told him so one Sunday after the weekly service, which was held in his rooms. Hearne ordered the youth to stay behind with Mr. Jefferson and another officer, who had read that day's sermon, and he reached for a book, Voltaire's *Dictionnaire philosophique*. "Here is my belief," he had said, holding up the slight volume of essays that had incensed civic and religious authorities in several European countries when it appeared in 1764. "I have no other."

David was eager to leave for another reason. Churchill was desolate year-round. The winter had been long, gloomy and severe, and the spring bore no resemblance to the idyllic season he had known in England. Here it was all mud and melting snow and treacherous ice. Once the land was free of winter's grip, which wasn't until mid-June, the mosquitoes appeared. Every puddle, every pool and pond spawned the voracious insects, which rose in roiling clouds to torment man and beast alike.

Fortunately, the weather had turned before he and his companions set out. The cold had suppressed the insidious swarms of insects and made the country bearable again. He slept that first night on an empty stomach and awoke chilled by the dew that had dampened his blanket. The Indians rose early, seemingly untroubled by the liquor they had consumed, and walked till sunset before shooting a goose and three ducks, which they plucked and cleaned and roasted for dinner.

The boy became accustomed to hunger and fatigue because his companions walked from morning till evening without eating. They followed a wet, muddy trail along the shore of the bay. When the tide was in, the sea lapped at their feet, but when it was out, immense flats littered with boulders stretched as far as the eye could see. And to their right were vast marshes and countless ponds now bustling with migrating waterfowl.

As he observed them, a question arose in the boy's mind. How was it, he wondered, that ducks and geese and swans could fly with such precision from their breeding grounds north of Hudson Bay to winter havens on the Gulf of Mexico, a journey of nearly three thousand miles? A European, schooled in the sciences, would say instinct. But who could say what instinct was? He had not seen it defined or explained in any of the books of natural history he had read, including those that Mr. Jefferson and the other officers had lent him. The packet Indians and their brethren believed the birds were guided by a manitou, a spirit that protected the flocks. And David reckoned that one explanation was as good as the other.

He was curious about many things he saw along the way. Each day they passed polar bears lounging a short distance from shore in groups of three to five. The beasts reclined with their heads close together and their bodies radiated outward, which seemed unusual, but the Indians assured him it was their habit. They told him to maintain a steady pace and pay no attention and the fearsome creatures would ignore them, a practice that worked on every occasion but one, when they encountered a solitary bear feeding on a beluga on the opposite bank of a creek. It roared at them, exposing its ferocious teeth and prompting the travellers to walk upstream a good distance before wading across the waist-deep stream.

Only once did David question his native companions. After walking for six days, they arrived at the mouth of the Nelson River, which drained into Hudson Bay just four miles from the mouth of the Hayes. They had only to cross the Nelson and the narrow peninsula formed by the convergence of the two rivers to reach York Factory, but a strong wind and a high tide grounded them for two days. Midway through the third, the Indians declared that they would silence the wind. They stood and began chanting and, after about half an hour, one said to David: "You see, the wind is calming. Such is the power of our songs."

"You see the ducks, the plover and other birds follow the ebb tide," he replied. "They know the wind is calming without your song. If you possess such power why did you not sing on the first day of our being here?"

But they did not answer.

The next day, September 15, 1785, the Indians delivered their charge to York Factory. The governor ordered a clerk to give each man goods equivalent to ten made beaver, a standard unit of measurement in the fur trade. Afterward, a clerk recorded the transaction in the post account book: "Gave as a gratuity to the two Indians, for the care they have taken of David Thompson,

"brandy 3 gals. 16 MB.

"tobacco 4 lbs. 4 MB."

Humphrey Marten, the governor, had his instructions but chose to ignore them. They had been written May 4, 1785, by the governor and committee of the Hudson's Bay Co., bundled up with all the other mail, packed in a leather pouch and sent to York Factory aboard the annual supply ship. "As an Assistant Writer is much Wanted We have ordered our Apprentice David Thompson to be sent to you from Churchill: he has been instructed in the Mathematicks and writes a good Hand. We recommend him to the attention of our Chief that he may be kept from the common Men & employed in the Writing accts. And Warehouse Duty, so that he may by degrees be made Capable of transacting Business, and become useful in our services, As he will be under the immediate Eye of our Chief. We hope his morals and behaviour will be diligently attended to."

Useless, Marten thought after reading it. The committee had sent another useless apprentice, and he would have to groom him so that the boy would, one day, become useful. The governor had seen many like this one. He had once been a novice himself. That was in March 1750, when he joined the company as a writer—a would-be clerk who recorded transactions in the account books and helped keep the post journal. He had trained many apprentices during his long career. But he had no interest in taking on another.

He had no patience. Not with all his ailments—gout, failing eyesight, disorders of the stomach and kidneys and old injuries that had never healed properly. His behaviour had become erratic, and unbearable to most of his associates, and he had been overbearing and domineering to begin with. He had thrown food in the face of his surgeon and tried to push him down the stairs of the officers' residence after the surgeon called him an old brute, a liar and a scoundrel. He and Hearne were barely communicating. William Tomison, who was in charge of the inland trade, criticized him for not putting sufficient effort into this side of the business. He had so abused the factory tailor that the man returned to England before his contract had expired even though he had a large family to support.

Few disliked Marten as intensely as Edward Umfreville, who served as his deputy at York between 1775 and 1782. The governor was despised at every post on the bay, according to Umfreville, and his reputation extended even to the Orkney Islands, where the company for years had recruited the labourers and ordinary employees known as servants. Umfreville accused Marten of mistreating the Indians to such an extent that the trade had declined annually at the post. In one case, in June 1780, an Indian who had come to trade at York had become so angry with the governor that he had tried to stab him. And in the fall of 1781, an old native man had arrived unexpectedly to claim his daughter and her two children, who were living with Marten.

The governor had always maintained relationships with native women, often keeping several at the same time, some of whom bore him children, and in the winter of 1785–86 he had two and sometimes three youthful Indian women living with him at York. There was no place in Marten's life for an apprentice who needed to be trained, so he sent young Thompson off with a party of hunters, who were expected to live in a tent and keep the factory supplied with fresh meat till spring. He supervised the work of the servants and ran the factory and turned to his women for solace when necessary. But they were unable to ease his loneliness, or alleviate his pain, which was clear from a letter to Hearne, dated March 30, 1786.

"You will see by this letter the writer is not well," Marten wrote. "Indeed, I am not so, nor do I think I ever shall be free from pain; a Bilious disorder Joined to a wandering Gout, which is continually flying from head to foot destroys the few Pleasures that might be expected by a Man in his 57th Year: yet a consciousness of being honest to my Masters doth as it must to you, sooth the pains of the Body and Blunt the points of Rancourous darts hurled at us by those bad Men, who think we injure them by being honest to our Masters. But whilst this feeble hand can hold a pen, untill these Eyes are closed for ever, or at least whilst You and I remain in the Service I will join with You heart and hand in preventing as much as in me lies all illicit practices."

When you hunt grouse with the net, the young hunter explained, you must kill them cleanly. Take a bird in your hands. Put the head in your mouth and snap its neck with your teeth. Do not break the skin or blood will drip on the net. The smell of blood always attracts foxes, even when it is dry, and they will chew the mesh until they have shredded it. The hunter reached for a bird and showed David Thompson how it was done. Then he picked up another and handed it to the apprentice.

Thompson learned this procedure during his first winter at York. Early in the season, they hunted the flightless grouse, also known as ptarmigan, shooting them as they fed on willow buds, but later, when the snow was deep and the birds gathered in large flocks, they used the net. The hunters drove four posts into a snow-drift and attached the net to the posts.

Some of the men herded a flock toward the trap and, when the birds were busy feeding on a mixture of gravel and willow buds, one of their companions pulled the rope and brought the mesh down upon them. On a good day they took a hundred and twenty grouse, and the young apprentice became proficient at dispatching them with his teeth, though it troubled him. They were beautiful birds, their plumage brilliant white, and hardy enough to survive winter nights of minus eighty-five by burrowing into the snow. But it was their gentle nature that struck him. Kneeling in a drift, holding them in his hands, he sometimes poked and prodded, but these creatures accepted their fate without stirring.

That first winter, Thompson was assigned to a hunting party of three men and an Indian woman, who was likely the companion of one of the men. They left York in late October after the fall goose hunt, accompanied by a strong, handsome Labrador dog. Each of them hauled a sled loaded with about seventy pounds of provisions and supplies, and the dog carried goods weighing a hundred pounds. They camped on French Creek, seven miles south of the factory, and lived in a tent twelve feet high and twelve to fourteen in diameter. It was sparsely furnished, with a three-gallon brass kettle for cooking, a smaller kettle for drinking water and pine branches spread beneath their bedding.

The men erected a crude log structure called a hoard, which was eight feet long, six wide and five high, to store their provisions and to keep out predators attracted by the smell of food. Game was plentiful that fall. They fished for trout, baiting hooks with the hearts of grouse and dropping them through holes in the ice, until the cold became extreme and drove the fish to the deepest parts of the river where they could not be caught. They snared rabbits, shot grouse and trapped martens, foxes and wolverines.

Every few days, the hunters sent sleds loaded with game back to the factory, and Marten duly noted each arrival in the post journal. On November 7, the governor dispatched two Indians to the camp on French Creek and they returned the next day with twenty rabbits, eighty fish and ten grouse. Two weeks later, Thompson and Robert Tennant went to York with fifteen rabbits, sixty pounds of fish, eighty grouse and three foxes. They sent a hundred and twenty grouse, ten rabbits, thirty-three pounds of fish and two foxes on November 29, and a day later Thompson went in with thirty-six pounds of venison and forty-four grouse.

Polar bears were prevalent until the bay froze up and they could hunt seals. They usually kept their distance, but one night a hungry bear showed up at the camp. Thompson and a companion had left for York earlier in the day with a load of game. Two other men, John Mellam and William Budge, and the Indian woman, who was not named in the surviving accounts of the incident, stayed behind. The woman was cooking dinner and the men were cleaning the guns when they heard the beast pacing around the tent. It circled until it found the entrance, then thrust its head in. Tent poles on either side stalled the bear.

Mellam grabbed a musket and tried to shoot, but the gun failed. He took the barrel in his hands and began smashing the bear's snout with the stock. The Indian woman struck it over the head repeatedly with a two-and-a-half-pound axe. The blows forced the bear to retreat, whereupon it began demolishing the hoard. Mellam loaded a fowling piece, fired two shots and killed the bear. Then he turned to find the woman threatening Budge, who had shinnied up a pole. Mellam disarmed her, but she never forgave Budge's cowardly retreat.

Christmas was quiet at York that year. The hunters came in from French Creek on December 23, hauling sleds laden with four hundred grouse, forty-eight rabbits, fifty-two martens, three foxes and ninety-two pounds of fish. A grateful Marten wrote in the post journal: "Blessed be God. The year hitherto hath turned out plentifull a great Blessing when we have so many mouths to feed and English provisions come so dear." But his entry for Christmas Day, addressed to his superiors in London, read: "I humbly wish your Honours the compliments of the Season. Am sorry to inform your Honours that the Extreme Pains I am in with the Gout prevents and hath prevented our having Divine Service now and for some time past."

The hunters returned to their tent in January, though the tremendous cold and short days made the work slow and difficult. They had to remove their mittens, which were lined with rabbit fur, the warmest available, to load and fire their guns. They would put the mittens on as quickly as possible, retrieve the game and search for more, before reloading. Nevertheless, by January 21,

John Mellam and David Thompson brought in three hundred grouse, some of them shot and some captured under the net, and two weeks later the young apprentice went in with another three hundred, all taken with the net. But on February 19, the governor decided that the youth had had enough of hunting. "Ordered David Thompson to bring his things in," Marten wrote, "he being much frostbitten in the face."

It was as hard a winter as any Marten could recall and he had spent most of the previous thirty-five years in the country. "Cold weather continues," he wrote on February 26. "This continuance of cold weather occasions a prodigious consumption of firewood, the officers declaring they cannot do without an almost constant fire. The firewood already consumed is I think as much as ever I Remember during a whole winter in any year since I have been in your honourable service."

The winter held until late April, when the river ice began to break up in front of the fort, but it was another month before the waterways were open and Indians arrived from inland to trade. The first group reached York on May 28. They announced themselves by firing their guns. Servants, tradesmen and officers rushed to the shore to see fourteen canoes coming down the river, one beside another, each paddled vigorously by strong, sure men seated in the bows and sterns, their women and children in between and the luggage stowed securely around them.

The head men came ashore first, leaving their subordinates and the women to empty the canoes and erect the teepees. They were escorted to the factory trading room, where the governor awaited them with pipes and tobacco. Each man smoked a bowl full in silence. Afterward, the governor and the leading chief exchanged greetings and news and then everyone joined in the conversation. Marten named three of the Indians captains and three lieutenants and, following the customs of the trade, presented the captains with hats, lace-trimmed coats and shirts, breeches and stockings while the lieutenants received caps, coats and shirts, minus the lace. Then he distributed food and liquor and the Indians returned to their camp. The following day, another thirteen canoes arrived. The ceremonial greeting was repeated and more liquor handed out. "The Indians as usual very drunk," Marten wrote, "and continually howling for Brandy."

Trading commenced after the Indians had finished celebrating, but Marten was disappointed with the outcome. He suspected that some of the natives had traded their best furs to the Canadian pedlars from Montreal who were roaming at will on lands awarded exclusively to the Hudson's Bay Co. in its royally granted charter of May 1672. "The furs of many appear to be the refuse of the Canadian traders," he wrote. "This will be the case, strive what we can, untill the Honourable Hudson's Bay Company Chartered rights to the country are vindicated and Interlopers terrified from the manifest encroachments made by those who acknowledge they have no right to the ground they occasionally occupy."

A few Indians came to trade over the next month, but the factory was quiet until the company's inland employees, thirty-five in all under the leadership of William Tomison and Robert Longmoor, arrived in a brigade of canoes on July 1. For several days, servants and tradesmen neglected their duties to celebrate with their compatriots who had wintered in the vast interior. But not the officers. They had to plot the next stage in their battle with the Canadians, who had taken so much of the trade away from the Company of Adventurers.

The company now had three posts inland: Cumberland House, established on Pine Island Lake, along the Saskatchewan River, in 1774; Hudson House, built on the north branch of the river in 1779; and Manchester House, established a hundred and twenty miles farther up the north branch in the spring of 1786. Tomison and Longmoor now proposed a fourth, this one on the south branch of the Saskatchewan where the interlopers were already operating. They would put Mitchell Oman, a capable

Orkneyman, in charge. But Oman could neither read nor write. He would need a clerk to maintain the post journal and the account book, and Humphrey Marten had the ideal candidate: he would send David Thompson inland.

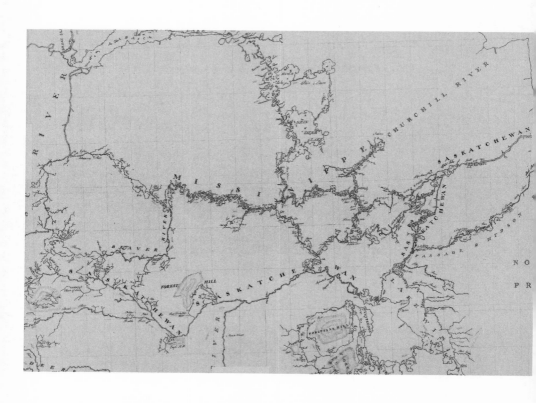

Thompson's travels, 1786–89: His masters sent the unpaid, teenaged apprentice from Hudson Bay to the foothills of the Rockies.

Into the Country

(1786)

DAVID THOMPSON WAS SUNBURNT AND SORE AND THE BACK OF his neck covered with insect bites, but after a day on the river he was too hungry and tired to care. The sun hovered over the highlands to the west and in these northern latitudes would remain visible for two, perhaps three hours. The canoes, eight of them, were overturned side by side on the shore and the cargo stacked neatly and covered with a leather tarp. He lined up for dinner with the rest of the servants, devoured the heap of food served by one of the Indian cooks, and afterward looked for a dry spot—sand, pebbles, moss, it didn't matter. He spread his blanket, crawled under and did not stir till he heard Robert Longmoor ordering everyone up. Overhead, the sky was dark and starry. He could hear the river, but could not see it, and the forest, denser here than on the coast, resembled heavy, black curtains. But just above the treetops the eastern horizon glowed faintly. Time to move.

That spring he had turned sixteen, and each day's travel left an imprint on him. His hands hurt when he tugged on his boots. His knees ached. His back was stiff. He rolled up his blanket and walked slowly to the river. He drank and washed his face, then joined the others. They loaded each canoe with six packages of trade goods, each package weighing ninety pounds, plus their luggage and the provisions—sixty pounds of oatmeal, twenty pounds of flour and thirty pounds of bacon per vessel. One after another they pushed away from shore, dipped their paddles into the water and glided silently into the current.

Thompson knelt in the middle of a canoe, a cross-beam supporting his weight, while two older, stronger, more experienced servants paddled before and behind him. He was unaccustomed to starting without breakfast, despite his trip a year earlier from Churchill with the packet Indians, and his stomach rumbled and ached, but he would not eat till mid-morning. Dawn was the time to paddle, Longmoor insisted, before the wind rose and the bugs came out.

They were travelling up the Hayes River on the first leg of an eight-week, seven-hundred-mile journey from York Factory to Cumberland House and from there to the northern fringe of what was then known as the Barren Grounds—the vast prairie that lay in the heart of the continent—where they would establish South Branch House. Longmoor, who was in charge of Manchester House, the uppermost company settlement on the Saskatchewan, had left York at one o'clock on the afternoon of July 21, with a party of twenty-three servants, and Tomison and his brigade of twenty-five departed on the twenty-second. Eight Indian women were among the two parties. Some were returning to their homelands after wintering at York. Some had come along as cooks and still others may have taken up with some of the men.

For the first hundred and twenty miles, the river crossed a coastal plain, but the current was so strong that they could make little progress by paddling and had to tow the canoes. The men worked in teams of three. Two strapped on harnesses, hitched ropes to the bow of their canoe and pulled from the shore while a third stayed on board to steer—a technique known as tracking.

Thompson found tracking easy enough, but the heat and the mosquitoes turned the work into a dreadful ordeal.

They next entered a portion of the river that left everyone exhausted but was especially arduous for a first-time traveller like Thompson. The coastal plain gave way to a higher, rocky country and the character of the Hayes changed so sharply that the Hudson's Bay men had named it the Hill River. It was swift and shallow, and full of rapids, waterfalls and portages. In the space of fifty miles, there were fifteen stretches of unnavigable water that forced the men to go ashore and carry or tow the canoes. Each evening Thompson was close to collapse.

He was relieved when they surmounted the Hill. The river changed again and they paddled over flat water, crossed tranquil lakes and proceeded up narrow channels, harassed by flies and mosquitoes and fickle weather that brought rain, hail, gales, stifling heat and, occasionally, a pleasant day. They followed the Hayes almost to its source, four hundred miles inland from York, then hauled the canoes over a short portage into a peaceful, tea-coloured stream that the Cree called Echimamish, the River That Flows Both Ways. It defied logic, but was nonetheless true. The source of this river was a pond in the middle of a swamp. The Echimamish sent water east to the Hayes and west to the enormous Nelson, which was permanently swollen by the cold, tawny water discharged by Lake Winnipeg.

On Lake Winnipeg, they paddled eighty-five miles around the treacherous north shore and down the western side, ever fearful of a south wind that could raise powerful swells capable of dashing canoes against the high clay cliffs at the end of the lake. They exited at the mouth of the Saskatchewan River and paddled two miles to the foot of the Grand Rapids.

The land rose 128 feet over the next twelve miles, and the river tumbled from ridges, raced headlong across channels littered with boulders and rubble and roared through deep, narrow gorges. They towed and carried the boats from the foot to the head of the

Grand Rapids, the most arduous stretch being a two-mile portage past the gorges. Sometimes, though not on this occasion, Cree or Saulteaux families were camped by these raging waters, spearing fish, and would trade a plump, tasty sturgeon for tobacco or a little brandy. At the head of the rapids, they embarked again and resumed their journey.

The Saskatchewan was the road to the interior, but even the most experienced of the English traders, men like William Tomison and Robert Longmoor, possessed only a sketchy understanding of this broad, swift stream. Tomison had first come inland nineteen years earlier, in 1767, and for the past decade had worked on the Saskatchewan. Longmoor entered the service of the company in 1771 and spent most of his time inland. He had wintered with Indians, travelled to the buffalo country and been robbed of his trade goods by Canadian pedlars—French-speaking interlopers from Montreal, who travelled to the interior via the Great Lakes and brought with them goods supplied by the town's British and Scottish merchants. Longmoor had helped establish both Hudson House, two hundred and eighty miles above Cumberland, and Manchester House, a hundred and twenty miles beyond Hudson.

Tomison and Longmoor knew that this big river and its south branch originated in the Rocky Mountains. They knew that both branches flowed through dry, open country. But they knew nothing of the tributaries that fed these rivers, or how much land the two branches drained, or how many Indian nations lived on these lands and claimed them as their own. And the best maps of the day offered no enlightenment. Between Lake Winnipeg and the Pacific, they were blank. The English traders had much to learn about the country, and much ground to cover before they caught up with their Canadian competitors, who were more numerous, had penetrated more deeply into the interior and had established more posts, most of them strategically positioned to cut off the flow of furs to the bay.

In the fall of 1786, the Hudson's Bay traders would push the company's presence farther inland. On September 13, fifty-five days after leaving York, Longmoor's brigade reached Cumberland House, two hundred miles up the Saskatchewan, and stopped just long enough to take on dried provisions. That day, David Thompson, serving as writer, made his first entry in the post journal he would keep over the winter. "Longmoor dispatched Mitchell Oman with 5 canoes and 13 men besides myself," he wrote, "to erect a Settlement in some convenient place up the South branch of the Saskatchewan there to trade with the Natives as seems best for your Honors Interest."

Mitchell Oman and his men spent a slow, quiet winter on the south branch. Their house, which they named after the river, stood high on a bluff above the swirling, sandy-coloured waters of the South Saskatchewan. It was snug—thirty-six feet by twenty-four—and warm. There were three sections: the master's quarters, which Oman shared with Thompson; the guard room, where the trading and business were conducted; and three servants' rooms, each twelve feet by eight. The traders had erected a pole outside the house and every morning one of them hoisted the Hudson's Bay Co. flag to declare their presence in the country.

South Branch House was twelve days beyond Cumberland, and about forty miles above the forks. They had towed the canoes a good part of the way up from Cumberland because the river was low and sandbars prevalent. Some days, the men were strapped into their harnesses for fourteen hours and advanced twenty-five miles, walking on wide, dry beaches. There were large herds of deer in the forest along the river, and as the traders trudged upstream they heard stags bellowing or locking antlers with rivals and fighting for turf, or females. Oman and his men arrived in late September and began building on October 2, about two hundred yards upstream and across the river from two Canadian posts, which were well stockaded and almost side by side.

They framed and enclosed the house with poplar logs, though straight ones were hard to find because the Canadians had used most of them. Afterward, they plastered the exterior with mud. Thompson worked alongside the servants. He learned how to square timber for the walls, how to saw floorboards, how to make a good mud plaster for the walls and a mortar of mud and grass for the chimney.

Oman kept some of his men busy that winter cutting and trimming timber for the stockades. The hunters periodically rode in with horses bearing loads of buffalo meat, and Indians arrived unannounced from the Great Plains. Thompson recorded all the activities in short, crisp journal entries: "2 Stone Indians came in for tobacco"; "received a Doe Moose from an Indian who was paid and left"; on November 24, "dismissed the Indian hunter had only killed 2 cows since Nov. 4"; "an old Indian and 2 Young Indian men engaged to hunt for us"; "3 men came from hunting tent with 6 Horse loads of meat"; "sent someone to Hudson House for hatchets ours all traded"; "3 Chief Indians and followers came in but poorly gooded"; "Indians quite drunk."

There were other visitors that winter. Several times, after the river froze up, the Montreal traders, Nicholas Monture, who was French, and William Thorburn, a British naval veteran, came across with their men. The traders in the three houses were competitors, but the isolation and a natural curiosity about their neighbours prevailed over commercial rivalry. The French Canadians wore long red or blue caps and grey capes tied at the waist with broad, multicoloured sashes. Monture spoke enough English to conduct business and converse briefly. He was polite and easygoing and always smiled when he spoke and bowed when he left, whereas the English traders remained stiff and serious.

Thorburn, who was in his mid-thirties, came over for the opportunity to speak English. From him Thompson learned much about the Canadian trade and how the French and the English had formed a productive partnership, and he later wrote down what Thorburn had told him. "At the time of the cession of Canada to the British, all the fur trade was in the hands of the French," Thorburn explained. "British merchants soon acquired a share of it and, at length, the whole of it, but by means of French traders to whom they furnished goods for the trade. Some of these were good characters, men of integrity. Where this was the case, the trade gave a decent profit to both the Indian trader and the merchant.

"Too frequently, it was otherwise. French traders had little, if any, education. They kept no books. When in their wintering houses, they passed the time in card playing, gambling and dancing, which brought on disputes, quarrels and all respect was lost. Goods beyond the extent of their wages were taken by the men to pay their gambling debts and every festival of the Church of Rome was an excuse to get drunk. The fisheries were neglected, starvation loomed and they returned to the merchants in beggary and distress."

To remedy these problems, the merchants had begun sending English-speaking clerks inland to manage the trade and they had begun forming partnerships rather than competing against each other. These were short lived and ever changing, but before sending their traders inland for the winter of 1786–87, a number of merchants had united to form a large partnership, which they had called the North West Co.

Business was poor at South Branch House that winter, and most of the servants blamed the Canadian traders. Mitchell Oman said no, it had nothing to do with them. The problem was that there were fewer Indians than there had been just a few years earlier, and Thompson was inclined to believe him. He worked closely with Oman and came to trust and admire the handsome, powerfully built Orkneyman.

Oman had served the Hudson's Bay Co. for sixteen of his thirty-four years. He was bright and inquisitive, despite his lack of education, and possessed an extraordinary memory. He had been at York when the French sacked the place and among the Indians when smallpox struck in 1780. He and some fellow servants had seen the effects of the plague while paddling up the Saskatchewan in the fall of that year, their canoes laden with a winter's supply of trade goods. One night, while enjoying the warmth of a fire, Oman told the men of South Branch House how they had come to a camp and seen people sitting on the beach, and Thompson later wrote an account of the story.

"When we came to them, to our surprise they had the marks of the smallpox. They were weak and just recovering. None of us had the least idea of the desolation this dreadful disease had done until we went up the bank to the camp and looked into the tents. In many, all were dead, and the stench was horrid.

"Those that remained had pitched their tents about two hundred yards from them and were too weak to move away entirely. They were in such a state of despair and despondence that they could hardly converse. From what we could learn, three fifths had died under this disease. They informed us that as far as they knew all the Indians were in the same dreadful state.

"When we arrived at the House, instead of a crowd of Indians to welcome us, all was solitary silence. There was no Indian to hunt for us; before the Indians fell sick, a quantity of dried provisions had been collected for the next summer's voyage, upon which we had to subsist, until at length two Indians with their families came and hunted for us. These informed us that the Indians of the forest had beaver robes in their tents some of which were spread over the dead bodies, which we might take and replace by a new blanket and that by going to the tents we would render a service to those that were living by furnishing them with tobacco, ammunition and a few other necessities and thus the former part of the winter was employed. The bodies lately dead, and not devoured by the wolves and dogs, we laid logs over.

"From the best information, this disease was caught by the

Chipaways, the forest Indians, and the Sioux, of the plains, about the same time. From the Chipaways, it extended over all the Indians of the forest to its northward extremity and by the Sioux over the Indians of the plains and crossed over the Rocky Mountains. More men died in proportion than women and children for, unable to bear the heat of the fever, they rushed into the rivers and lakes to cool themselves and the greater part thus perished.

"The natives allowed that far more than one half had died and, from the number of tents which remained, it appeared that about three fifths had perished. Despair and despondency had to give way to hunting for provisions, clothing and all the necessities of life for, in their sickness, they had offered almost everything they had to the good spirit and to the bad to preserve their lives and were destitute of everything. All the wolves and dogs that fed on the bodies of those that died lost their hair, especially on the sides and belly, and even after six years many wolves were found in this condition and their fur useless."

The Indians who came to South Branch House—Crees and Stoneys along with a few Atsina and Saulteaux—were survivors of the plague. They brought an assortment of furs, about one-third of them beaver and the rest a mix of fox, wolf, lynx and badger. Trading finished for the season in early April, when the Indians began leaving their winter camps and moving to the plains to hunt buffalo.

The men spent the rest of the spring erecting stockades around the post, or sorting and packing the furs. On May 21, four servants departed for Cumberland House in two canoes. Oman left six men to guard South Branch House over the summer and set off May 27 with four others, including Thompson. Both branches of the Saskatchewan were swollen with runoff and the powerful current carried the British traders down to their destination in a mere three days.

At South Branch House, the traders had lived on buffalo and venison, but at Cumberland they ate fish three times a day—mostly pike and sturgeon. Cumberland stood on the south shore of Pine Island Lake, an irregular body of water fed from the southwest by the silt-laden Saskatchewan and from the north by a clear but smaller river that flowed out of rocky, forested terrain. The Hudson's Bay men fished with nets three hundred feet long and six feet deep and caught the tastiest sturgeon where the Saskatchewan joined the lake. They called this fish the water hog because it liked to wallow in muddy alluvial deposits, and the voracious pike was known as the water wolf: it seized other fish by the back and held tight till they expired. Pike ate whitefish, perch, pickerel and even smaller members of its own species. Sometimes the traders would slice open one of these sharp-toothed predators and find mice in the stomach.

Thompson remained at Cumberland in the summer of 1787 with three other servants while William Tomison led the annual brigade of canoes down to York Factory with a cargo of furs. He helped the men set the nets and take them. He became adept at making and repairing nets and learned to extract oil from the sturgeon, which was used to light the lamps at night. He was an enthusiastic apprentice who quickly mastered these tasks and other skills necessary to become a successful trader.

In his leisure hours, he yearned to read, but there were no books at Cumberland, not even a Bible, and for this he blamed the master, George Hudson, like himself a former student at Grey Coat School. Hudson had entered the service in 1775, at age thirteen, and had been in charge at Cumberland since 1781. The years of isolation at the wilderness post had, in Thompson's opinion, sorely affected his character. He smoked tobacco mixed with weed, and he never exercised. He kept the post journal and accounts, but writing was a struggle. He rarely conversed with the men, and provided almost nothing that might keep them entertained in their spare time.

The only diversion was a checkerboard, and Thompson played often. If he could not coax one of the others to sit for a game, he would play both sides himself, and this led to a strange experience, one that he would never forget. "I was sitting at a small table with the chequer board before me," he later wrote. "When the devil sat down opposite to me.

"His features and color were those of a Spaniard, he had two short black horns on his forehead which pointed forwards; his head and body down to his waist (I saw no more) was covered with glossy black curling hair, his countenance mild and grave; we began playing, played several games and he lost every game, kept his temper but looked more grave; at length he got up or rather disappeared.

"My eyes were open. It was broad daylight, I looked around, all was silence and solitude, was it a dream or reality? I could not decide. Young and thoughtless as I was, it made a deep impression on my mind. I made no vow but took a resolution from that very hour never to play a game of chance, or skill or anything that had the appearance of them and I kept it."

William Tomison and his men completed the annual spring journey down to York Factory without any notable incidents and remained there for several weeks. He and the governor plotted strategy for the upcoming winter, and the servants packed the goods they would take back inland. They left on July 25 and reached Cumberland House on August 28 after a journey filled with hardship and loss. Tomison and his men endured a wild assortment of weather—rain, hail, oppressive heat, high winds and swells on the lakes—and they buried three comrades along the way.

On August 6, one of the Indians complained to Tomison that he had been suffering from a violent pain in his head for three days. He passed away twenty-four hours later. "He was a stout, able and good-natured man as could be found in a hundred," Tomison wrote in his journal, "aged about 30 years, and will be a great loss to Cumberland House."

A servant named William Saunders died one evening while making camp. He was covering the trade goods with a sheet of leather when a gun—left leaning against the merchandise—slid to the ground and discharged. The ball hit Saunders in the stomach, knocked him over and exited by his left shoulder. "God have mercy on me," he said as blood surged from his wounds. "Lay hold on me for I am gone." And he was, in six minutes.

The third man, John Lynklyter, died at the Grand Rapids on the Saskatchewan River. He and his partner, George Short, were towing a canoe and had almost reached the carrying place at the foot of the big falls when the current pushed the canoe back and pulled the two men into the river. Short broke free of the harness, but Lynklyter could not escape, and his twisted, broken body washed ashore downstream a short time later.

Tomison spent a week at Cumberland, allowing his men to rest and repacking the trade goods for the posts farther up the river. He left September 5, 1787, with fourteen canoes, and noted in his journal: "The misfortune that has happened and so many lame men obliges me to take David Thompson as a third man in my canoe."

Tomison had received from Mitchell Oman favourable reports of the character and capabilities of the young apprentice, who was then seventeen and had acquired a working knowledge of Cree by conversing with the Indians who passed through Cumberland during the summer. This had so impressed Tomison that he sent Thompson out from Manchester House with a party of six to winter among the Piegan Indians, who were sometimes called the Peekanow, both being derived from *Pikuni,* a name bestowed on them by others, for it meant the people who wear badly dressed robes. If Thompson could learn one Indian tongue, Tomison reasoned, he could surely learn another, in this case Blackfoot, the language of three allied nations: the *Siksika,* or the Blackfoot, the *Kainah,* or the Bloods, and the *Pikuni,* who were the most westerly and lived on the prairie, along the eastern flank of the Rocky Mountains.

The party left Manchester House in late September, each man

with two horses—one to ride and a second to haul the trade goods—except for Thompson, who had only one horse. It carried his outfit—an extra shirt, a leather coat, a blanket, a buffalo robe, forty rounds of ammunition, two knives, six flints, awls, needles and various other items. After travelling for a month, at a rate of fifteen miles a day, most of which Thompson walked, the Rocky Mountains appeared—like shining white clouds on the horizon, as he would later recall. A short time later, they crossed the Bow River and met a dozen mounted, well-armed Piegan warriors, who welcomed them and led them to their camp.

The elderly men came forward to meet the strangers and each extended his left hand to greet them. They invited the visitors into their camp and made room for them in their lodges. Thompson's host was named Saukamappee, a Blackfoot word that meant young man, though Saukamappee was, in the winter of 1787–88, very old. He was six feet tall, his frame erect and his strength still evident though his once lustrous black hair had faded to grey. Thompson judged him to be near ninety, though he had no way of knowing for sure.

The young white trader and his native host spent many evenings together that winter, on opposite sides of the fire, the Indian sitting and talking, a buffalo robe pulled snugly around his shoulders, and his companion lying between robe and blanket, listening intently. Often, they began after dinner, always a tasty, filling stew of wild meat—bear, venison, antelope and the best parts of the buffalo, simmered and nurtured from early morning by the women—and they continued talking till the others were asleep and the night quiet, except for the wind and the wolves.

The old man was delighted with his guest. He listened unusually well, especially for someone so young and especially for a white man. And he understood Cree, Saukamappee's mother tongue. Saukamappee explained many native customs, like the habit of using the left hand to greet people. "If one of our people offers you his left hand, give him your left hand, for the right hand is no mark of friendship," he said. "This hand wields the spear, draws the bow and pulls the trigger of the gun. It is the hand of death. The left hand is next to the heart and speaks truth and friendship. It holds the shield of protection and is the hand of life."

During their evenings together, the old man talked of politics and spirituality. He told stories of famous chiefs and of the long war between the Snakes and the Piegan, which he had learned about as a boy because his father had left their village one day at the head of a party of twenty warriors to fight with the Piegan.

Then, the Piegan had lived farther north and east, closer to the Saskatchewan River and the partly wooded divide between the northern forests and the Great Plains. They had always been the frontier tribe of the *Siksika* confederacy and the first to confront their common enemy, the Snakes, a division of the Shoshoni people who lived west of the Rocky Mountains. The Snakes came over the mountains to hunt buffalo, first on foot and later on horses, and they became fearsome warriors. They wore armour of wood and leather, carried shields and charged at their foes wielding short-handled stone clubs.

The Piegan had never seen horses and had no word to describe these wondrous beasts, so they called them big elk. Mounted warriors filled the Piegan with terror and they turned to their neighbours for help. Saukamappee's father, for one, had responded. By the time Saukamappee reached manhood the Piegan had acquired guns from the white traders and no longer needed reinforcements, but he had gone to war anyway because his father-in-law made it known that he desired a Snake scalp for his medicine bag.

Saukamappee said that he, two other young Cree and seven Stoney Indians set out from their camps, each armed with a gun, and soon came to a Piegan village. After several days of feasts, dances and speeches, a large war party departed in search of the Snakes, and their scouts quickly found an encampment, though this band owned no horses and the only guns among the Piegan belonged to Saukamappee and his friends.

"When we came to meet each other as usual," the old Indian told his youthful guest, who would later write an account of this conversation, "each displayed their numbers, weapons and shields, in all of which they were superior to us, except our guns which were not shown, but kept in their leathern cases. For a long time they held us in suspense; a tall Chief was forming a strong party to make an attack on our centre. We prepared for battle as best we could. Those of us who had guns stood in the front line, and each of us had two balls in his mouth, and a load of powder in his left hand to reload.

"Our eyes were all on the tall Chief and his motions, which appeared to be contrary to the advice of several old chiefs. All this time we were about the strong flight of an arrow from each other. At length the tall chief retired and they formed their usual long line by placing their shields on the ground to touch each other, the shield having a breadth of full three feet or more. We sat down opposite to them and most of us waited for the night to make a hasty retreat. The War Chief was close to us, anxious to see the effect of our guns. The lines were too far assunder for us to make a sure shot, and we requested him to close the line, which was gradually done, and lying flat on the ground behind the shields, we watched our opportunity when they drew their bows to shoot at us. Their bodies were then exposed and each of us, as opportunity offered, fired with deadly aim, and either killed, or severely wounded, every one we aimed at.

"The War Chief was highly pleased, and the Snake Indians finding so many killed and wounded kept themselves behind their shields; the War Chief then desired we would spread ourselves by twos throughout the line, which we did, and our shots caused consternation and dismay along their whole line. The battle had begun about noon, and the sun was not yet half way down when we perceived some of them had crawled away from their shields and were taking flight.

"The War Chief seeing this went along the line and spoke to every Chief to keep his men ready for a charge, of which he would give the signal. This was done by himself stepping in front with his spear and calling on them to follow him as he rushed their line and in an instant the whole of us followed him. The greater part of the enemy took flight, but some fought bravely and we lost more than ten killed and many wounded. Part of us pursued and killed a few, but the chase had soon to be given over, for at the body of every Snake Indian killed, there were five or six of us trying to get his scalp, or part of his clothing, his weapons, or something as a trophy of the battle."

Saukamappee and his companions remained with the Piegan after the battle to hunt and because they were anxious to see a horse. "At last as the leaves were falling we heard that one was killed by an arrow shot into his belly, but the Snake Indian that rode him got away. Numbers of us went to see him, and we all admired him. He put us in mind of a stag that had lost his horns and we did not know what name to give him. But as he was a slave to man, like the dog, which carried our things, he was named the big dog."

The Piegan chiefs implored Saukamappee and the others to stay, offering to adopt them as sons and promising each a wife, but they were eager to see their families and so set off for home. They arrived after a journey of five or six days. "My mind was wholly bent on making a grand appearance before my wife and her parents and presenting her father the scalp I had to ornament his medicine bag. Before we came to the camp we had dressed ourselves and painted each other's faces and were proud of ourselves. On seeing some of my friends I got away and went to them and by enquiries learned that my parents had gone to the low countries of the lake and before I was three moons away my wife had given herself to another man and that her father could not prevent her and they were all to the northward, there to pass the winter.

"I said nothing, but my heart was swollen with anger and revenge and I passed the night scheming mischief. In the morning my friends reasoned with me upon my vexation about a worthless woman, and that it was beneath a warrior's anger. There was no want of women to replace her, and a better wife could be got. Others said if I had stayed instead of running away to kill Snake Indians, nothing of this would have happened. My anger moderated. I gave my scalp to one of my friends to give to my father, and renouncing my people, I left them and came to the Piegan, who gave me a hearty welcome. Upon informing them of my intentions to remain with them, the great chief gave me his eldest daughter to be my wife. She is the sister of the present chief and, as you see, now an old woman."

Thompson listened night after night as the snow fell and the others slept, never tiring of such tales, and he remembered them for the rest of his life, though he did not record them until he was an old man writing the story of his travels in the northwest. He was sorry to say farewell to Saukamappee.

Winter was nearly spent when they arrived back at Manchester House, and they soon received their assignments for the summer. Tomison left six servants, including Thompson, at Hudson House to look after the company's horses, about forty all told. He allowed them a month's dried provisions and for the remainder of the summer they provided for themselves. They spent their days on the prairie, hunting deer, antelope and buffalo, and in early August, Thompson witnessed the migration of the buffalo northward across the river—herd after herd, day and night, as he later wrote, until these solitary plains became a moving mass of black cattle.

Winter again, this time at Manchester House, and William Tomison filled the post journal for 1788–89 with the remarkable events and ordinary occurrences of daily life on the frontier: "Six men out hunting buffalo . . . Tailor making clothes for the men . . . Smith working at hooks and hinges for the door   Making them out of ice chisels . . . 2 men sawing boards . . . 2 men making candles . . . Gilbert Laughton repairing old Hatchets and making nails for putting parchment in the windows and the rest collecting firewood . . .

Gilbert Laughton making a Candlestick out of a tin Cannister . . .

"Four Sarcee Indians arrived carrying a few skins on their back . . . They complain much of the depth of Snow which prevents them from travelling with Horses. . . In the Evening 2 lads arrived here from the Hunters Tent for men to fetch meat which is very agreeable news there not being 1/2 day's Provisions in the House. . .

Traded with the Indians that came Yesterday and have made them small presents as usual They have brought 60 Whole and 40 half parchment Beaver, 26 Wolves and Provisions of sorts 290 lbs."

The entries were routine until December 23, a clear, sharp day. Tomison had sent some men out to cut firewood. In early evening, the servants he had dispatched to the hunters' tent the previous day returned with nine sledloads of meat. But an otherwise ordinary day ended badly. "David Thompson unfortunately fell coming down the River Bank about one Mile from the House by which his leg caught between a stick and the Sled which fractured the bone and otherwise bruised his leg very much. I set it and put splinters around it with bandages in the best manner I could but such accidents would require a more skilful Person than I am."

He had broken the thigh bone in his right leg, and Tomison recorded his slow, painful convalescence. December 25: "David Thompson has had tolerable good rest the last 24 Hours as can be expected of a person in his situation." December 31: "David Thompson has been but indifferent for these three days past." January 12: "David Thompson has so far recovered as not to want any attendance in the night." January 17: "Took the bandages off David Thompson's leg and looked at it then bound it up again he has but little pain in it but still very weak I would not have opened it so soon but being so swelled and has now fallen and become loose." March 29: "David Thompson was out of bed for the first time but had not set long before his foot and ancle swelled a good deal so that he was obliged to lie down again God only knows how it may turn out."

Thompson's fate was still uncertain as spring approached and everyone began preparing for the annual trip down to York. The men sorted, graded and packed the furs into bundles. Tomison took an inventory of the trade goods. He chose eight men to stay behind to protect the post from Indians and the Canadian traders. On May 16, about a dozen men departed in six canoes loaded with sixty-four bundles of fur and three hundred pounds of pemmican. The following day, Tomison and three able-bodied servants loaded two canoes with twenty bundles of fur and three hundred pounds of pemmican. They brought Thompson out in a stretcher, laid him amid the luggage and embarked. "By his own desire," Tomison wrote, "I am taking David Thompson down but God knows what will come of him."

Thompson was bedridden at Cumberland House most of the summer. He sat up for three hours on August 11 and one week later walked a little on crutches, assisted by Malcolm Ross, the master of the house. His condition had improved significantly by August 25, as Ross noted in the post journal: "David Thompson by the help of his crutches walked out of the warehouse where he has lain all Summer into the Mens' House which is the first he has attempted since he came here in the spring."

But he was unable to participate in the work of the house. On August 29, fifteen canoes, manned by company servants, arrived from York Factory with trade goods for the winter, and the next day four canoes of Indians, hired to bring merchandise inland, reached Cumberland. Over the next week, the goods were sorted and repacked for the journey upriver to South Branch and Manchester Houses. And every few days throughout the month of September, Indians arrived with furs or provisions, or to acquire goods on credit, and, afterward, paddled off toward their winter camps.

The post was quiet between such brief bursts of activity, and Thompson foresaw a long, slow winter. Besides himself and Ross, who had his Indian wife and two children with him, there were only seven men at Cumberland. He expected to fill the idle hours playing checkers or reading the Bible, if one were available. But everything changed with the arrival of Philip Turnor on the seventh of October.

Turnor had come up from York with three canoes and eleven men, including George Hudson and Mitchell Oman. He was articulate and well dressed and had about him an air of importance. He had just returned to the country after nearly two years in London and had been sent by the governing committee on an assignment that could, he said, shape the future of the company.

Turnor was the company's inland surveyor—the first person to hold the position. He had been appointed in 1778 and visited most of the company's posts, making observations in order to calculate latitude and longitude, and determining the distances between the settlements. He had travelled from York to Cumberland, and beyond to Hudson House and Manchester House, and then went back down to the bay and surveyed the posts around James Bay—Fort Albany, Henley House, Gloucester House, Eastmain House and Moose Fort. As well, he had established two inland posts and served as master of both.

Back in England, Turnor produced maps based on his travels, and advised the committee on the necessity of finding a route from the Saskatchewan River to Lake Athabasca and the country around it, which the Montreal-based trader Peter Pond had opened for the Canadians in 1778–79. Since then, the Hudson's Bay men at Cumberland had witnessed these interlopers returning each spring from Athabasca in canoes laden with lush, high-quality fur.

The pedlars were trading with the Chipewyan Indians, who for nearly a century had journeyed down the Churchill River to Hudson Bay to trade their furs with the company's servants. But over the past decade, the flow of furs to Churchill Factory had dried up. The company needed to reach Athabasca, and sent Turnor to find a route.

Thompson listened to all that Turnor said. He would stand near the dinner table and lean on his crutches, or hover in the

Hunting in the Athabasca country: Montreal-based traders got there first and tapped a rich source of lush, high-quality fur.

shadows just beyond the glow of fire and candles. He had many questions, but apprentices took no part in conversations between officers. He was willing to wait until the surveyor was alone or unoccupied, and then he would ask about the Athabasca expedition or the shiny brass instruments, which Turnor kept in secure, cork-lined wooden boxes.

Thompson was intrigued by these devices—a sextant, a telescope, a thermometer, several watches and a compass. It seemed wondrous that a surveyor could observe the motion of the sun, the moon, some of the brighter stars and other celestial objects and, on the basis of those observations, calculate the precise position of a trading post, or a lake, or the junction of two rivers, or any other landmark. These positions were expressed as geographical coordinates—degrees of latitude north of the equator and degrees of longitude west of the prime meridian, which ran through the Greenwich Observatory in London. These coordinates could be used to produce maps that would make this vast wilderness intelligible and accessible and replace the trader's quaint but colourful language of travel—the post is three days beyond the mouth of the river, the first carrying place is half a day above the lake, beware the rapids below the falls.

Turnor used his instruments daily, and Thompson was always there to assist or to ask a question. The surveyor would use his sextant to observe the sun at midday and from its altitude above the horizon, which varied by place and season, could ascertain latitude. On clear evenings, after the sun had set, he and Thompson would stand outside the house, the wind rustling the last of the birch and poplar leaves, the air crisp and dry, the sky bejewelled with stars.

Turnor would take out his telescope and locate Jupiter. He would find its moons—stormy, gaseous Io and her ice-bound sisters, Europa, Ganymede and Callisto—and then let Thompson observe them slip out of view behind the giant planet. This was one way to observe for longitude, but it was not very accurate. The more reliable method was to observe the motion of the moon as it travelled past certain fixed stars.

Turnor had decided to teach his craft—practical astronomy— to Thompson because the company needed surveyors and maps to keep pace with changes in the fur trade. For the better part of a century, while the company enjoyed its monopoly, the business had been static and predictable. Competition had now made it fluid and dynamic. The British traders and their Canadian adversaries were advancing up the great rivers of the interior. Officers like Tomison and Longmoor and Ross could decide where the next post went. The committee, its members resident in England, had to set policy and plot strategy. But how could they do either when their vast lands remained uncharted wilderness? The country had to be surveyed, but one man could not do it alone, so Turnor was pleased to train the eager young apprentice.

Turnor saw in Thompson, now nineteen years old, the qualities required of a good surveyor. He was bright, meticulous and patient. And still recovering from his broken leg, he had time to learn. Thompson devoted himself to making observations and mastering the complex calculations required to determine latitude and longitude, even after he resumed his duties as a fur-trade clerk on February 15, 1790.

He worked during the day and spent as many nights as possible observing—five during the month of February, eight in March, six in April and two in May. All told, he took thirty-five observations for longitude alone. Afterward, while others slept, he would sit at a table, well into the early hours of the morning, performing his calculations by candlelight. Determining the latitude of Cumberland House was comparatively easy. Longitude was much more difficult, and a single calculation could take three to four hours.

Longitude is based on the notion that the earth makes one complete revolution—360 degrees—every twenty-four hours, moving 15 degrees each hour. At the equator, a degree of longitude is equivalent to about seventy linear miles. At sixty degrees north, it is equal to thirty-five miles. The distance becomes shorter as the lines converge at the North Pole. The key to calculating longitude was to determine the position of a celestial body on a certain day and its movement over the course of hours, minutes and seconds local time. The surveyor then compared his observations with the position of the same object Greenwich time by consulting the *Nautical Almanac,* a hefty reference work published annually and containing tables giving the positions of the sun, the moon, the larger planets, the moons of Jupiter and a number of prominent stars each day of the year and at different intervals daily, all in Greenwich time. The difference between Greenwich and local time could be converted to degrees, and degrees could be converted to distance. The surveyor also had to factor temperature into his calculations, because the light of a heavenly body was refracted, or bent, upon entering the earth's atmosphere, and the degree of refraction depended upon the density of the atmosphere.

Thompson was enthralled by this work. It was challenging and stimulating compared to the humdrum business of handling merchandise and keeping ledgers, and it was a new science. Practical astronomy was based on recent technological advances—the invention of the sextant in England in 1757, and the development of precise, reliable watches—that made possible for the first time the accurate measure of longitude. The result was a race among explorers and their governments to survey the globe and to produce accurate maps. And Thompson could be part of this grand endeavour if he could just make himself useful to Turnor, useful enough to join his Athabasca expedition.

As spring approached, the surveyor had not set a date of departure, nor had he chosen all who would accompany him. His plans became even more unsettled when George Hudson, who was to serve as his assistant, died April 19. The death was noted in detail in the post journal: "Mr. George Hudson departed this World in a sudden kind of Manner   he had for some weeks past been much indisposed   in the latter of last Month his legs began to swell violently and never settled down but began to swell about the belly and breast with a dropsical appearance but not so as to confine him to his bed until the 18th Instant when he said he would lay and indulge himself   about the last 7 days he had a violent cough which at last took him suddenly and carried him off almost instantaneously without a struggle."

Some of the men built a coffin the following day and on April 21 they buried George Hudson. His death meant that Turnor would have to select another assistant, and Thompson considered himself capable and qualified. But the surveyor had his doubts. He wondered if the young apprentice's leg, though nearly healed, would withstand the rigours of the Athabasca expedition. Turnor had other reasons to be concerned. In mid-May, Thompson developed an infection in his right eye that impaired his vision, a malady caused by working late at night under candlelight.

Turnor chose as his assistant Peter Fidler, a labourer who had joined the company two years earlier and had spent the previous winter at Manchester House and South Branch House. Fidler arrived at Cumberland on June 3 and immediately began training under Turnor. Thompson, dejected and angry at being passed over, left six days later with a brigade of canoes destined for York Factory.

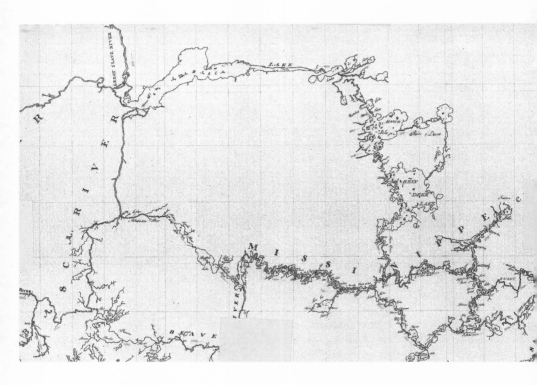

Thompson's travels, 1790–96: The young clerk nearly drowned on a journey of discovery to the Athabasca country.

By Star and Compass

(1790)

MAIL MOVED TWICE A YEAR WITHIN THE HUDSON'S BAY CO.
Each spring the committee sent out bundles of correspondence
with the supply ships, which arrived in late summer and were sent
ashore as soon as the anchor was dropped. The officers and servants sent journals, ledgers, letters and other documents to London when the supply ship returned in early autumn. The departure
of the ship, with furs and mail stowed securely, represented the end
of the business year at a trading post and the start of another, an
event always acknowledged on the final page of the daily journal.

So it was that on September 7, 1790, Joseph Colen, who had
succeeded gout-ridden, pain-racked Humphrey Marten as governor of York Factory, signed off on another year with the short
entry: "North Wind   part Clear   part Cloudy   sharp frost
this Morning   upwards of sixty families of Indians on the
Plantation   About Noon closed the Packet and delivered it to
Capt. Ganwell   pray God send the Ship Sea Horse in safety
to England   Amen."

Among the documents contained in the York packet was
Philip Turnor's journal and a letter he had written to the

honourable gentlemen of the committee, dated July 9. "In my Journal," Turnor wrote, "which contains my Observations, I have inserted some Observations made and worked by Your Honours' unfortunate apprentice David Thompson   I am fully convinced they are genuine and should he ever recover his strength far enough to be capable of undertaking any expedition I think your Honours may rely on his reports of the Situation and of any place he may visit and should he not be capable of travelling he may be very usefull in giving others instruction."

The packet also contained a letter from David Thompson— his first to the committee. "It being usual for apprentices when their terms of years were nearly expired to write to their Honors Employers, I have taken the same Liberty and assure your Honors I have served you with the utmost Fidelity during my apprenticeship which will expire May 20, 1791   I had the Misfortune to break my Leg December 23, 1788 which has disabled me from serving you on Inland Duties but am now acting in the Station of Writer at York Factory where I hope I give Satisfaction

"The last Winter I passed at Cumberland House with Mr. Turnor of whom I learned the Theory and Practise of Practical Astronomy   my improvement in that Science I hope my work will show   I am willing to go to make Observations for the Latitude, Longitude and Position &c of any part of the Sea Coast you may send me and doubt not to give your Honors satisfaction

"Besides those observations which are enclosed with Mr. Turnor's I have sent your Honors a Copy of Observations I made in my Passage from Cumberland House to this place Shall send your Honors a Draught of the Lakes, Rivers &c from here to Cumberland House next Year and I have not had time since my arrival to make one but have the Rough draft by me

"Your Honors specified in the Terms of my Indenture to give me at the Expiration of my term a compleat Set of Clothes both Linen and Woollen   In lieu thereof shall be obliged to your Honors to let me have a Brass Sextant . . . likewise a good

Magnifying Glass   I hope your Honors will also send me out a pair of Parallel Glasses 3 1/2 Inches by 3 1/2 Inches made to fold in a Case and Nautical Almanacs for the Years 1791, 1792, 1793 and 1794 without which I cannot work any observations I may make, and please to place them to my account as likewise the Value of the Sextant may be (if any) above the Suit of Clothes

"I leave my Terms to your Honors Generosity trusting my 7 Years apprenticeship and the faithful Discharge of the Duties required of me will give your Honors a favourable opinion of Your most dutiful Servant David Thompson."

He had taken up his position as writer at York Factory in early July 1790 and, while he awaited his response to the letter, spent his days recording transactions and keeping track of inventory. At night, he sat at a table, working by candlelight on the map he had promised the committee the following year. This work would be based on observations made with a sextant, compass and watch, all borrowed from another servant, a Mr. Stayner, before leaving Cumberland, and recorded in the journal he had begun keeping the previous October.

He observed for latitude and longitude at seven places during the twenty-eight-day, seven-hundred-mile journey and recorded these in his journal: "In the Lake Winnipeg about three-quarters of a Mile west of the Mouth of the Lake"; "On a Point of Rocks in Buscuscoggan Lake"; "On the north east end of the White Fall Carrying Place"; "At the Bottom of the first Rapid in Trout River where we stopped awhile"; "At the first small Sandy Bay in the upper Narrows of the Knee Lake"; "In a Small Bay on a Small Island in the Knee Lake"; "At the Last Sandy Bay in the Swampy Lake near the Head of the Hill River."

But to produce a map, he needed a record of every twist and turn in the waterways between these fixed points, and he relied on a technique known as the tracking survey. Kneeling in a canoe, paddle in hand, he kept a watch, a compass and a notebook in front of him. He jotted down each change of direction, noting in his mind the approximate speed of the current, and used the watch to determine how long they paddled before switching courses again. He could then estimate distance travelled on the basis of time elapsed.

His record keeping began June 9: "At 10 a.m. embarked Cumberland House Lake North 55 degrees   E 1m into a small River NE 1/2m into the Muddy Lake   E10 degrees N 3m   at Noon entered the Saskatchewan River   ENE 6 m   NE 2 m   NE & E 5 m   North 1 m   passed the Fishing Weir   N&E 4 m   E by N 4 m   N by E 3 m   SE 1/2 m   SE 1/4 m   E by S 1/2 m   SSW 1 m at 7 3/4 PM put up fine day."

On July 6, the brigade's last full day on the water, he recorded a forty-three-mile jaunt, turn by turn: "Wind Easterly   Weather Clear   at 2 3/4 AM embarked   NE 3m   NE by N 3m   N by W 12m   S by E 1m   NE by N 1/2m   ENE 1/2m   E by E 1/2m   at 5 AM entered the Hayes R   NNE 1/2m   N by E 1m   NE 2m   N by E 1m   NE by S 1/2m   North 3m   NNE 1/2m   NE by S 1/2m North 1/2m   NNW 1/2m   NW 1/2m   NNE 1/2m   NNW 1m NW by W 1/2m   WNW 1/2m   SSW 1/2m   passed Pennycutaway River   NNE 1m   NNW 1m   NE by S 1m passed the 10m Island NE by N 2m   NNE 2m   NE 1m   NE by E 4m about 7 1/2 PM put up at Dram Point."

He made a final observation for latitude and longitude at York Factory on July 17, then returned the instruments to Mr. Stayner, who was going back inland. He would not be able to view the motion of heavenly bodies—not until the committee sent out a sextant, compass, watch and *Nautical Almanac* on the next supply ship—and anyway he was preoccupied that fall with a more earthly problem.

The post was infested with mice, which were more numerous than anyone remembered because of a mild winter. Thompson and some of the men moved much of the merchandise to the upper level of the warehouse, though this did little to halt the damage caused by the rodents. Indian children killed enough to fill bushel baskets, seemingly without reducing their numbers.

The arrival of winter suppressed the mice, and by year end Joseph Colen reported that an air of contentment had settled over York Factory. "The men finished their Holiday diversions," he wrote in the post journal on January 1, 1791. "God be praised we begin the New Year with more pleasing prospects than for three years past. Health is our attendant   Kind providence smiles on us   We abound in every plenty which we enjoy with thankful hearts."

The package arrived on the supply ship of 1791, and after the anchor had been dropped and the big vessel had come to rest in Five Fathom Hole, out in the bay just beyond the mouth of the Hayes River, it was sent ashore on the factory sloop, along with the rest of the mail. A labourer brought the package to the warehouse and placed it on a table. It was a wooden box, securely sealed and addressed to DAVID THOMPSON, YORK FACTORY. There was an accompanying letter, and Thompson broke the wax seal, lifted the flap and removed a single, carefully folded sheet of paper.

"We have received your Letter of the 30th of August last, are well pleased with your Services and the Account of them which we receive from others," it began. "We are sorry for the Misfortune you met with in the Service   as you are now got to the Factory where you have the assistance of a Surgeon, we hope he may put you on such a Course as may give strength to your leg and enable you, in Time, to proceed in any further necessary Discoveries inland, but if that cannot be, we shall be glad to make your abilities useful in some other way.

"We have at present appointed you a writer in the Factory at 15 pounds per annum for three years. If you continue to make yourself useful to us you shall not fail of further Encouragement. To convince you of this we send you a sextant and the other things you Desire and mention in your Letter as a present and not to be deducted from the Value of the Cloaths which your interest gives you a Right to.

"We have received the Copy of your Observations, which together with Mr. Turnor's are put into the hands of Mr. Wm Dalrymple, from whom we doubt not to have a good account of them, shall be glad to receive your Obs. Of the Lakes and Rivers from York to Cumberland House every information that can tend to form a good Survey & Map of the Country Inland will always be particularly acceptable to us."

The letter, unsigned, had come from the committee, and before the supply vessel departed for England, Thompson dashed off a response. "Accept my sincerest thanks," he began, "for your truly Generous present." He declared himself ready to go wherever their honours should choose to send him, though at present he was limited by the injury he had suffered nearly three years earlier. "My Leg is pretty well recovered," he wrote, "my ancle not quite so well and will not permit me to travel above 10 or 12 Miles a day."

He could stand for several hours to observe for latitude and longitude, however, and first used his sextant on the night of September 8. He stood in the inky blackness around York Factory, listening to the wind and the river racing down to meet the sea, and gazed at the dazzling canopy overhead. He trained his instrument on Capella, the she-goat on the back of Auriga, the charioteer of the ancient Mesopotamian and Greek astronomers. Capella was bright and strong and outshone almost every other star in the sky—an ideal beacon for a novice astronomer.

He observed twice in October, three times in November and once in December, using as his reference points Arcturus, Aldebaran, Regulus and other stars that rivalled Capella's brilliance. There were only so many nights suitable for observing—those occasions when the skies were clear and it was not too cold and he had eaten well enough.

Most days that winter, the men at York Factory ate poorly. Fresh fish and meat were available only once or twice a week because game was scarce in the surrounding countryside. Joseph Colen had assigned fourteen hunters to four locations, but they could barely take enough to support themselves. The men were surviving on salted food, and, by Christmas, Colen feared an outbreak of scurvy. "To prevent any bad effect arising from the Men's eating such a quantity of salt Meat," he wrote on December 24, "I offered them in lieu of one day's salt venison to give two quarts of Scotch barley and one quart of molasses which they one and all thankfully accepted   I hope to keep off that dreadful malady felt at the factory for years past."

The barley and molasses were not enough. "Nine men on surgeon's list," Colen wrote on February 13, "part of whom begin to be so disabled in their legs by the scurvy as to prevent their walking." Five days later, he noted that some of the sick were "so very decrepit in their Limbs they can scarcely crawl about with the assistance of crutches." There were men sick until mid-March, but David Thompson remained in good health and continued observing periodically through the winter.

By late April 1792, he had determined definitively the latitude and longitude of York Factory. With that, he had nothing more to accomplish at that place and was eager to travel. Coincidentally, there was talk among the officers of an expedition that summer. Men would be sent to the muskrat country immediately west of the bay to investigate the incursions of the Canadians and to find a remedy. Thompson was delighted, and let it be known that his leg was strong and his ankle fully healed.

For years, the officers had been seething over the depredations of the Canadians. It was bad enough that these audacious Scotsmen and their French-speaking partners had established posts hundreds of miles in the interior on lands granted exclusively to the Hudson's Bay Co. Now, they had infiltrated the muskrat country, for all intents and purposes the backyard of the bayside posts. In May 1786, shortly before he retired from the service, Humphrey Marten had railed against the interlopers and "their manifest encroachments."

Joseph Colen was equally flustered by the Canadians. "2 Canoes of N. River Natives are come in," he wrote on June 26, 1790. "A great number had assembled in spring   were making canoes to come to the factory at Duck Lake   Six Canadian pedlars arrived on foot just before the ice broke up distributed two large rundlets of double proof spiritous liquor and collected all the furrs   These Incroachers came so near this Factory as the Gull Lake, not more than 120 miles distant and collected all the furrs of the home guard natives who wintered there.

"They persuaded many of the natives that dealing with them was the same as dealing with the factory as the furrs were all carried to one common stock   These natives further tell me the Pedlars have collected large quantities of furrs from the Masqua Rat and North River Indians who usually brought great trade to York."

The Canadians were formidable competitors. They matched or exceeded every move the company made on the Saskatchewan, and they were well established in the Athabasca country. In 1789, one of their men, Alexander Mackenzie, had travelled north from Lake Athabasca, paddled downriver to an even larger lake that flowed into an enormous river and had followed this river all the way to the Arctic Ocean. And even then Mackenzie was planning another epic journey, this one to the Pacific. Meanwhile, other enterprising Canadians were capturing the trade within a few miles of the bay.

The London committee of the Hudson's Bay Co. was pressing its senior officers, William Tomison, who was in charge of the inland trade, and Joseph Colen at York, to fight back by establishing operations in the fur-rich Athabasca country. But Tomison was determined to challenge the Canadians on one front—the Saskatchewan—and nowhere else. Colen, meanwhile, put up with the antics of these rivals until he could endure them no longer. In 1790, he sent men to Split Lake, on the Nelson River, to establish a post and the following year he ordered them to build another, farther inland. They travelled up the Grass River, a tributary of the

Nelson, and built Chatham House, on Wintering Lake. Twelve months later, in the summer of 1792, Colen and Tomison agreed to put additional men into the fight against the Canadians.

They would send out a small party to investigate reports, obtained from Indians, of a shorter, more direct route north and west from York to Athabasca. The explorers left on September 5, and Colen recorded their departure: "David Thompson with 7 men in 2 Large Canoes loaded with Trading Goods set off up the Nelson River to proceed on a Journey of Discovery toward the Athapescow Lake."

The trip up the Nelson to Sipiwesk Lake, where they planned to spend the winter, took thirty-four days. They travelled two hundred and fifty miles on waters that had fallen as rain or snow in the Rocky Mountains and flowed from the mountains to be collected by the north branch of the Saskatchewan River, by the Red Deer River, by the Bow and the Oldman. These rivers flowed across the prairie, the Bow falling into Red Deer to become the South Saskatchewan, the Oldman falling into the south branch and this southerly stream flowing on its own for three hundred miles before merging with the north branch for the descent to Lake Winnipeg, where these waters joined those of the Assiniboine, the Red and the Winnipeg Rivers. And this great lake, which seemed as broad and stormy as a sea to the early fur traders and explorers, discharged its waters into Playgreen Lake, which sent them on to the Nelson, and there they became a broad, powerful, cataract-filled river charging through its bed of granite and down to the bay.

Thompson and his men paddled and pulled their canoes against these waters. They lifted their vessels, as well as the luggage, provisions and trade goods, twenty-seven times to portage around waterfalls and rapids, and did so amid rain, sleet, snow and strong winds. It took a team, four-strong and tight, to keep a canoe on course, so Thompson could not record every change of direction as he had done on more peaceful rivers.

Thompson observing with the sextant: he could read the stars better than most men could read a book.

But he did observe for latitude and longitude: on the north shore, about three hundred yards below the end of the lower Seal Island; at the lower end of the Gull Fall carrying place; and at five other sites, and he estimated the length, breadth and position in the river of every island, details to be included in the maps he would one day draw.

He and his men reached Sipiwesk Lake on October 8 and erected their tents. The next day, Thompson started a meteorological journal, noting that the wind was out of the northeast at two knots, accompanied by moderate rain. He left two columns blank—one for the temperature and the other for the hour at which he had observed the weather—but in the margin added the following note: "put up and looked for a place to build on."

A note on November 3 read: "Removed into the House from the Tents; 3 Tickameg 3 Suckers and 2 Jack." The nets, set in the lake, had yielded eight fish for eight men—a typical catch at Sipiwesk. And the surrounding countryside, bereft of game, was adding nothing to their larder. His men could starve in this place, but on November 8, before such a prospect loomed, Thompson acted, and made a record of it in his journal: "7 1/4 AM Peter Brown Wm Flett and myself left the house in a canoe and set off for Chatham House to get a supply of provisions our little flour &c being almost expended and no hope of relief appearing."

Chatham House was north of them, on Wintering Lake, how far north they did not know, but they knew it could be reached by portaging and paddling through a series of lakes and creeks using an Indian trail. They paddled until noon on November 8 and completed the first portage only to discover that the next lake was frozen. They abandoned the canoe, made sleds and departed at eleven the following morning. They soon came to a small, round lake, about three miles in circumference and covered by a thin sheet of ice.

They crossed this lake and followed a creek to a larger body of water, Susquagemow Lake, but it was open. "This unexpected accident much dejected us," Thompson wrote. "However we comforted ourselves with this Reflection   that we could not find a Place worse than that which we had left." They made camp on a point, set their net and two days later hauled out five fish, a huge relief, as Thompson noted: "God be Thanked we have enough for a good Meal which we have not had these several weeks past."

They spent ten days waiting for the lake to freeze, left at daybreak on November 19 and reached Chatham House, under the command of Thompson's friend William Cook, at three o'clock that afternoon. Five days later, he set off for Sipiwesk House, accompanied by an Indian guide and carrying sixteen pounds of meat. The two of them arrived on the morning of November 26. The five men who had remained at Sipiwesk had caught only enough fish for one good meal. Their provisions had dropped to one quart each of flour and oatmeal. They assumed that Thompson and his companions had lost their way and perished. Desperate for relief, they were preparing to set off for Chatham House.

Thompson determined that the distance between the two posts was only thirty miles. He and the seven men with whom he left York spent the winter at Sipiwesk, scratching out a living and, when provisions were low, dashing to Chatham House over icebound lakes and through the snowbound forest.

On May 28, 1793, Thompson left Sipiwesk on his journey of discovery accompanied by John Harper, a company servant, and a Cree guide named Kisathinis. They travelled north on an Indian road, paddling across three labyrinthine lakes full of islands and deep bays and channels, and portaging on the muddy, swampy trails between them. From the last of these lakes they hauled their canoes and goods over a height of land to the Weepooskow, or Burntwood, River and paddled up this stream, encountering a rocky, rugged country and many waterfalls. The first, which he described in his journal, was about forty feet high: "The whole River which is deep and about 300 yards wide is here contracted into about 150 yards and falls down the Precipice with a Milk White foaming Torrent and with that Force . . . the Water below ascends like a heavy Rain about twice the height of the Falls."

Kisathinis guided them until June 6, when they met twenty-three canoes of northern, or Chipewyan, Indians. Thompson hired two of these, a man and his wife, who led them, without incident, for ten days, until the river widened and in places resembled a lake speckled with islands and a confusing array of channels. In one of these channels, they encountered schools of sturgeon leaping and splashing in the current and, nearby, a shrine of sorts. "We passed a set of tent poles and a Painted Stone set up for a God to which they had offered several things   among them were several Sturgeon

Spears   our Religious Pilot went ashore and being in need of a good Spear made fine to take the best one and in return made him an offering of a few willow poles."

On June 19, they passed a former Canadian settlement on the Missinippi, or Churchill, River, one established by a trader named Baldwin, and the next day they discovered another Canadian post. It was in a large bay, and here they witnessed something sinister. While crossing the mouth of the inlet, they observed a fire and two canoes of Chipewyan Indians paddling along the left shore. Thompson's Chipewyan guide and his wife went with John Harper to investigate. They returned two and a half hours later.

They had glimpsed an Indian standing in the doorway of the trading post. The man had ducked out of sight as their canoe approached, but three dogs came down to the edge of the water and followed them partway as they paddled past the house to examine the fire. They then returned to the house. The dogs and their owner had disappeared and the post was deserted, but the traders' belongings were strewn on the ground.

"These with many other Circumstances made our Pilot not hesitate to pronounce the Chipewyans had murdered the Canadians and plundered the House," Thompson wrote. "This accident gave me much trouble as they were for returning fearing they might be killed by those Indians and plundered of our goods."

He persuaded his men to continue, but the next day the female guide led them up the wrong branch of the river and did not realize her mistake until they came to a waterfall and were forced to turn around. At that point, Thompson's journey of discovery had ended.

"Our woman pilot, who has guided us from the upper Neestowyaks declared herself unable to guide us further   her knowledge of the Road these past three days has been very superficial and no ways trustworthy   Thank God for conducting us thus far in safety   I pray he may return us safely back   All our provisions consist now of a little Bear Meat and that very bad."

The journey back to York took one month. They arrived July 22, and Thompson reported his findings to Joseph Colen and William Tomison. He had located three Canadian posts. He had travelled up the Burntwood to a place called Duck Portage. There, he and his companions had hauled their canoes over the height of land to the Churchill River—a potentially valuable discovery. Thompson informed his superiors that they could move men and supplies from the Nelson River to the Burntwood to the Churchill and from there to the Athabasca country to challenge the Canadians—a shorter and quicker route than the long, circuitous path of their Canadian rivals.

Perhaps he hoped his superiors would authorize another exploratory journey so he could travel farther up the Churchill. Or perhaps he expected they would send him back to the district where the Canadians were in order to compete against them. Whatever his expectations, they were not met. Colen informed him that for the winter of 1793–94 he would be going to Buckingham House, the company's newest establishment on the North Saskatchewan and its most distant, 550 miles above Cumberland House.

William Tomison, a man Thompson liked and admired, was in charge at Buckingham House and from there he managed the inland trade. The young surveyor recalled fondly how Tomison had treated him—with the tenderness of a father—in the winter of 1788–89 when he broke his leg; Tomison had done everything possible to alleviate his suffering. He knew his friend to be kind and honest. But he had begun to question Tomison's ability as a leader.

Tomison was waging a good fight on the Saskatchewan, had established the company's presence on the south branch and advanced more than five hundred miles beyond Cumberland House on the north branch. And all the while he was perennially short of men. England and France were at war, and the British military had taken the best available men from the Orkney Isles—the company's principal source of labourers.

Still, Thompson believed that Tomison was too narrowly

focussed on the Saskatchewan. This winter, 1793–94, Tomison was again at the forefront of the fight against the Canadians who had built a post—Fort George—a few hundred yards downstream from Buckingham House. Yet he ignored the wealth of the Athabasca country. He would not be persuaded to send an expedition out to challenge the Canadian monopoly there. Thompson had tried. So had Malcolm Ross. And the committee in London had urged Tomison to throw Ross and Thompson into the fray, but he had ignored their directives.

Thompson saw another shortcoming in his friend: an inability to deal satisfactorily with the Indians. He was a parsimonious man who showed no enthusiasm for the lavish generosity of the natives or the gift giving that preceded every trading session. He did not get along well with them, and he was incapable of doing anything when they became truculent and menacing that winter.

The trouble started early in the season, for reasons that were unclear, and both the Canadians and the Hudson's Bay men felt the effects. "A very disagreeable affair happened last night," Tomison wrote in the post journal on October 12. "Several Blackfoot Indians being in at both houses those at the other House Quarrelled among themselves and one of them was killed by a South Indian and all the rest fled off in the Night and left everything they brought."

Ten days later, he reported another incident. "At noon Robert Linklater arrived and brought the disagreeable News of Manchester House being robbed of everything belonging to the Company and the Men stript of everything they possessed by the Fall Indians who came to the House on pretence to trade   having sent for tobacco 3 days before, they began on the Canadians first and took a number of Horses and stript many of their Men."

Things were quiet at the Hudson's Bay and Canadian post until January 18. "Blood and Blackfoot Indians arrived & behaved very rudely so that I was obliged to disarm them before they came into the House   one of those that went to the Canadian House fired upon those that were aiding their arrival without any provocation whatsoever   such behaviour I cannot account for."

Another disturbance occurred three weeks later, on February 5. "At noon 4 Men returned from the Island House brought 3 Kegs of Powder 28 Gallons of brandy being all that was saved of what was left at Manchester House   they inform me that there has been a large band of Blackfeet and Fall Indians in number 150 armed men   these brought 1200 Wolves which they traded and went away tolerably peaceable & the next day returned and took 52 Horses 6 of which they had just traded & had they not seen 50 Armed Men at the Canadian House it is not known what lengths they would have gone to."

The Hudson's Bay traders closely guarded their horses for the rest of the season, but the trouble with the Indians ceased as quickly and inexplicably as it had begun. In mid-May, when it was time to begin the long journey downriver to York Factory, Tomison left nine men behind to guard the post and set off with a brigade of thirty men in thirteen canoes. Thompson travelled with them as far as Cumberland House. There, he obtained permission from Tomison to depart with a small party to explore a series of rivers and lakes northeast of Cumberland that led him to the Burntwood and Nelson Rivers. He surveyed this alternative route to York and satisfied, in part, his enormous desire to see new country.

In the summer of 1794, Thompson's first three-year contract with the Hudson's Bay Co. expired and a new offer of employment arrived aboard the annual supply ship. "I am directed by the Honourable Committee to inform you," wrote Alexander Lean, the company secretary, "that . . . they are extremely well pleased with the Attention which you have shown, on all occasions, to the Duties of your Station, and being persuaded of a Continuance of that Zeal in such Operations as may be, in future, committed to you, they do not hesitate to advance your salary to 60 pounds per Ann . . . The two Watches which you sent home to be repaired are now returned together with a new one of Twelve Guineas value made by Jolly. The Charges of repairing the old & Cost of the new are at the Company's expense."

In one stroke, the company had quadrupled his salary. He was now earning more than his friend Malcolm Ross, who was fifteen years older and had an additional six years' service with the company. He was, of course, flattered that his employers thought so highly of his work, and was grateful for their generosity. But the letter was, in one respect, disappointing. The committee provided no hint of what his future duties might be. They did not even encourage him to think that he might one day be made an official surveyor. He would continue to take orders from Joseph Colen and William Tomison, and they sent him to Reed Lake House, north of Cumberland House, in the fall of 1794, where he spent a quiet, uneventful season working under Malcolm Ross.

The following summer he and Ross left York Factory together and travelled up the Nelson and Burntwood Rivers to the Churchill, where they were to recover the trade lost to the Canadians. Thompson and four servants went as far as a place called Duck Portage on Sisipuk Lake, while Ross and a slightly larger contingent ventured farther up the river. Thompson and his men had been at their wintering place for about a month, building a house and trading with both Cree and Chipewyan Indians, when a party of seven Canadians arrived. They erected a post thirty yards away and siphoned off a good portion of the trade.

To make matters worse, five fellow Hudson's Bay employees from Churchill Factory, who were wintering about two days' journey below them on the Churchill, showed up in mid-January. George Charles, the officer in charge, claimed they had come to collect debts from the Indians and to build a house, a notion David Thompson found preposterous given the weather. On successive days shortly before their arrival, he had recorded temperatures of minus thirty, minus twenty-six, minus forty and minus forty-nine Fahrenheit, at which point the mercury in his thermometer froze solid after an hour's exposure.

Charles departed with one of his men after a couple of days, but left the other three men behind for the rest of the winter. They declared that they were free to compete for the trade at Duck Portage because they worked for the governor at Churchill Factory and were not under the command of Tomison and Colen. Thompson was thoroughly exasperated and in late May 1796 drafted a letter of complaint to the committee. "From a review of the Proceedings of the Churchill People and from private Intelligence," he wrote, "I cannot help being of the opinion that they are very much averse to our coming into the Northward Country consider themselves of a different Interest and have accordingly privately opposed us to their utmost."

But he had no time to brood on the experience. Before leaving York Factory the previous summer, he had asked for and received permission from Joseph Colen to undertake in 1796 a journey of exploration from the confluence of the Reindeer and Churchill Rivers west to the eastern end of Lake Athabasca. As soon as the waterways were clear of ice that spring, he left for Fairford House, Malcolm Ross's post on the Reindeer, where he hoped to obtain men and materials.

Thompson learned a hard lesson about the workings of the company that summer. Senior officers might approve an expedition; that didn't mean they would ensure there was support for it. At Fairford House, Malcolm Ross had informed him that he could not spare anyone. This was discouraging news. Most men would not proceed on a journey of exploration unless supported by a large party, but Thompson was driven by an uncommon desire and an iron resolve to see new lands and, by chance, he found two Chipewyan Indians who were willing to accompany him. One was named Kozdaw. He was strong and possessed a carefree, adventurous spirit, while his friend, whom Thompson nicknamed Paddy because he could not pronounce the man's name, was quiet and introspective. They had come in with a party to trade at Fairford House. Both had some familiarity with the country ahead, having hunted on it for two winters, but they had no knowledge of the lakes and rivers in the summer, nor had they any experience in guiding a canoe through swift water or powerful currents.

Thompson also received little in the way of materials and supplies at Fairford House. There were no extra canoes at the post, so he built one that was seventeen feet long and thirty inches wide at the middle beam—large enough to navigate in big, unruly bodies of water. He and his companions set out on June 10, equipped with the bare essentials for survival: a gun for shooting waterfowl, forty lead balls, five pounds of lead shot, five pounds of gunpowder, a fishing net a hundred and thirty feet in length, three flints, a small axe and a grey cotton tent.

The first leg of the journey took them up the Reindeer River, sixty-four miles long and three hundred yards wide in many places, to a vast lake of the same name. The waters of this lake were clearer than any he had ever seen and pitted with rocky, spruce-covered islands. They paddled a hundred and eight miles up the west shore of Reindeer Lake and entered a small, shallow stream known as Paint River, and then travelled fifty miles west through a low, swampy, mosquito-infested country that brought them to Manitou Lake.

No white man had visited these lands and their waters, and not many Indians had either. "That these countries are unknown, even to the natives," Thompson wrote, "can excite no surprise; their canoes are small and when loaded with their Wives, Children and Baggage, are only fit for calm water, which is seldom seen on these Lakes; The east side of these two Lakes, have a range of full six hundred miles, on which there are no Woods, all is Rock and Moss."

Manitou Lake brought a striking change of scene. "All around," he wrote, "as far as the eye could see, were bold shores, the land rising several hundred feet in bold swells, all crowned with Forests of Pine." The Indians believed this lake had special powers because it sent forth its waters in two directions, east toward Reindeer Lake and west toward Athabasca, and so had named it Manitou. It, too, was a large and splendid body of water, and they coasted eighty miles along its western shore, without incident, till they arrived at the head of the Black River, which would carry them down to Lake Athabasca.

Thompson determined the length of the Black River to be 162 miles and described the land around it as "a wretched country of solitude, broken only by the large Gull and the Loon." There were many rapids and waterfalls on the Black, which absorbed the waters of several streams and lakes and grew in volume as it descended, and they spent a good part of the journey in the water, naked from the waist down, guiding the canoe past rocks and shoals and other obstructions.

But their exertions were rewarded. On July 2, 1796, they reached the mouth of the river and paddled into the long, narrow east end of Lake Athabasca. Thompson made an observation and later determined his position at fifty degrees, sixteen minutes and twenty-two seconds north of the equator and a hundred and five degrees, twenty-six minutes west of the prime meridian.

Having ascertained this, he was able to estimate that Lake Athabasca was some five hundred miles west of Churchill Factory, as the crow flies, and he had answered a question pondered and debated within the Hudson's Bay Co. from the early days of the fur trade, the days when the company's monopoly was intact and the northern Indians, whom the Cree called *Chi pu wi an*—the People Who Wear Pointed Skins (though they called themselves *Dene*—the People), would appear at Churchill or its predecessor, Prince of Wales's Fort, sporadically, unannounced, almost mysteriously, their canoes laden with rich, lustrous, high-quality beaver pelts harvested from the myriad streams and ponds of the Athabasca country.

That question—was there a direct route from Churchill Factory to the eastern end of Lake Athabasca?—had now been answered in the affirmative. But that only raised another question in the mind of David Thompson: What would the honourable company do with this most useful discovery?

Twice during their journey, they came to Indian camps, the first on June 25, while descending the Black River. They met five Chipewyan families who were hunting moose. The Chipewyans extended their usual hospitality and invited Thompson and his companions into their lodges to share a meal and spend the night, and the next morning the travellers left well fed and refreshed. The second occasion occurred on the return trip and was a godsend because by then all three were ragged and starving.

They had stayed only a short time at Lake Athabasca before turning back to ascend the Black River. About midway there was a waterfall with powerful rapids both above and below. They portaged around the falls and put the canoe back in the water. Thompson instructed his companions to tow it upstream with a rope. He remained in the stern, steering the vessel near the shore and out of the current. They had advanced about eighty yards when Kozdaw and Paddy encountered a birch tree at the edge of the water. An argument ensued. They could not decide whether the rope should pass to the left or the right of the tree.

The oncoming water pushed the stalled canoe to the centre of the river and the current swung it sideways. Thompson waved frantically at them to release the rope but they did not notice. He leapt to the front of the canoe and cut the rope with his pocket knife, but had no sooner done so than the canoe went over the falls, which were about twelve feet high, and dumped him into the roiling water below. He came to the surface with the canoe on top of him. He kicked it off, dragged it to shore and collapsed, bruised and exhausted, the sole of his left foot gashed from heel to toe.

Everything had been thrown from the canoe except his gun, an axe, a pewter basin and the tent. The Chipewyans searched downstream and retrieved the paddles, as well as his sextant box, which contained his instruments and papers. Thompson had saved his pocket knife, to the astonishment of his Indian companions, who thought it a sign of avarice to have held on to such a trifling item while facing death, but he now used it to start a fire by striking the blade against a flint to create sparks.

After drying their clothing and repairing the canoe with pine gum, they advanced a short way upstream that day. Once they had put up for the night and warmed themselves by the fire, Thompson thought about their situation. "It was now our destitute condition stared us in the face," he later wrote. "A barren country, without provisions, or the means of obtaining any, almost naked, and suffering from the weather, all before us very dark, but I had hopes that the Supreme Being through our great Redeemer to whom I made short prayers morning and evening would find some way to preserve us."

They would have to forage for food because they could not hunt or fish. They found nothing the next day, but the following afternoon, in a grassy bay off a small lake, they located a nest containing three young gulls, which yielded about four ounces of meat and merely sharpened their hunger. A day later, on another small lake, Kozdaw climbed a tree and plucked two baby eagles from their nest, while his companions hurled rocks to ward off the parents. Afterward, they divided the fat and flesh into three equal portions. Thompson and Paddy ate the fat first, saving the flesh for the next day, while Kozdaw consumed the flesh and rubbed the fat on his body. That night, Thompson and Paddy awoke violently ill with dysentery from eating the fat.

For the next several days, they survived on crowberries, which were bland and devoid of nutrition, and their morale sunk. "To the sixteenth of July, both Paddy and myself were now like skeletons," he wrote, "the effects of hunger and dysentry, from cold nights, and so weak that we thought it useless to go any further but die where we were." Thompson even used charcoal to etch a statement on a piece of birchbark so Kozdaw would not be accused of murder if they did not return. In the morning they decided to embark one last time, and that afternoon they were saved when they came upon two tents of Chipewyans, who nursed them back to health.

Thompson spent many hours during the winter of 1796–97 brooding about his future with the company. He was in the final year of his three-year contract. A new offer of employment would arrive on the annual supply ship and, coincidentally, Malcolm Ross planned to sail with that vessel when it returned to England.

The previous summer, while Thompson was off on his Athabasca expedition, Ross had given the standard one year's notice of his intention to retire from the service. He had held discussions with Joseph Colen and William Tomison about his successor and they had decided to appoint Thompson the new chief to northward, supervisor of the inland trade in the northern district. Ross had informed Thompson of these changes and they were not at all to his liking. He could see what lay ahead. He would be forced to devote most of his energy to the trade. There would be no time for exploration and surveying. As he contemplated these matters, a thought, once inconceivable, began to form in his mind: perhaps he should join the Canadians.

But what did he know of them? For a while not much—only what he heard from the officers of the company. That they were interlopers trespassing on lands granted to the honourable company by royal charter. That they were lowly pedlars, unlike the British traders, who were adventurers and gentlemen. That they were profane. That they lied to the Indians. That they debauched them with alcohol. That they were wild, unbridled men.

For a time, he accepted these views, but slowly he had begun to form his own opinions. In the winter of 1786–87, when he had been posted at South Branch House, he had met one of these men, William Thorburn, who was personable and forthcoming. He had encountered canoe brigades of Montrealers and admired the camaraderie that flourished among these men of very different cultures and temperament. Within their ranks, there were French Canadians, Englishmen, Scots and Americans. They enjoyed more freedom and autonomy than the employees of the Hudson's Bay Co. They displayed more daring and initiative, and all these things had made them dynamic and formidable competitors.

The Canadians had another advantage: they had organized. They had formed a powerful interest called the North West Co., based in the colonial town of Montreal, hundreds of miles and dozens of portages away. They had first challenged and then wrested control of the fur trade away from an imperial enterprise backed by the British Crown and the financial might of the City of London. He was impressed with them, but could he really desert from the Hudson's Bay Co. to join them, or should he do the safe thing and sign on for another three years with the only employer he had ever known?

These questions preoccupied him throughout the winter, which he spent at Reindeer Lake working under Ross. They had come up together from Fairford House in the last days of August with fourteen men, two Indian women and three children. He had chosen a site for a settlement near the mouth of the Paint River, but intended to go on and winter at a lake on the Black River, and Ross agreed to send him out with two canoes and five trustworthy young men.

They set out for the Black River on September 8, Thompson, Ross and ten men, five of whom would travel a short way and return with Ross to Reindeer Lake. Ross agreed to travel part of the way to Thompson's proposed wintering ground in order to see for himself this new route to Lake Athabasca, though he questioned the wisdom of this venture from the start. The Paint River was shallow and fed only by swamps; it had nearly dried up in many places. It was narrow and windy and strewn with deadfalls, and they spent nearly as much time carrying and pulling their canoes as paddling them.

On September 10, Ross noted in his journal, they got under way at 5 a.m., paddled one hundred yards and portaged three-quarters of a mile, paddled two miles and carried three-quarters of a mile, paddled three-quarters of a mile and carried half a mile, paddled a hundred and eighty yards and carried one mile. Two days later, Ross convinced Thompson that it was hopeless to proceed farther. They all returned to Reindeer Lake, and Ross glumly noted: "I am at a loss how I shall winter so many people in such a poor country."

They spent a hard, miserable winter on the shore of the big, crystalline lake. Their house, a mere twenty by twenty-four feet, was cramped and often smoky because the chimney of grass and mud would not carry the smoke aloft. The cold was deep and unrelenting. Snow fell on October 17 and remained. Reindeer Lake— deep, broad (one hundred miles wide in places) and long (two hundred and thirty miles)—was completely frozen over by mid-November. On December 15, the temperature fell to minus forty-two Fahrenheit and six days later it slipped even further, to minus fifty-six.

Food was scarce, as Ross noted in several journal entries: "17 Tichameg and 4 Trout which is small allowance for so many people," he wrote of the catch one November day. "How it will be with us before winter is out I do not know." Four days before Christmas, he noted: "24 Tichameg 5 trout, two Pike from the nets a very small allowance for 15 Englishmen and two women and 3 Children and very little likelihood of Relief from those cursed, useless Indians the more encouragement they get the more indolent they turn."

Thompson travelled many miles on Reindeer Lake hunting and fishing that winter and learned what he could from the Chipewyan. Once, he cut five holes in the ice, which was six feet thick, dropped a line with a baited hook down each, but caught nothing over two days. He then watched as an old native man, fishing about a hundred yards away, hauled out two trout in the space of an hour, each weighing around thirty pounds.

"He remarked to me that I came too soon and staid too late," Thompson would later write, "that the trout took bait only for a while after sunrise to near sunset, but that about noon was the best time; it has always appeared strange to me that a Trout in forty fathoms water, with a covering of full five feet thickness of ice, on a dark cloudy day, should know when the sun rises and sets, but it is so."

Most of what they knew about fishing, the Chipewyans would not share with him, though he gleaned some things by observing. "The bait for the Trout, the largest fish of the Lakes was the head half of a White Fish, well rubbed with Eagles fat, for want of it, other raw fat; but not greese that had been melted by the fire. The Pike and Pickerel take almost any thing, even a red flag; but the pride of these people is to angle the white Fish, an art known to only a few of the Men; they would not inform me of its composition, the few baits I examined appeared to be all the same, and the castorum of the Beaver worked into a thick paste, was the principal item; around were the fine red feathers of the Woodpecker, a grain of Eagles fat was on the top of the bait, and the hook was well hid in it."

Somewhere in his travels on Reindeer Lake he encountered traders of the North West Co. A small brigade of six men, led by Alexander Fraser, arrived in mid-April and established a post on the lake, about eighty miles south of the Hudson's Bay house. Where they met and how often, Thompson kept to himself; he committed nothing to his journal. But at one of their meetings, Fraser offered him employment.

The North West Co. needed someone with precisely his skills: a surveyor who was an experienced wilderness traveller, comfortable dealing with diverse Indian nations and capable of learning their languages. The Nor'Westers wanted lands surveyed from Lake

Superior west to Lake of the Woods and beyond to the Red River. Indians had been the sole occupants for longer than anyone remembered until early in the eighteenth century, when French-speaking fur traders began travelling an Indian road through this country to the interior, a road later adopted by the Nor'Westers.

Then, in 1783, after the War of Independence, British and American diplomats had partitioned these lands without ever seeing them or consulting the occupants. The Treaty of Paris defined the boundary between British and American possessions from the Bay of Fundy to the Lake of the Woods. The pertinent part of the treaty, for the Nor'Westers, was the clause stipulating that a border would be drawn "through Lake Superior Northward of Isles Royal & Phelipeaux to the Long Lake; Thence through the Middle of said Long Lake, and the Water Communication between it & the Lake of the Woods . . . Thence through the said Lake to the most North-westernmost Point thereof."

The North West Co. established trading posts between Lake Superior and Lake of the Woods in the years after the treaty was signed. They were scattered over hundreds of square miles of territory, and some stood on lands that might one day become American territory, though the Nor'Westers could not be certain because the langauge of the treaty was vague and confusing. None of this mattered much until 1794, when Britain and America signed Jay's Treaty, named after the lead U.S. negotiator, John Jay.

The treaty gave British interests until June 1, 1796, to evacuate what were then considered western posts, situated south and west of Lakes Erie and Michigan. It also gave British and American citizens joint access to lands drained by the Mississippi, and the future boundary was extended west of Lake of the Woods to the Mississippi. Taken together, the treaties meant a partitioning of lands on which the Nor'Westers were operating and shared access with American citizens.

The prudent thing to do, they decided, was to have a survey done to determine the location of their posts, as well as the major rivers and lakes, and so they extended an offer of employment to David Thompson. He readily accepted.

Thompson broke the news to Malcolm Ross on May 21, 1797, and Ross made a typically dry entry in the post journal: "2 Geese from the Indians   Mr. David Thompson acquainted me with his time being out with your Honours' and Thought himself a free born Subject and at liberty to choose any Service he thought to be more to his advantage and was to Quite your honours service and Enter the Canadian Company's Employ."

Two days later, at three-thirty in the morning, with snow falling and a hard northerly wind blowing, Thompson left the company house on Reindeer Lake with two French Canadians and two Indians. That night, camped with his companions on the shores of the snowbound lake, he made a brief entry in his journal that did no justice to the magnitude of the decision taken. "This day left the Service of the Hudsons Bay Co and entered that of the Company of Merchants from Canada   May God Almighty prosper me."

PART TWO

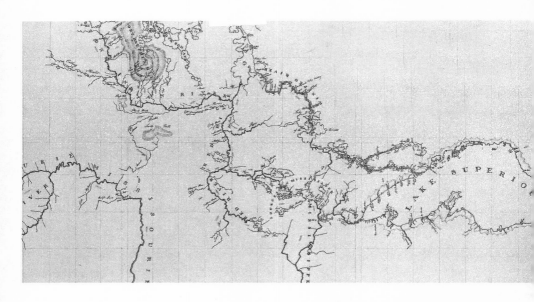

Thompson's travels, 1796–97: He covered 4,000 miles in 10 months and made a wintry trip to the Missouri River to meet the Mandans.

With the Nor'Westers

(1797)

THE EVENING MEAL WAS A LIVELY AFFAIR. CLERKS, GUIDES AND interpreters clustered around their tables, agents and partners at theirs—a hundred Nor'Westers most nights—and each plate was heaped high with an assortment of meats—beef, pork, ham and venison—as well as peas, corn and potatoes, with bread and butter on the side, all washed down with a choice of tea, wine or milk. There was always milk.

David Thompson sat at one of those tables, eating heartily but drinking slowly from his metal cup filled to the brim with thick, rich milk. He had not tasted milk in thirteen years, not since leaving Grey Coat School as a fourteen-year-old apprentice to the Company of Adventurers. He savoured each sip, poured a second cup and a third, and by then the meal was finished and the tables cleared. The revelry had begun.

There was liquor at every table and talk and laughter— enough to fill Grand Portage's large, rough-hewn dining hall—and music too, lively jigs and reels played by men on flute, fiddle and bagpipe. Graceful Indian women, who lived in the immense forests surrounding this wilderness depot on the northwest shore of Lake

Superior, came dressed in their finest attire and danced with the men. Thompson, a newcomer making his first visit, mostly watched and marvelled at the gaiety around him.

He had arrived July 22 with a brigade that set out a month earlier from Reindeer Lake, a thousand miles to the northwest. Canoemen, most of them French Canadian *hivernants,* or winterers, had paddled, and he had undertaken tracking surveys and, while portaging, had observed for latitude and longitude. They travelled down Reindeer River and a short way on the Churchill before turning south and paddling and portaging to the Saskatchewan, paying a brief visit to Cumberland House.

They continued downriver to Lake Winnipeg, crossed to the east shore and travelled south some two hundred miles to the mouth of a short, surly river of the same name. Thirty-two times in the space of 125 miles they were forced ashore to portage around raging rapids and thunderous waterfalls. The Winnipeg brought them to Lake of the Woods—all islands and channels in the north, but a broad, clear bay in the south, which they crossed to reach Rainy River. Beyond the Rainy was a land that seemed equal parts rock and forest and water, and beyond that was the Pigeon River and the start of *le grand portage*—the great carrying place.

Here, they left their canoes, sleek, sturdy *canots du nord,* twenty-four feet long, four to five feet wide and capable of carrying 2,900 pounds of furs plus five men, their luggage and provisions. Every man hoisted a ninety-pound bale of furs to his back. These they carried to the first staging place, where they stopped, returned to the canoes and brought forward the rest of the things. Then they repeated the process: advancing to a staging place and going back for another load. They hauled everything to the summit of a long, steep ridge, crossed a valley and surmounted another ridge—taking five days to cover nine miles—before Lake Superior's cold, blue waters came into view.

Thompson first saw Grand Portage from above. He saw the post standing on the shore of a small bay and beyond that the lake stretching to the horizon. He saw the steep-pitched roofs of the buildings—there were sixteen of them protected by stockades—and, on the shore, dozens of overturned canoes, beautiful thirty-six-foot-long *canots des maîtres,* up from Montreal, each paddled by eight to ten men and big enough to carry 4,500 pounds of merchandise, including liquor. On the grounds outside the stockades, he saw a crowd, more people in one place than he'd seen since leaving London.

More than twelve hundred men—almost the entire workforce of the North West Co.—had assembled for the annual rendez-vous at this otherwise solitary wilderness post. There were the voyageurs—wind-burned, carefree French Canadians who wore red caps and brightly coloured sashes and provided the muscle that moved the entire enterprise. There were also the comers and goers, or pork eaters, so called because they mainly ate a dish called hominy—corn that had been boiled, dried, boiled again and mixed with fat to make a pudding. The pork eaters paddled the *canots des maîtres* up from Montreal and they camped alongside the voyageurs in tents outside the stockades or slept under their vessels and spent their days drinking, singing, talking and sometimes quarrelling among themselves while awaiting orders to leave for Montreal or the interior.

There were clerks, guides and interpreters, along with the partners, or shareholders who controlled the company, and they enjoyed comfortable lodgings and fine meals inside the post. By day, they were preoccupied with business. Furs were sorted and repacked for transport to Montreal. Merchandise was divided into ninety-pound packs, or pieces, for the journey to the interior. Accounts were settled. Contracts renewed or terminated. Strategies for expansion of the trade were discussed and debated and men were assigned to the various districts of the northwest. When the day's work was done, the Nor'Westers took their places in the dining hall for the evening meal.

Thompson resided among these men while he was at Grand Portage, and he was full of questions about the company and its operations. From the guides, he learned about treacherous rapids, long portages and dangerous lake crossings. From the interpreters, he heard about the ways and habits of natives unknown to him— the Ojibway, the Sioux and the Stone, or Assiniboine Indians.

He met the traders who had come in from all corners of the North West Co.'s vast network of trading posts: from the Nipigon country on Superior's north shore; from the Muskrat country on the west coast of Hudson Bay; and from the major rivers of the interior—the Red, the Assiniboine, Saskatchewan and the Churchill. He met the partners who wintered in the interior and he met William McGillivray, nephew of the imperious Simon McTavish, and Alexander Mackenzie, the renowned explorer.

McGillivray and Mackenzie were the Montreal-based agents of McTavish and his firm, McTavish, Frobisher and Co., which held a controlling interest in the North West Co., and several times Thompson was summoned to the fireplace in the dining hall where these men and the wintering partners plotted their next move in the battle against the Hudson's Bay Co.

Seated amongst them, Thompson had no regrets about switching sides. He had been a faithful and productive servant of the Company of Adventurers for thirteen years, had earned the trust of his superiors and conducted business profitably despite all the attendant risks. He had been deemed useful, and the men who ran the company conferred no higher praise upon employees. For a time, he had been flattered.

Gradually, that word—*useful*—had become distasteful. He knew he could never aspire to anything more than being useful. He would remain a trader preoccupied with accounts and ledgers, revenues and profits so long as he was employed by the Hudson's Bay Co. He could dream of exploring and surveying and of one day creating a grand map of all the lands he had seen and surveyed, but he would never fulfill his dream.

Things were different here, very different, he thought, among these bold, ambitious merchants from Canada. They aspired to more than turning a profit and paying a dividend. They were moved by what he called a liberal and public spirit. They were committed to exploration and discovery. They were determined to extend their operations as far and wide as possible. They wanted their lands surveyed. They wanted to know the courses of the rivers they used, the size and shapes of the lakes they crossed and the positions of their trading posts.

To achieve all these things, they made David Thompson astronomer and surveyor of the North West Co. and, during his first, short stay at Grand Portage, they gave him an assignment that went beyond anything he could have hoped for with the Hudson's Bay Co. He was to find the source of the Mississippi River and to delineate the forty-ninth parallel west from Lake of the Woods to at least the Red River, which had come to be accepted as the divide between British and American territory in the northwestern interior. He was to extend his surveys below the forty-ninth to the Missouri River and visit the villages of the Mandan Indians in order to persuade these fair-skinned farmers of the Missouri to come north to trade at company posts. He was to make enquiries of the Indians about fossilized remains of large animals and was given papers instructing trading-post commanders to back his endeavours with men and materials.

Thompson left Grand Portage on August 9 with a brigade of four canoes under the command of Hugh McGillis, a senior employee in charge of the company's Swan River district. Over the next three months, Thompson travelled hundreds of miles. He returned to the interior via the voyageurs' road—Pigeon River to Rainy River to Lake of the Woods and down the Winnipeg River to the big lake of the same name. They crossed Lake Winnipeg, paddled up the Dauphin River to Lake Manitoba, which they crossed, and then portaged to Lake Winnipegosis. They paddled up the west shore of this lake, and on September 19 the party split up.

McGillis and some of his men took one river, the Red Deer, to their wintering place while Thompson ascended another, the Shoal, to Swan Lake and on to the company's Swan River post, where he put up his canoe and travelled by horse. He visited trading houses in the district, determined the position of each post by astronomical observations and got to know the men in charge, most of whom he had scarcely met at Grand Portage.

He stayed with McGillis, William Thorburn, John McDonell, Cuthbert Grant and the Frenchman Belleau and he met the Indians—the Nehiayawaks, or Cree, to whom this country belonged, the Ojibways, or Chippeways, from the forests north and west of Superior, and a sprinkling of natives from the forests of Canada: Nipissings, Algonquins and Iroquois. All of these peoples were prosperous. Many wrapped themselves in scarlet cloaks and wore fine, brightly coloured attire. Men, women and children wore silver earrings and other jewellery and adorned their garments with brooches.

The Indians harvested the pelts, which the traders hauled down to Superior each spring. Beaver were plentiful here and powerful. These sagacious animals, Thompson wrote, were in full possession of the country. He speculated that he was seeing things as they were before the European discovery of Canada some 320 years earlier when two classes of beings—mankind and the beaver—dominated the northern half of the continent from the Atlantic to the Rocky Mountains and north to the margins of the Arctic.

Frequently, he and his guides had to cross flooded terrain or detour around ponds the size of small lakes created by beaver dams. One such diversion added forty miles to a trip of a hundred and eleven miles. Another time, Thompson and his guide were crossing a beaver dam a mile long, which was covered with earth and overgrown with grass and appeared to be a strip of land. They walked their horses across and looked out over a body of water one and a half miles square in which there were fifty-two beaver lodges clustered together to resemble a village. Along the way, they met an elderly Indian, a man of about eighty, who invited them to spend the night in his teepee, which he shared with another elderly man as well as several women and children. They were Cree, and Thompson spoke their language, so they spent the evening in conversation.

The old men told him that the beaver were being destroyed and this was happening because the great spirit was angry with them, as he had been once before in ancient times when these animals were a people and lived on dry land. "They were always beavers, not men," Thompson recalled one of the old Indians saying. "They were wise and powerful and neither man nor any animal made war on them.

"They were well clothed as at present and as they did not eat meat they made no use of fire and did not want it. How long they lived this way we cannot tell, but we must suppose they did not live well for the great spirit became angry with them and ordered Weesaukejauk, the trickster, to drive them all into the water and there let them live, still to be wise but without power; to be food and clothing for man and the prey of other animals, against which his defence shall be his dams, his house and his burrows.

"You see how strong he makes his dams. Those that we make for fishing weirs are often destroyed by the water, but his always stand. His house is not made of sand or loose stones, but of strong earth with wood and sometimes small stones and he makes burrows to escape from his enemies and he always has his winter stock of provisions. When he cuts down a tree you see how he watches it and takes care that it shall not fall on him. But if he is so wise, for what purpose does the beaver cut down large trees of which he makes no use whatever? We do not know; perhaps an itching of his teeth and gums.

"I have told you that we believe in years long passed away the great spirit was angry with the beaver and ordered Weesaukejauk to drive them all from the dry land into the water and they became and continued to be very numerous. But the great spirit has been and now is very angry with them and they are now all to be destroyed. About two winters ago, Weesaukejauk showed to our brethren, the Nipissings and Algonquins, the secret of their destruction; that all of them were infatuated with the love of the castorum of their own species, and more fond of it than we are of fire water. We are now killing the beaver without any labour. We are now rich, but we shall soon be poor for when the beaver are destroyed we have nothing to depend on to purchase what we want for our families. Strangers now overrun our country with their iron traps and we and they will soon be poor."

Thompson knew that the old men were correct about the destruction of the beaver. He knew why it was happening, though he did not know what could be done about it. He had seen the power of iron traps baited with castorum—a reddish brown substance with an oily feel and a bitter taste. It was extracted from the groin of the beaver, ground into a paste with aspen buds and spread on willow branches, which were placed at the edge of the water. A trap was set just beneath the surface and the beaver were caught as they came ashore to take the bait. Once, he and some companions found a trap with a severed leg in it, the beaver having gnawed its limb off in order to escape, but two nights later the same animal was caught again. On another occasion, a beaver managed to swim away with a trap fastened to its thigh and was later found caught fast in another trap.

Indians of the east coast had first begun baiting their traps with castorum a few years earlier, and the method quickly displaced other, more laborious ways of killing beaver. Indians elsewhere adopted the trap and rapidly wiped out the beaver in their hunting grounds. By the time Thompson had joined the Nor'Westers, natives of the eastern forests—Nipissings, Algonquins and Iroquois—had begun moving onto the prairie with their traps. "Every intelligent man saw the poverty that would follow the destruction of the beaver," he later wrote, "but there were no chiefs to control it; all was perfect liberty and equality."

The French Canadians and their dogs created an awful ruckus out there on the prairie. There were seven men and thirty dogs hauling sleds loaded with trade goods, a little caravan travelling south to the Missouri River and the villages of the Mandan. They had acquired the dogs—strong, feisty mongrels—from the Stone, or Assiniboine, Indians, who were always rich in dogs but poor in horses. The beasts were used to carrying goods on their backs when the Indians moved from camp to camp, but were unaccustomed to wearing a harness and pulling a sled. They yelped and snarled, barked and balked, and their masters hurled obscenities and lashed their flanks to keep them moving.

Thompson liked these tough, good-humoured, illiterate men who routinely consumed eight pounds of meat a day, but found the din they created unbearable. He rode or walked two to three miles ahead—accompanied by his personal assistant, Joseph Boisseau, the guide René Jussome and the interpreter Hugh McCracken, an Irishman who had lived several seasons among the Mandan—while the French Canadians and their dogs followed the trail across the frozen, snowbound plain.

The snow was three inches deep and the temperature minus twenty when they set out November 27 from a company post near the confluence of the Assiniboine and Souris Rivers, a hundred and sixty miles west of the southern tip of Lake Winnipeg. They followed the Souris, or Mouse, southwest across the prairie, travelling in the broad, shallow valley of this modest stream, which was rarely more than fifteen yards across. Here and there, they found groves of poplar and aspen, as well as ash, elm and oak, to provide firewood and shelter from the wind.

The wind always blew in this part of the country. It hummed. It howled and sometimes it hit the prairie with a roar that sounded to Thompson like the sea crashing upon a rocky shore. It gave the cold a harsh bite. On successive days at the end of November and the start of December, he recorded temperatures of minus twenty-seven, minus thirty-two, minus thirty-seven and minus thirty-six. But the weather could change quickly and catch travellers exposed and vulnerable.

This happened on December 5, when Thompson and his men set off across open prairie for a wooded upland called Turtle Hill. It was minus thirteen at seven-thirty in the morning, but by early afternoon the temperature had risen to near freezing. The wind had grown to a gale and their destination was nowhere in sight. "All before and around us a boundless plain and Mons. Jussome could not say where we were," Thompson later recalled. "The weather appeared threatening and preparing for a storm. Our situation was alarming and anxiety was on the face of every man for we did not know to which hand to turn ourselves for shelter."

Thompson mounted his horse and rode to a slight elevation. He scanned the horizon in every direction with his telescope, but saw nothing except a few black specks in the northwest, which he took to be trees. He decided to proceed that way, relying on his compass to guide them. The French Canadians did not believe in such devices and went their own way, but soon turned back and followed him. They walked against the storm all afternoon. Darkness fell and they had to shout to each other to ensure that no one got lost. At seven o'clock, having travelled thirteen miles in six hours, they finally reached the woods and erected their tents.

Five days later, Thompson and his men again came close to perishing in a storm as they attempted to reach Turtle Hill. They broke camp at seven-thirty in the morning. It was minus twenty, and they had to cross twenty-two miles of barren prairie. "We walked at a good pace for some time," he wrote. "A gentle south wind arose; and kept increasing; by 10 AM it was a heavy Gale, with high drift and dark weather, so much so that I had to keep the Compass in my hand, for I could not trust the Wind.

"By Noon it was a perfect Storm, we had no alternative but to proceed, which we did slowly and with great labor, for the Storm was ahead, and the snow drift in our faces. Night came on, I could no longer see the Compass, and had to trust to the Wind; the weather became mild with small rain, but the Storm continued with darkness; some of the foremost called to lie down where we were, but as it was evident we were ascending a gentle rising ground, we continued and soon thank good Providence, my face struck against some Oak saplings, and I passed the word that we were in the Woods, a fire was quickly made, and as it was on an elevated place it was seen afar off.

"As yet the only one with me, was my servant who led the Horse, and we anxiously awaited the others; they came hardly able to move, one, and then another, and in something more than half an hour, nine had arrived; each with Dogs and Sleds, but one Man, and a Sled with the Dogs were missing; to search for the latter was useless: but how to find the former, we were at a loss: and we remained so for another half an hour, when we thought we heard his voice, the Storm was still rageing, we extended ourselves within call of each other, the most distant man heard him plainly, went to him, raised him up, and with assistance brought him to the fire. At 7 1/2 PM Ther 36 being four degrees above the freezing point . . . making in little more than twelve hours a difference in temperature of fifty six degrees. I had weathered many a hard gale, but this was the most distressing day I had yet seen."

On December 30, after travelling 238 miles in thirty-three days—a journey of ten days in good weather—Thompson and his men reached the Mandan villages, which were surrounded by stockades to defend against roving bands of armed and mounted Sioux warriors. The Mandan lived in dome-shaped dwellings of wood and mud, about eighteen feet high and thirty to forty across, roomy enough for an extended family and their horses. They welcomed the visitors—Thompson, who had come on business, and the French Canadians, who had made this arduous journey for other reasons that soon became apparent.

———

The next day, Thompson stood before the men of the principal Mandan village, his interpreter at his side, and made a brief speech. He had come, he said, as a representative of the North West Co. of merchants of Canada, a distant land beyond the big lakes to the east, and had come in peace and friendship. His men, the French Canadians, most of whom had stopped at the uppermost village on the Missouri, had brought sleds laden with tobacco and ammunition, axes and wool clothing and many other goods that the Mandan would find useful and pleasing.

The merchants of Canada wished to supply them with such things, but the journey was long and perilous and they could not come often. He hoped they would consider bringing their furs and hides and any surplus food to the company house situated where the Assiniboine and Souris Rivers came together. Afterward, he presented a three-foot roll of tobacco and a fine lace coat to the leading chief, Big White Man, who passed the coat around for all to inspect.

There were five Mandan villages and two camps of Fall Indians, allies of the Mandan, within a few miles of each other. Thompson visited each of them. He counted the houses and estimated the total number of inhabitants at just under three thousand. At one of his stops, he met a French Canadian named Manoah, who had lived with these Indians many years, married a Mandan woman and in every way had become one of them.

Manoah informed him that the Mandan had previously inhabited the partly wooded country east of Red River and north of the headwaters of the Mississippi, but had been driven from these lands, in the time of their grandfathers, by the Chippeway Indians, who would emerge from the forests armed with guns, knives and axes obtained from the white fur traders. The marauders would attack their villages, then return to the forest where they could not be pursued.

Thompson found the Mandan villages clean and the inhabitants polite and orderly, but was shocked by what he learned of

*Mandan buffalo boats and village: Thompson came to trade,
his men to avail themselves of the Indian women.*

their sexual practices. Jussome and McCracken described a ceremony that took place each summer, one they had both experienced, and more than once, though neither could explain its
meaning. It lasted three days. On the first two, the men and women
wandered about aimlessly shrieking and feigning grief. This continued again on the third day until the men assembled and sat in a
line on the ground. The women came together opposite them. One
by one, the women selected partners other than their husbands
and led them away and lay with them.

Jussome and McCracken hinted that the French Canadians
had been enjoying the company of the Mandan women since their
arrival, and upon inquiring Thompson found this to be true. "The
curse of the Mandans is an almost total want of chastity," he later

wrote. "This the men with me knew and I found it was almost their sole motive for their journey hereto: The goods they brought, they sold at 50 to 60 per cent above what they cost; and reserving enough to pay their debts, and buy some corn; the rest they spent on women."

Snowshoeing through drifts three feet deep on Reindeer Lake, at the fifty-eighth parallel of latitude, was discernibly different from doing the same thing ten degrees farther south in the valley of the Red River and its tributaries, as Thompson learned later that winter when he embarked on a journey of discovery to the headwaters of the Mississippi. Farther north, the snow was dry and powdery and disappeared slowly during the long, frost-filled spring. He had once melted a cubic foot of tightly packed snow at Reindeer Lake and it yielded two inches of water in a pot, whereas the same amount of denser, heavier Red River snow produced four to five inches. It melted quickly in the spring and flooded mile upon mile of flat, low-lying land.

Thompson, with three of his men and an Indian guide, had left from the Souris River post on February 26, 1798, about three weeks after returning from the Mandan villages. The others stationed there advised against a mid-winter expedition, and he too had his doubts, which he expressed in a journal entry: "The gentleman"—John Macdonell, the master of the house—"laughed at this scheme as a piece of Quixotism. How far I shall succeed Heaven knows."

The small party travelled down the Assiniboine River to the Red and proceeded up this river. They were travelling south and the journey soon became arduous. "Very deep Snoe, which supported by high strong Grass renders it almost impossible for our Dogs to haul the Sleds," Thompson wrote in his journal on March 3. Two days later, he noted: "At 3 1/2 PM put up   exceeding heavy deep walking and very bad hauling   the Snow wet." The following day, both he and the Indian fell through the ice, and on March 8 his journal entry read: "Gale NE wind   thick driving snow very bad night   we exposed to it got all our Bedding & clothes wet   no way to dry them."

On the twelfth, they came to an Ojibway camp of four lodges, but the Indians were inhospitable and did not ask them in to warm themselves. The men cleared a place in the snow to build a fire and at noon Thompson took out his instruments to observe for latitude. Curious, the Ojibway inquired about the strange white man. The guide told them he knew as little as they did, except that this adventuresome individual had travelled all over the world and was highly respected by everyone.

"Their superstitions got the better of their reason," Thompson wrote, "the largest and best lodge was cleared out for me and I was ushered in with all ceremony   not a soul dared to speak or stir for fear of me and my Instruments   in the evening all the Men to about 35 with my guide came in and set down about 5 feet from me forming 3 Ranks   as I was vexed with their illiberal treatment of me and my Men I took no notice of them and such was the power of their Fears that they did not dare to speak till they saw me laying my head down to sleep when a venerable old Man in a trembling voice begging me not to be offended for presuming to speak begged pardon for their not having received me better and begged their Lives with the lives of their women & Children and that the Animals might be permitted to remain on their Lands or they would die of hunger."

The old man spoke for half an hour before Thompson assured him that he was mortal, and as weak as they, and that they would not be harmed provided they worshipped only the great spirit and no man.

Thompson and his men next visited three company posts, all of which were south of the forty-ninth parallel and therefore beyond recognized British territory according to his observations. They stayed a week at the third house with Jean Baptiste Cadotte and his wife, then continued on their way, but conditions got worse. On March 30, Thompson's journal entry read: "Almost the whole of our Road has been from the ancle to the calf of the Leg in Water   the sleds floated along."

The prairie had become impassable. He and his men retreated to Cadotte's post, which was east of the Red on a tributary river. This time, they stayed nine days, and during their visit an Ojibway chief named Sheshepaskut, or Sugar, arrived with several of his men. Thompson judged Sheshepaskut to be about sixty but his physical vigour and handsome countenance made him appear younger.

Thompson inquired about his people and their customs, but was especially interested in the warfare between them and their southerly neighbours, the Cheyenne and the Sioux. He addressed Sheshepaskut in Cree. The Indian responded in Ojibway, a language very similar to Cree, but Thompson did not understand, and Cadotte, a well-educated man who spoke French, English and Ojibway and understood Latin, interpreted.

Thompson had heard about a massacre of Ojibway at Sand Lake on the Mississippi in February 1797. Sheshepaskut explained that the people had ventured from their forested homelands in the spring one year before that to draw syrup from a rich stand of untapped maples. The Sioux ignored the first incursion into these lands, which were on the margins of their own. But when it happened again, three hundred Sioux warriors fell upon the sixty-seven Ojibway and slaughtered every man, woman and child. The incident had rekindled Ojibway hatred of the Sioux, but vengeance was impossible because the Sioux had horses and were now masters of the plains.

The Ojibway had been at peace with the Cheyenne for several years and even traded for the squash and corn they grew until an Ojibway hunting party disappeared one summer. Sheshepaskut's people assumed the Sioux were responsible. But while on a trading mission, an Ojibway woman saw a Cheyenne hunter with a scalp taken from one of the missing men.

The following summer, Sheshepaskut led a war party of a hundred and fifty men to avenge this act. He explained to Thompson all the preparations that were made, their journey to the Cheyenne camp and how their scouts had watched for six days. They attacked after a large party of men had departed on horseback to hunt buffalo.

"We entered the village and put everyone to death, except three women," Sheshepaskut told Thompson. "After taking everything we wanted, we quickly set fire to the village and with all haste retreated for those that fled at our attack would soon bring back the whole party and we did not wish to encounter cavalry in the plains."

Sheshepaskut stopped there and lit his pipe, and Cadotte took over. He said the Ojibway made prisoners of the three women, one of whom had an eight-month-old infant. Instead of taking scalps, they decapitated the corpses of twelve men left behind to guard the camp and carried the heads in sacks back to their camp at Rainy River. A day after their return, a war dance was held to celebrate the victory.

"The war circle being made by the men, their wives and children standing behind them, the three prisoners were placed within the circle," Cadotte said. "The heads were taken out of the bags and preparatory to their being scalped, the whole circle of men, women and children with tambours, rattles and flutes shouted the war whoop and danced to the song of victory.

"The prisoner woman with her infant in her arms did not dance but gently moved away to where the head of her husband was lying, and catching it up, kissed it and placed it to the lips of her infant. It was taken from her and thrown on the ground. A second time she seized it and did the same. It was again taken from her and thrown on the ground. A third time she pressed the head of her husband to her heart, to the lips of herself and child. It was taken from her with menace of death. Holding up her infant to heaven, she drew a sharp pointed knife from her bosom, plunged it into her heart and fell dead on the head of her husband."

Sheshepaskut added: "The Great Spirit had made her a woman, but had given her the heart of a man."

By early April, the country was still not fit for travel. The winds were cold, the trees bare, the waterways clogged with jumbled, broken ice and the land flooded. But what did it matter? Cadotte gave them an eighteen-foot *canot du nord* and they set off. They had to break a path through the ice with hatchets and poles. Elsewhere they trudged through frigid, knee-deep water and towed the canoe and luggage. Perseverance was the motto of the North West Co., and Thompson would persevere.

He was eager to impress his new employers. The Nor'Westers had posts on the headwaters of the Mississippi, though the returns were scant because beaver and other fur-bearing animals were scarce and the natives poor. The company's access to these lands was in jeopardy because of events that had occurred since the signing of the Treaty of Paris in 1783. A number of commercial disputes, including the retention of British fur-trading posts in the Ohio River valley, the Michigan territory and around Lake Michigan on the American frontier, had brought the two nations to the brink of war by the early 1790s. Most of the outstanding issues were resolved in Jay's Treaty, signed in 1794, which stipulated that British posts south of the Great Lakes had to be abandoned by June 1, 1796, though the Mississippi was open to citizens of both nations.

The Nor'Westers anticipated that their posts south and west of Lake Superior might be on contested land, or on land clearly granted to America by treaty. They feared the U.S. government would dispatch representatives to assert its sovereignty and were depending on Thompson to determine, by astronomical observations, whether their posts stood in British or American territory. Duty pushed him on, but so did his enormous desire to see new lands. He would never wait for good weather, or choose comfort over exploration.

Thompson and his companions left Cadotte's house on April 9, and on April 27, after an arduous journey of only fifty-six miles, reached what he took to be the source of the Mississippi, a body of water called Turtle Lake, which was four miles long by four wide and so named because its shoreline resembled the profile of a turtle. His observations placed the lake at forty-seven degrees, thirty minutes latitude north of the equator, about a hundred and fifty miles south of where the British and American diplomats assumed it to be based on a 1755 map of North America. He also determined that several of the company posts were well below the forty-ninth parallel, the generally accepted limits of British territory, and therefore were at risk of being lost if America were to begin claiming more territory or asserting sovereignty in this part of the continent.

From Turtle Lake, Thompson and his men followed the sinuous Turtle Creek that flowed to Red Cedar Lake, where the Mississippi became more robust. They covered sixty-eight miles in three days and stopped at the Sand Lake River, near the site of the Sioux massacre of the Ojibway the previous year. Here they turned east toward Superior and began a remarkable leg of their journey.

On May 19, they reached a company post at the mouth of the St. Louis River, at the westernmost tip of the lake, and exchanged their small *canot du nord* for a twenty-eight-foot vessel outfitted with oars and sail. Nine days later, they arrived at the falls of St. Marie at the southeast corner of Superior, where the lake discharged its waters. They had travelled 671 miles, and Thompson had taken astronomical observations and conducted tracking surveys along the entire shoreline.

Alexander Mackenzie was at the falls, en route from Montreal to the rendez-vous at Grand Portage, and upon receiving a report of Thompson's efforts, and learning that he had travelled nearly four thousand miles since the previous autumn, the celebrated explorer declared: "He has performed more in ten months than I expected could be done in two years."

In September 1798, while travelling to his wintering ground, Thompson stopped at a company post at Isle a la Crosse, near the headwaters of the Churchill River, and was introduced to a strong, capable Cree woman. She was the wife of a former trader named Patrick Small and worked there to provide for her three children: Nancy, Patrick Jr., who was employed in the trade, and bright, perky Charlotte, who had just turned thirteen.

Small had spent about fifteen years in the trade. He had come to Canada from his native Scotland in the mid-1770s, carrying with him a few bags, and in one of them a letter of introduction to help him get started. The letter was from a great-uncle, Gen. John Small, to an old friend and fellow Scot, Simon McTavish, then an ambitious and talented Montreal merchant and a rising power among the colonial town's enterprising fur-trading houses.

Small arrived at an opportune moment. The Montrealers were enjoying a triumphant decade in the northwest. Their traders and canoemen had taken a good chunk of the Hudson's Bay Co.'s business. The lustrous furs flowing from the interior were beginning to produce handsome profits, and the merchants realized that by joining forces, and reducing the competition among themselves, they could increase those profits, which led, in 1779, to the formation of the original North West Co., a partnership of eight trading houses, each with two shares.

Small advanced rapidly. He became a partner in McTavish and Co. and in 1778–79 was sent west to winter on the Churchill River. He resided in the interior for the next thirteen years, mostly at Isle a la Crosse Lake, one of the North West Co.'s remotest outposts. He became a very capable trader and was rewarded with two of sixteen shares issued in the reorganized North West Co. of 1783. And when, in 1787, another restructuring took place, and the number of shares increased to twenty-four, Small retained his holdings.

Soon, he was prosperous. His shares rose in value and he had saved most of the salary he had earned during his wilderness years. In 1791, Small sold his shares, collected his savings and retired from the fur trade. He left the northwest for a comfortable life in London and abandoned his Cree wife and their three young children.

Thompson's initial encounter with Small's family was brief. He and his brigade of twelve French Canadians spent only a day at Isle a la Crosse, but he thought often of Charlotte Small that winter and was tempted to write, though he suspected she could not read. He wondered how such a fleeting acquaintance could have made such a powerful impression. They had exchanged just a few words but he had been struck by her and she by him. He was certain of that because he had seen her eyes fastened upon him and she had come down to the water to see him off.

He had started up the Beaver River in one of three canoes paddled by the French Canadians. They travelled south for several days before the river took a big turn west. They arrived at Lac La Biche, their destination, in early October, a month after their stop at Isle a la Crosse and almost three months after leaving Grand Portage.

The snow and cold had arrived ahead of them, and the men were irritable and quarrelsome as they erected their houses at the new Lac La Biche post, but the winter passed quietly and in the latter half of March 1799 Thompson set off to explore and survey this part of the country.

Over the next two months, he and a small entourage of five or fewer travelled more than seven hundred miles on horseback and by canoe and followed a roughly circular route that took them south to the North Saskatchewan River, west to the Pembina River, north on the Pembina to the Athabasca, and down the Athabasca to the point where the Clearwater River emptied into it. From there they went east on the Clearwater and over the Methy Portage, which brought them into the watershed of the Churchill and down to Isle a la Crosse.

In the final days of this journey, Thompson was anxious and excited. It was the prospect of seeing Charlotte Small again that stirred him up. They arrived May 20 and he was relieved that she had not taken up with someone else.

He began courting her immediately, and she was taken with this man who was handsome and sincere and different from most she had known. He wanted a partner for life, not a country wife to be left behind when he retired from the trade. He would not have children and abandon them like so many others—even her own father—had done. But life with him would not be easy and he was honest about that. They would travel farther and more frequently than her Cree forefathers and would encounter hazards and hardships, but all this she was prepared to accept.

On June 10, 1799, Thompson married Charlotte Small without fanfare or celebration, according to the customs of the Cree. Each consented to the union, her mother approved it, and they became man and wife. He was twenty-nine, his bride thirteen. Shortly afterward, they set off down the Churchill River on the long journey to Grand Portage, and their life together had begun.

In autumn 1800, David and Charlotte were preparing to winter at Rocky Mountain House, the company's most westerly post on the North Saskatchewan River. Charlotte was pregnant with their first child and stayed close to the house after they arrived in late September. Her husband and Duncan McGillivray (William's brother) were instructed by Simon McTavish, McGillivray's uncle and the most powerful individual in the North West Co., to cross the mountains and establish a trade with the Indians of the western slopes. For twenty-five years, the Nor'Westers had been trying to remain one step ahead of the Hudson's Bay Co. on the Saskatchewan. The race had brought the rivals from Lake Winnipeg to the rolling, forested foothills of the Rockies, which stood—majestic and formidable—on the horizon.

The competition for furs had intensified with the formation of the New Northwest Co.—commonly known as the XY Co. because its packages of furs and trade good were marked with the letters XY to distinguish them from those of the North West Co. The new firm was a partnership of two Montreal trading houses that was as well financed as the original North West Co., though not as strong in the field. And one district after another to the east had been trapped out, forcing the Nor'Westers to look beyond the mountains.

Thompson left on October 5. Old Bear, his Piegan guide, rode at the head of the line, followed by Thompson, five Canadians, a Cree named He Dog and three pack horses. Old Bear led them up the Clearwater River, a tributary of the North Saskatchewan, and overland to the Red Deer River. They followed the Red Deer west toward the Rockies to meet a party of Kootenay Indians coming across the mountains to trade.

On their second day out, as he and his companions trekked up the Red Deer, Thompson observed that the river was once five hundred yards wide and had carved different channels, separated by gravel banks, but now was no more than fifty yards across in most places and rarely exceeded two hundred. This aroused his curiosity. That night, as he sat near the fire recording the day's events in his journal, he speculated about the powerful and mysterious forces that had so changed the river.

"Let us ask the Cause of this," he wrote. "Is it that the heavy Rains and melting of the Snows have carried away such Quantities of the Particles of the Mountain as greatly to have diminished it's height and therefore does not attract the Clouds & Vapours so strongly as formerly; or that the Earth and Oceans in these climes do not yield the Vapours so freely as of Old; or if they do, are they driven by some unknown Cause to break and dissolve before they reach the Mountains? Whatever opinion we may form, the Fact is certain, that at present and for several Years past the Mountains do not send forth above two thirds of the Water they did formerly, for we see upon the Banks of all the Rivers large Trees that have been carried down by the Stream, and left either a great way from their present Boundaries, or a great Height upon the Banks far above the greatest known level of present Times."

Nine days after setting out, Thompson and his party met the Kootenays. Twenty-six men and seven women, led by four elderly males, had made the journey. They were poorly dressed and had with them eleven horses, but complained that they had been harassed by Piegan warriors, who had stolen most of their horses. The Piegan were hard, fierce people. They lived on the western frontier of Blackfoot country, and were responsible for protecting their brethren, the Blackfoot and the Bloods, from enemies who came over the mountains.

The Piegan had no intention of letting the Kootenays pass unmolested through their lands to Rocky Mountain House, where the white traders would supply them with guns, knives, hatchets and other goods that would make them strong in battle. A large party of Piegan warriors shadowed the traders and the Kootenays and sometimes confronted them.

In his journal entry of October 15, Thompson noted: "We arrived at the Camp, about an Hour after Sun Set, very much fatigued by the Badness of the Roads. The poor Kootenaes were hardly arrived when one of the Pekenow Scoundrels took a Fancy to a Black Horse belonging to them, & wanted to take him by force—but the Kootenaes bravely springing upon their Arms, he was obliged to relinquish his Prize."

Overnight, the Piegan stole five horses, including Thompson's and another belonging to one of his men. Later that day, three young Piegan blocked the trail, took hold of the horse of the leading Kootenay and tried to force him to turn back. But the Kootenays were courageous souls, as Thompson noted in his journal.

"I cannot help admiring the Spirit of these brave, undaunted, but poor Kootenaes," he wrote. "They have all shown a courage and Fortitude admirable—not the least sign of Weakness or Cowardice, altho' they are in the Power of a large party of Indians, who are at least 20 to one. They are conducted by four old Men who seem worthy of being at the Head of such People. This day when the young Pekenow Men seized the Heads of their Horses, they all acted as if by one Soul bent their Bows, got ready their Weapons, and prepared to make their Oppressors quit their Horses or sell their Lives."

They arrived at Rocky Mountain House on October 20. The Kootenays traded their furs—a hundred and ten beaver, ten bear, five fishers and two wolverines—and departed two days later. Thompson sent two men, French Canadians whom he identified as La Gassé and LeBlanc, to winter with the Kootenays and he pressed the Indians to come again in the spring to guide him to their country.

From the outset, Thompson and the others had grave doubts about the guide. His name was The Rook and he was a Cree. He lied so often, about matters large and small, that the traders believed nothing he said. Had anyone else been available, Duncan McGillivray would never have hired him to lead an expedition across the Rocky Mountains. McGillivray promised The Rook substantial rewards if he succeeded and harsh punishment if he failed. And McGillivray had him smoke to the great spirit and declare that he would bring the wrath of this mighty power upon himself, his wife and his children if he did not fulfill his promise.

The party of eleven, commanded by James Hughes with Thompson as his second, left Rocky Mountain House on horseback June 6, 1801, and followed the North Saskatchewan west for twenty-two miles. All went well till The Rook led them up a tributary swollen with spring runoff and several weeks of unusually heavy rains. Fallen trees made the already muddy trails nearly impassable. They crossed bogs in which the horses sunk to their bellies. Several times, horses lost their footing and tumbled down the steep, high banks of the river. Most days, it rained, sometimes in torrents. Crossing creeks, or the river itself, was difficult and dangerous because the water was moving so fast.

By the evening of June 10, The Rook was in poor spirits. Hughes served rum to him and his wife, who was accompanying them, and they got drunk. The next morning, the guide had a hangover. He summoned his wife from the fire where she and the Nor'Westers were warming themselves, and he used a sharp flint to open a vein in her arm. He filled a wooden bowl with blood, raised it to his lips and drank heartily. Thompson, standing nearby, later recorded the conversation that followed.

"What," exclaimed one of the appalled Nor'Westers who witnessed this, "drink warm from the vein the blood of your wife? I have eaten and smoked with thee but henceforward thou and me shall never eat and smoke together."

"Oh, oh my friend," The Rook replied. "Have I done wrong? When I find my stomach out of order, the warm blood of my wife in good health refreshes the whole of my body and puts me to rights. In return, when she is not well, I draw blood from my arm. She drinks it. It invigorates and gives her life. All our nation do this and all of us know it to be a good medicine. Is this the first time you have seen it? From whence comes your surprise, my friends?"

The next evening, after a day spent travelling up a deep, narrow valley with mountains towering above them, The Rook pleaded with Hughes to be allowed to return. Hughes assured him he had nothing to be afraid of except mountain goats.

"This is the way of all you white men," The Rook replied. "You joke at everything till you are fairly killed. For my part, I am certain there are strange Indians near us who will kill us. I dream continually of them."

Hughes and Thompson refused to consider returning.

"We cannot go much further," The Rook told them. "Some of your horses are already quite feeble and others nearly crippled and we still have the worst of the mountain to pass."

"That is nothing to you," Thompson said. "We will go on while we have a horse left."

"Oh, but I will not follow you to be killed," he replied. "It is true I drank your rum. You have given me a good horse, but I love my life better than this."

The next day, June 13, they trudged through hard, crusty snow two to three feet deep and came to a narrow lake about a mile long and a quarter of a mile wide and flanked by mountains that rose straight from the water's edge to the clouds. The men were relieved. They had given enough and were ready to quit. But not Hughes and Thompson. They interrogated The Rook. Had he really been here once with horses, as he had claimed before leaving Rocky Mountain House?

"Oh, we had no horses with us," he said. "We left them with our families at the entrance to the mountains."

"Why you scoundrel," said Hughes. "Did you not tell us at the fort that you had horses with you the whole of the road across the mountains?"

"I thought where we had gone on foot horses might possibly go, but I forgot this part of the mountain. You see plainly as well as me that if we go further, we must leave our baggage and horses."

Hughes and Thompson proceeded on foot, without luggage, but could not advance beyond the end of the lake because of the roughness of the terrain. They now set out on the return journey. At the Saskatchewan River, Hughes went east toward Rocky Mountain House. He left Thompson with eight men and instructions to examine the country ahead. They spent ten days building a canoe and waiting out heavy rains and three days poling and pulling their vessel until they could no longer advance against the current.

"Here then for the present was my last hope destroyed," Thompson wrote. "I felt this more keenly than ever from seeing before me for a great distance westward a country not very mountainous but covered with green hills which seemed to promise a much better road."

They reached Rocky Mountain House on June 30 and Thompson learned that he had become a father. Three weeks earlier, Charlotte had given birth to their first child, a daughter whom they named Fanny.

What happened to Jean Baptiste Cadotte? That was the subject of many a conversation at the rendez-vous of 1803. The facts were there for all to see in the minutes of the partners' meeting of July 19: he had indulged in drunken and riotous behaviour since becoming a partner in 1801; had neglected his duty the previous winter; had caused a severe loss to the company; had rendered himself unworthy and unfit to remain a partner; had been deprived of his two shares; and, finally, had been expelled by a unanimous vote of his peers as "fully and effectually as if he had never been a partner."

This the men knew. Still, they wondered: what had come over Jean Baptiste? The loneliness and isolation of a trading post could do strange things to a person, but they had not expected such conduct from an educated man, and not from a Cadotte, a name associated with the fur trade of the northwest for fifty years. His father and namesake had been employed at Sault Ste. Marie as far back as 1751, before the British conquest of New France, and had worked there until 1796, when he turned the business over to Jean Baptiste and his younger brother Michel. The company had sent Jean Baptiste west to the interior, where he had worked as a labourer and a clerk before becoming a partner and then he had slipped.

Cadotte was out, but Thompson was in. At a meeting on July 9, the partners had agreed to award their surveyor and astronomer two of the ninety-two shares issued under the most recent reorganization of the company, which had taken place the year before. But Thompson was not present to accept the offer. After his stint at Rocky Mountain House, he and Charlotte had moved north to Peace River in the Athabasca District. They had spent the winter of 1802–03 on the Peace and remained during the summer of 1803.

Thompson was working mainly as a trader but found time to survey and explore long stretches of the Peace. He observed for latitude and longitude and recorded in his notebook every change in direction so that he could, one day, produce an accurate image of the river to go along with all the others he had surveyed, in whole or in part: the Hayes, the Nelson, the Churchill, the Saskatchewan, the Athabasca, the Red Deer, the Bow, the Assiniboine, the Souris, the Red, the Winnipeg and the Rainy.

In early June 1804, Thompson led a brigade of canoes on a journey of more than a thousand miles from the Peace country to Lake Superior for the annual rendez-vous. Charlotte and the children, three-year-old Fanny and their son, Samuel, born three months earlier, accompanied him. When they arrived, Thompson learned that he had been awarded Cadotte's shares and was now a partner. He was honoured and elated, but soon learned that the North West Co. was a financially troubled enterprise.

One of Thompson's first acts as a partner was to discuss with his fellow proprietors a resolution that began with the declaration: "the great sacrifices occasioned by the Opposition carrying on against the North West Company for five years successively and other causes, have considerably diminished the profits on the shares, and seems to point out the necessity of adopting every measure . . . that can tend to retrench expenses and introduce a system of Economy throughout the country."

Among the other causes was the cost—more than ten thousand pounds—of moving the inland headquarters. The partners had decided that Grand Portage would likely be on the wrong side of the future international border, so they had abandoned the place and built a new terminal, Fort William, named after William McGillivray. It was located thirty-five miles north, safely within British territory at the mouth of the Kaministiquia River. But the principal problem was the rivalry with the XY Co.

Everyone knew the two Montreal-based competitors should end their foolish fight and combine forces against the Hudson's Bay Co., but personal animosity between two men—Simon McTavish, who was known as the Marquis, and Alexander Mackenzie, who was nicknamed the Knight—made such a practical solution impossible. Mackenzie had left the North West Co. in 1799 and gone to England, where he published an account of his epic voyages to the Arctic and Pacific Oceans and was knighted by King George. He returned to Canada in 1802 and immediately put his resources and prestige behind the upstart XY Co.

The two firms waged commercial warfare in the fur country. The war was fought with booze and the casualties were almost all natives. In many places, the two firms, along with the Hudson's Bay Co., had posts within a musket shot of each other and dispensed liquor freely to bring in the Indians. In 1803, the Montreal companies alone hauled sixteen thousands gallons of liquor into the interior, and the Nor'Westers shipped three gallons for every one of the XY Co.

Alexander Henry, a partner stationed at a North West Co. post on the Pembina River, recorded the awful results in his daily journal. In one eight-month period, he made the following entries:

"Tabashaw stabbed a near relation of his own, Missistaygouine, in six different places in the breast and sides; every stab went up to the handle; the poor fellow lingered an hour and died. . . .

"Water Hen, in fighting with another Indian, was thrown into the fire and roasted terribly from his neck to his rump. . . .

"Le Boeuf quarreled with his wife and knocked her senseless with a club, which opened a gash on her head six inches long and down to the bone. She laid so long before she recovered her senses that I believed her dead. . . .

"Mithanasonce was so troublesome that we were obliged to tie him with ropes to prevent his doing mischief. He was stabbed in the back in three different places about a month ago. His wounds were still open and had an ugly appearance; in his struggling to get loose they burst out afresh and bled a great deal. . . .

"What a different set of people they would be were there not a drop of liquor in the country," Henry concluded. "We may truly say that liquor is the root of all evil in the North West."

After the rendez-vous of 1804, the wintering partners of the North West Co. returned to their posts in the interior to fight it out with their rivals for another year. But a decisive event had already occurred. McTavish had died July 6 at the stone cottage on his Montreal property where he was having a huge mansion constructed. He was, at fifty-four, wealthy and powerful, but was brought down by an illness that had seemed no more serious than a cold.

With McTavish gone, his nephew William McGillivray took charge and quickly entered negotiations with the XY Co. By early November they had agreed to amalgamate, although Mackenzie was barred from further participation in the trade. The principals to the deal immediately sent packets from Montreal to the partners wintering in the interior. Henry received the news in early January, but Thompson, who was residing on the Churchill River, about two hundred miles inland from Hudson Bay, did not learn of these events until June 1805.

The merger ended a destructive rivalry and allowed the company to breach the final frontier of the northwestern fur trade—the land beyond the Rocky Mountains—and they chose two men to lead the effort. One was Simon Fraser. The other was David Thompson.

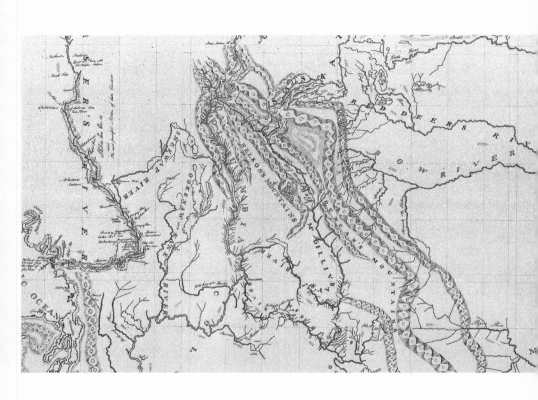

*Thompson's travels, 1807–1810: He crossed the Rockies
to seek the great river of the west.*

Over the Mountains

(1807)

WHERE WAS THE RIVER OF THE WEST? THAT WAS A QUESTION that perplexed a restless, outward-looking minority within the North West Co. The mouth of this river had been discovered fifteen years earlier, in 1792, by an American sea captain, Robert Gray, who was cruising up the west coast of North America on a trading mission financed by Boston investors. His objective had been to load up on sea otter pelts by trading with the Indians and then to sail to China, where he would exchange the pelts for tea. On May 12 that year, at forty-six degrees latitude he entered an inlet at the mouth of a river that, he noted in his journal, "extended to the ne as far as eye cou'd reach." Gray named this river the Columbia, after his ship the *Columbia Rediviva,* or Columbia Reborn, and proceeded to sail fifteen miles upstream.

After returning to the sea, he sailed north and encountered Capt. George Vancouver, who was charting the coast on behalf of the British Crown. Vancouver had earlier come upon the mouth of the same river, but chose to bypass it. After hearing Gray's account of his discovery, Vancouver turned his vessels, the *Discovery* and the *Chatham,* south to examine the Columbia himself. The *Chatham,* captained by William Broughton, dodged the sandbars at the mouth of the river and sailed a hundred and fifty miles inland. There, according to his journal, Broughton "formally took possession of the river, and the country in its vicinity, in his Britannic Majesty's name, having every reason to believe, that the subjects of no other civilized nation had ever entered into this river before."

But a fundamental question remained: Where was the source of the Columbia? Those ambitious Nor'Westers told themselves the river of the west must begin as a spring or a brook high on the western slopes of the Rockies and gain strength and stature as it descended and collected snowmelt and the waters of other creeks and streams. The river, they believed, would meander for hundreds of miles, flowing bold and strong through forests and valleys, across plains and plateaus. It would absorb the substantial flow of other rivers that had themselves travelled hundreds of miles and, by the time it reached the Pacific, it would be a mile wide or more.

The river would not only be long and mighty. It would be navigable. They would be able to put their canoes in near the headwaters and ride its waters, allowing for portages around rapids and waterfalls, all the way to the sea, where they would meet a ship that would take their furs to the Orient and leave behind goods from China or Britain.

Distance made the traders of the North West Co. dream of such a river, the ever-increasing distances they had to travel from their posts to the inland terminal on Superior. Distance made their masters—the fur barons of Montreal—contemplate an alternative to the vast transportation network that sustained their enterprise. Distances increased costs, reduced profits and gave their old adversary, the Hudson's Bay Co., a significant advantage.

Both companies had to transport goods across the North Atlantic from Britain. But the Hudson's Bay Co. landed its merchandise on the west coast of the bay—five hundred miles from the interior. North West Co. goods came ashore in Montreal—a thousand miles from the head of Superior and twenty-five hundred miles from the remotest posts. Distance was the curse of the Nor'Westers and it kindled ambitions to find the great river that would provide a western outlet to the sea.

Alexander Mackenzie was the first to search for it, and he made two attempts, beginning in 1789, three years before Captain Gray made his discovery. On June 3 that year, Mackenzie left Fort Chipewyan, at the western end of Lake Athabasca, with four French Canadians, two of whom brought their wives, a German, an Indian known as the English Chief and his two wives, and two young Indians. They followed the Slave River north to Great Slave Lake and then entered a major river that flowed west for more than two hundred miles. Mackenzie was certain he was on his way to the Pacific, but then the river turned north and continued for a thousand miles before emptying into a polar sea. The explorer's reaction was evident in the name he conferred upon this waterway. In a letter to his cousin Roderick Mackenzie, he called it the River Disappointment.

Mackenzie tried again three years later. He left Fort Chipewyan on October 10, 1792, and this time went west, up the Peace River, wintered on the Peace and resumed his journey in the spring, accompanied by six voyageurs, two Indians and his dog. Mackenzie found a big river west of the Rockies, one that he called by its Indian name, Tacouthe Tesse. This river flowed north in a trench between two mountain ranges before turning west and then south. Mackenzie and his men embarked at the bend in the river and followed it south till they encountered rough, dangerous waters Indians had warned them of, at which point they turned up a tributary that flowed in from the west. They reached the Pacific on July 22, 1793, by a route so difficult and strewn with obstacles that it was of no commercial value.

Mackenzie returned, having earned the distinction of becoming the first person to cross the continent by land, and believing that he may have found the great river. He supposed that the Tacouthe Tesse and the Columbia might be the same waterway and said so in the book he published about his travels nearly a decade later. Mackenzie did no more exploring for the North West Co. in part because of his deepening differences with Simon McTavish. The company itself sponsored no further expeditions for fifteen years because of the competitive pressures of the Hudson's Bay Co. and later the XY Co., which eroded the profits and consumed the energies of the partners.

But with the 1804 union of the North West and the XY companies, and the rapid elimination of the beaver east of the Rockies, the partners again turned their attention to the territory beyond the mountains. They sent Simon Fraser up the Peace River from the Athabasca District to open a trade and to test Mackenzie's theory about the Tacouthe Tesse and the Columbia. They dispatched Thompson up the North Saskatchewan from Rocky Mountain House, primarily to trade, but also to find the river that would lead the Nor'Westers to the sea.

In late April 1807, a party of twelve Kootenay men and three women, laden with pelts, arrived at Rocky Mountain House. They had spent fifteen days crossing the mountains and were, understandably, exhausted. The snow in the passes, they told Thompson, was deep enough to bury a tall pine. But around the trading post, there were signs of spring.

On April 26, Thompson heard the first frogs. Three days later, he saw a small plover. And on May 4, he noted: "The River gave way below us   Much Ice along the Shores   The Snow nearly all out of the Woods." The following day, six men departed for the mountains in two canoes. Next, three French-Canadian voyageurs left by land. The party included the wife and three children of one of the French Canadians, a young Kootenay woman returning to her j131

people, two Saulteaux hunters and their families, and Charlotte Thompson and her children: Fanny, now almost six; Samuel, two; and Emma, who was fourteen months old.

The traders had begun preparing to cross the mountains the previous autumn. Jaco Finlay, an experienced clerk and interpreter and the son of a Nor'Wester and a Chipewyan woman, had travelled with three other men to the headwaters of the Saskatchewan to clear an old Indian trail and to build canoes that could be launched on the west side of the Rockies. Thompson had had his men move goods upriver in stages throughout the fall and winter to ensure that they could travel quickly and lightly in the spring.

When they at last departed, the traders were blessed with a stroke of good luck. The Piegan who normally patrolled the Saskatchewan, the Red Deer and the Bow Rivers had formed a war party and headed south for the Missouri River. They were looking for the Americans who had been involved in a skirmish with their brethren, the southern Piegan, in the summer of 1806.

Accounts of this incident had drifted north from one Indian camp to another and reached Rocky Mountain House in the autumn. Piegan and Blackfoot told them that a large and well-armed contingent of Americans, perhaps forty or fifty men, had come up the Missouri River, gone over the mountains and down to the sea. On their return, four of these Americans were exploring a tributary of the Missouri. They had encountered eight southern Piegan—boys and young men with a herd of thirty horses.

The two parties had spent an amicable evening together, but in the morning some of the younger Indians, who were barely out of boyhood, had tried to steal the guns of the still sleeping Americans. There had been an altercation, and the whites had shot and wounded one of the Indians and fatally stabbed in the chest a youth named He-That-Looks-at-the-Calf.

The Americans were members of the Lewis and Clark expedition, led by Meriwether Lewis and William Clark, who had been commissioned in 1803 by President Thomas Jefferson to explore the Louisiana Territory, more than eight hundred thousand square miles of land acquired from France and stretching from the mouth of the Mississippi to the headwaters of the Missouri. Jefferson had instructed the explorers to search for "the most direct and practicable water communication across this continent for the purposes of commerce."

Thompson was intrigued by the story. He may not have known exactly who the Americans were, but he did know that others would inevitably follow in their footsteps. Sooner or later, the North West Co. would face competition for furs and territory, which stiffened his resolve to cross the mountains and to establish a trade ahead of the Americans.

Thompson started on May 10, a Sunday and a very fine day, as he noted in his journal. "At 9 1/2 Am sent off Mr Finan McDonald & 5 Men in a Canoe with Goods & Necessaries to the expedition across the Mountains on which I pray the blessing of Heaven," he wrote. "At 10 Am I set off with Bercier on Horseback—we arrived at the Horse Tent, but could not get the Horses 'till 2 1/2 Pm, when with very hard riding thro' thick woods very much fallen down we arrived at the Round Plain."

The mountains reverberated day and night with the thunder of avalanches, which occasionally startled the poor, bony horses and frightened Thompson's infant daughter, Emma. He was fascinated with the power of these slides and the devastation they caused. One day, while hunting, he came to a small lake that had recently been pounded by avalanches. "In one place in particular the Snow, in rushing from the Side of the Mountain, had swept & broken all the Trees to a considerable distance & carried them all before it clean, except a Fir Pine of abt 3 fm [fathoms] round, beautifully made. It alone had withstood the ravage & the other broken Trees were piled about it to a height of about 12 or 15 feet—it stood most majestically erect amidst such vast Ruins."

By early June, the party had advanced about seventy-five miles west from Rocky Mountain House and reached the Kootenay

Thompson's sketch of the Rocky Mountains,
east of Kootenay House, winter 1808–09.

Plain—flatlands on either side of the Saskatchewan River, but well within the first ranges of the mountains. The plain contained a mix of forest and meadows, springs and ponds and was a favourite haunt of Stoney Indians, who came to hunt deer, elk and bison, which were plentiful here. The men on the river had towed the canoes most of the way, often wading through frigid water that numbed their legs since they could not paddle or pole against the current. The others had ridden along a reasonably good trail obstructed here and there by swamps and deadfall.

They travelled a day and a half beyond the Kootenay Plain before the trail became impassable with the snow. Thompson sent everyone back to the plain until the way was clear, but he stayed upriver with a voyageur named Bercier and two others.

They were stalled about three weeks. Thompson and his companions occupied themselves cutting and splitting pine wood and constructing boxes, twenty-three inches square and eight and a half high, and they packed the goods in them for the crossing. By June 22 Thompson was anxious to inspect the pass. He and Bercier left on horseback at 5:40 a.m. The ascent took four hours. They travelled nearly twelve miles until reaching a marshy meadow in a bowl flanked by two peaks.

Springs rose from the earth and mingled with melting snow. These waters trickled down a slight incline to form a creek just two yards wide—a wondrous site for Thompson. He had spent twenty-two years in the country and travelled thousands of miles on rivers and lakes that flowed east or north toward Hudson Bay. This creek flowed west toward the Pacific. He was standing on the continental divide, and paused to pray to the Lord: "May God in his Mercy give us to see where it's waters flow into the Ocean, & return in safety."

Back at the camp, Thompson sent one of the men to the Kootenay Plain for the others, and at 6 a.m. on June 25, they began the trek across. They reached the height of land without difficulty, but the descent was an ordeal. They had to hack their way through a trail too narrow for the pack horses and littered with deadfall. During one three-day stretch, they advanced only two and a half miles. In many places, the trail crossed the stream, and they soon had to take special precautions even though it was not very wide and not very deep.

"The water being far too violent to ford the horses," Thompson noted on June 29, "we examined the Brook upwards & found a place where a Bridge might be thrown across (which with some Trouble we got done) of 2 large Fir Pines. We then crossed all the Goods & horse Furniture on our Backs; we then crossed the Horses one at a time, by tying a strong Halter to them & 3 or 4 Men hauling them in the Water—for alth' not more than 3 ft deep, such was its extreme descent & velocity, that our best Horses were immediately thrown off their Legs & swept under."

The stream brought them, on June 30, to a large river that flowed north. Here, Thompson halted the expedition. He observed for longitude and latitude and found that they were a hundred and sixteen degrees, forty-seven minutes and eight seconds west of Greenwich and fifty degrees, seven minutes north of the equator. These calculations, together with Vancouver's account of his

The Rockies, Kootenay House: Here Thomspon found the source of the Columbia, a long, narrow lake fed by subterranean springs rather than the surrounding mountains.

coastal explorations, which Thompson had read, enabled him to determine that they were some five hundred miles from the Pacific and more than a thousand miles from the mouth of the Columbia.

He named the river the Kootenay, after the local Indians. In fact, this was the Columbia, the great river of the west, but he had no way of knowing that. This river flowed north. The mouth of the Columbia lay hundreds of miles to the southwest and he knew nothing of the country in between. Besides, he had more immediate concerns: which way should he go? He chose to travel south, since some of the men had heard the Kootenays speak of a large lake in that direction. But the canoes that Jaco Finlay had built the previous autumn were damaged. They spent twelve days building two smaller canoes and a large one and soon found themselves short of provisions.

"Very much in want of Food," Thompson wrote in his journal on July 5. "Sent word to the 2 Saulteaux that are here, that if they did not pay me part of the Meat they owed me, I would kill one of his Horses for Food—on this he brought me abt 30 lbs of a small Deer & a small Beaver." On the tenth of July, Finan McDonald and the others arrived with the goods, and Thompson concluded his journal entry by noting: "Shared last morsel with them." The next day, he sent McDonald and two others to search for the Kootenays they had hired to hunt for them. They could not find them, he noted, and added: "nothing to eat."

Things did not improve much as they began advancing up the river. Thompson, several men and the women and children went by canoe, while a French Canadian named Michel Boulard and three young Kootenay men took the horses. "I went up a Lake & fortunately killed 9 Swans," he wrote on July 13. "Thank Heaven for this relief." A few days later, they met six Kootenay men and their families and traded for six pounds of dried meat and a goose and advanced the men some ammunition.

They travelled eighty miles upriver. There were mountains to the east and west, six to twelve miles apart and, in the flat bottom of the valley, which rarely exceeded two miles in width, there was water—more water, it seemed, than land. The river meandered past marshes and small lakes, around ponds and islands. This place should have been blessed with an abundance of fish and fowl, but they could find nothing to eat. On July 18, they reached a long, narrow lake, one that seemed suitable for a settlement, and the work of the expedition began: securing provisions, selecting a site for a post and establishing relations with the Indians.

By late August, a new North West Co. post called Kootenay House was nearing completion. It stood on the west side of the valley on a bluff about twenty feet above a creek that flowed into the river. Thompson and his men had built a warehouse first and then a dwelling for him and his family. After that, they constructed a trading house and were at work on a residence for the single men when the Piegan arrived.

There were twelve young men and three women. They declared themselves happy to see that white men had crossed the mountains to establish a trading post among the Kootenays, but Thompson knew better than to believe this. The Piegan were old enemies of the Kootenays. The hostilities between them extended back two generations, to the days when a branch of the Kootenays left their ancestral homelands west of the mountains and settled on the grasslands to the east where they could pursue the vast herds of buffalo. They were content with their new lives and would have remained there had it not been for the Piegan and their brethren, the Bloods and the Blackfoot.

These nations, who spoke a common language and constituted a political and military alliance known as the Blackfoot confederacy, had emerged from the partly forested margins of the prairie and begun to move south and west. The fearsome and aggressive Piegan led the advance. They had horses and guns, knives and axes, whereas the Kootenays, without access to the white trading posts, did not have firearms or metal weapons, though they did have horses. The Piegan pushed farther and farther west, seizing land and driving the Kootenays before them until they had nowhere to go but over the mountains and back to the forested valleys whence they came.

The conflict did not end there. The Kootenays returned to the prairie most summers to hunt buffalo and occasionally tried to reach a white trading post to acquire the goods that had made their enemies so powerful. The Piegan guarded against these forays and often crossed the mountains to harass and intimidate the Kootenays and to steal their horses.

Thompson had known the Piegan for almost twenty years, from his days as a young apprentice with the Hudson's Bay Co. He was certain they would be displeased that he was supplying the Kootenays with guns and knives and altering relations between them. "They have it in their Power to be very troublesome to us, & even to cut us off," he wrote in his journal the day they arrived. "We however hope in the Care of good Providence."

The unwelcome visitors stayed four days. One of them admitted they had come to steal horses, but Thompson had hidden the company horses in hilly country north of the post. "On their going away they stole 3 of the Horses of a poor old Kootenay Man," Thompson noted; "2 Kootenays went after them, came up with them & had much altercation with them, but the Piegans listened to no Arguments, chased the Kootenays away & kept the Horses. The Kootenays in return fired on the Piegans, without effect, then flew back to the Ho[use] & put all their Goods &c under our Protection, camped close to the Ho[use] & kept themselves under Arms, with a continual good lookout for their Enemies."

That day, a Kootenay named Le Muet arrived with news that a larger party of Piegan was not far off. Thompson and his men prepared themselves by erecting sturdy fences on two sides of the post. The third remained unprotected and the fourth faced a steep embankment that dropped down to the creek. Three Piegan showed up on September 2, and the main party—twenty-three men and several women—arrived three days later. They stayed a week and spent one day gambling with several Kootenay men who had been engaged as hunters. The rest of the time, they threatened and harassed the Kootenays who arrived in small parties to trade.

Lack of food finally forced the Piegan to pack up and leave, but a few who loitered behind let it be known that they had come looking for trouble and would have plundered the post had either the white traders or the Kootenays provoked them. "I assured them," Thompson wrote afterward, "that whenever they might think proper to begin they would meet a warm reception, however numerous they might be."

On September 16, four days after the Piegan left, a large party of Kootenays came to trade. They brought with them another group of Indians who spoke the same language and appeared to be a division of the Kootenay nation, but dressed differently and lived on a large lake many days' journey to the southwest, so Thompson called them Lake Indians.

He asked the Lake Indians many questions about the geography of their country, which he found complex and perplexing. He had determined that the big lake his party had reached in mid-July was about eight miles long by two wide. Twenty miles farther south he had found a second body of water of similar dimensions, which was, he realized, the source of the river they had followed into the country. About two miles beyond the head of the second lake, he had come upon another large river. It originated in the Rockies on the east side of the valley and flowed south, and he had named it McGillivray's River, after the brothers William and Duncan.

The Lake Indians provided Thompson with an intriguing piece of information. They lived on a lake beyond the mountains to the west and near the place where these two rivers—the north-flowing Kootenay and the south-flowing McGillivray's—came together. This raised two questions in Thompson's mind: Was one of these rivers actually the Columbia? And was either navigable?

At the end of September, the Lake Indians prepared to depart. They refused Thompson's request to accompany them, but he finally found a willing guide in one of their leading chiefs, Ugly Head, so named because he had curly hair. On October 2, Thompson and the chief set out on horseback. They communicated through sign language and a few words and followed trails that took them down McGillivray's River. They had travelled about eighty miles when Ugly Head took another trail that departed from the river and led west, toward the mountains.

Thompson assumed the road would veer back to the river, but it didn't, and Ugly Head managed to convey that they would be eight or nine days on this course before reaching his country and the junction of the rivers lay still farther off. Thompson realized that so late in the season he could never get there and back. His travels were over for the year, but he had satisfied himself that McGillivray's River was navigable, and he could return in the spring.

The Kootenays were gambling again. They were packed into a lodge that stood just outside the stockades of Kootenay House. They were on their knees, hunched over, watching closely. The game was quick and intense. Two principal players—the pointers—faced one another at the centre of the lodge and the others, both men and women, lined up alongside them in opposing rows. The pointers started the play. Each held two small pieces of bone—one marked, the other plain. They shuffled the bones from hand to hand behind their backs or under a hat or a shawl. Both pointers held out their hands. Each took a turn trying to guess which of his opponent's hands held the unmarked bone. The winner took the bones, four in all, and gave two each to skilled handlers on each side of him. They shuffled, and the opposing pointer had to guess which held the unmarked bones.

And so it went: control switching from side to side; a set of pointed scoring sticks moving back and forth to record wins and losses; each side singing game songs, or pounding on logs, or cheering and laughing, and everyone betting heavily on the skill of their pointers and handlers.

The Kootenays had arrived at the North West Co. post toward the end of January 1808. They had come to trade, but then the game had started and for several days nobody gave any thought to commerce. They played from morning till night.

The match ended February 6, and Thompson recorded the outcome in his journal: "After a long gambling match, one Kootenay has gained near the whole. His gains are 17 Red Deer Skins - 24 Chevreuil [deer] - 1 Gun - 3 axes - 10 Knives - 350 Balls - 7 lbs. Of Powder - 6 Horses & Saddles - Saddle Stuff &c. - 1 Robe - 1 Blanket & many small Article besides 2 good Tents. The others have only their Wives Children, and old leather clothing left."

The Kootenays almost always gambled when they were around the post—a practice that seriously concerned Thompson. This venture west of the Rockies had to produce a profit for the company and it certainly wouldn't if the Kootenays frittered away the winter playing games of chance.

On several occasions, he tried to persuade them to end their games and to go off and hunt beaver. Once, he had a chief deliver a stern lecture to his people about how they needed to bring in furs if they expected trade goods, and another time he sent Michel Boulard to a Kootenay camp to warn them he would not stay on their lands if they did not hunt.

Having injured his knee in the fall, Thompson spent most of the winter at the desk he had built in the sixteen-by-twenty-foot dwelling he shared with Charlotte and the children. He calculated the expenses incurred for provisions and wages and optimistically projected a profit for the year. He wrote a progress report for his fellow partners, extolling the potential of the country and arguing for two seasons to develop the trade.

Thompson performed his duties conscientiously, but he did not have a deep or abiding enthusiasm for business. His was driven by a desire to observe, to explore and to make some sense of the wild, chaotic lands where he had spent most of his life. He dreamed of creating a map of the northwestern interior of North America. With this map, he would produce coherence out of chaos, and that winter, while his knee mended, Thompson began drawing images of the rivers he had travelled. He went through the notebooks in which he had hastily jotted down the courses he had followed up and down the waterways of the interior. These he transcribed in tidy columns, and alongside the columns he wrote his observations for latitude and longitude.

Then he set to work on the sheets of paper sent to him from Montreal. The observations became points on paper and the courses became squiggly lines that ran from point to point. He recorded his progress in short, spare journal entries. January 28: "Deer R to Grand Portage." February 4: "Finished the Road from Trout Portage to Cumberland Lake." February 7: "Drawing— Trout Portage to Isle a la Crosse." And then a new element—the arrival of spring—appeared in the journal entries. February 9: "Drawing   2 Days on This sheet and not yet done   Ducks a plenty   Water standing in all the Plains." February 27: "Draw-ing—Saw 1st Geese."

Thompson was always eager to move in the spring, and this year he was unusually restless. In December, five Piegan visitors had informed him that the Cree were making war on the Bloods and Blackfoot. This conflict would likely prevent the latter from attacking their enemies west of the Rockies over the summer, and would give Thompson the opportunity to explore McGillivray's River without worrying about an assault on Kootenay House.

Thompson was also aware of American advances to the south. Nor'Westers east of the Rockies had obtained a long letter by Meri-wether Lewis containing an account of his journey over the moun-tains and down to the Pacific. A copy was sent to Thompson, who transcribed it into his journal and studied closely the explorer's description of the lower Columbia.

Indians brought him another letter, a strange and menacing one, purportedly written by a "U.S. Lieutenant Jeremy Pinch." Dated September 29, 1807, it was addressed "To the British Mercht trafficking with the Cotanaiss." The writer, whom historians have never been able to identify, demanded that Thompson pull out, a demand backed by a threat. "We have more powerful means of per-suasion in our hands than we have hitherto used," the letter read. "We shall with regret apply Force . . . You will see Sir the necessity of submitting and with good grace."

Thompson dashed off a dismissive reply and sent a copy of the letter to his partners. He was not one to be intimidated by bluff and braggadocio. Yet he could not deny that the explorers Lewis and Clark had breached the mountains and that independent American traders had quickly followed in their wake.

By mid-April, he was ready and determined to extend the reach of the company by exploring the big south-flowing river he had named for the McGillivrays. "Gummed the canoes & got all ready to be off the Morrow Morning, please Heaven," he wrote on the nineteenth. "Thank God for his good Protection."

Moss bread was black, with a faintly bitter taste, and was not very filling or nutritious. The Kootenays made it of strands of lichen, thin as hair and about six inches long, which hung from the branches of fir trees. They collected tangled clumps of it, removed twigs and debris, and soaked it in water until it became flexible. They patted it into cakes, baked it overnight on hot rocks and ate it in the morning. On a good day, one in which Thompson and his men had an adequate supply of dried provisions, or a freshly killed mountain goat to roast on the fire, they would have passed on the moss bread. But such days were few during their journey down McGillivray's River.

The day before they first sampled moss bread, they had come upon an eagle ripping into the carcass of an antelope. "It was almost putrified," Thompson wrote in his journal, "but as we were without Food, we were necessitated to take what remained, altho' we could hardly bear the smell. At 6 1/2 Pm put up as the Men had tasted nothing all day & were much fatigued. Boiled our rotten Meat—we eat of it but all of us became quite sick, (& fatigued as we were, they could not sleep)."

Thompson travelled that spring with four men in a large canoe, looking for suitable places downriver to erect another trading post. He was eager to meet again with the people he knew only as Lake Indians and to visit their country. He also wanted to make contact with a people called the Flat Heads, who lived southeast of the Kootenays.

McGillivray's River was broad and smooth, its waters swollen by melting snow and the current very strong. Thompson's party paddled south for a week through mountainous country that gave way to hilly, wooded terrain and, in places, beautiful meadows. Game was plentiful at first. On their second day out, they saw six or seven mountain goats, two small herds of deer and many ducks, as well as several wolves, but the wildlife soon became scarce.

Thompson halted the expedition on April 26 near a trail and a recently occupied campsite. He sent three of the men to search for the Indians while he rested. His injured knee was stiff and swollen and he could hardly walk. Nevertheless, they travelled a short distance the following day and again on April 29, and then stopped for three days to hunt and to await a band of Kootenays who had agreed to take them to the Flat Heads, so named by Meriwether Lewis, though they called themselves the Salish.

The meeting did not take place, but a Kootenay named Le Monde arrived unexpectedly with his family, and Thompson was grateful. He gave him powder, ten balls and six inches of tobacco and sent him off hunting, and Le Monde soon returned with what Thompson thought was a kind of tiger—a fawn-coloured cat with a white belly, about three feet tall with strong legs and sharp claws. "Found the Tiger very good Food, (white,)," he remarked, "& yields as much Meat as a Chevreuil."

They travelled about two hundred miles south, crossing the forty-ninth parallel, according to Thompson's observations, all the while paddling on smooth, fast-flowing water, not once having to portage. The river then made a sharp turn west. Rounded, wooded mountains—still snow-covered—rose five to six hundred feet from the water's edge. About thirty miles beyond the big bend, they encountered a powerful waterfall. The river dropped twenty to thirty feet and careered through a narrow, S-shaped gorge. The north side seemed to offer a passable portage.

"We began carrying at 3 1/4 PM," he wrote later that day, "with light Loads & went abt 1 Mile over a terrible Road, along Side of a steep Hill nearly perpend, walking wholly among small fragments of black broken Rock that had rolled from the Summit. Our Height at times was abt 300 feet above the River, ascending and descending as the steep Rocks obliged us; (the least slip would have been inevitable destruction, as the steepness of the Rock allowed no return, or if once falling, to stop 'till precipitated into the River.)"

They arrived on May 8 at a camp of Kootenays and Lake Indians, ten lodges in all. These natives were out of provisions and surviving on moss bread. They were also short of horses. A party of nearly fifty Piegan had recently raided their camp and had stolen thirty-five horses. An elderly chief had managed to kill one of the thieves.

Thompson and his men spent four days hunting and trading and, in one of the lodges, he met Ugly Head, who greeted him like an old friend. Once again, the Lake Indian chief proved willing to assist Thompson, agreeing to visit the Flat Heads in order to persuade them to come north and trade. Meanwhile, Thompson and his party continued their journey on McGillivray's River, which now flowed northwest. They proceeded about fifty miles, recrossing the forty-ninth parallel, and by mid-May had arrived at a long, narrow lake, which Thompson had been particularly eager to visit. Ugly Head's people, the Lake Indians, lived there, and Thompson saw them as potential customers. Equally important, he hoped this lake might lead him to the Columbia.

The Lake Indians lived in lodges of bark and rushes and ate mainly fish. They welcomed the visitors, traded a few furs and informed Thompson that they were a division of the Kootenay nation but they were widely known as the Flat Bows, a name given them by the Blackfoot, who admired their powerful, stylish bows. They also provided Thompson with useful information about the geography of the country.

The outlet of the lake where they dwelt was about midway up the west shore. There, the river resumed and flowed west down to an even larger river whose waters travelled south. Thompson reasoned that this had to be the Columbia and judged from his host's description that it was only about fifty miles beyond the lake. He was sorely tempted to keep going, though there was a series of waterfalls and five portages on that leg of the river. But here the desire to explore conflicted with his duty as a trader. He still had to return to Kootenay House and move his furs over the mountains and down to Superior. Time would not permit him to do both, and so with regret he turned back.

By May 17, they were at the original camp, although the Kootenays had moved to higher ground because the river had overflowed its banks and flooded the shoreline. On his return, Thompson learned from Ugly Head that his trip to the Flat Heads had been unsuccessful. They could not make the journey north because of the flooding. There would not be the furs Thompson had counted on to make the year a profitable one. "Thus all my fine Hopes are ruined," he wrote, and began planning his return trip.

The Kootenays frequently travelled from the lower to the upper reaches of the big U-shaped river that ran through their country, but they usually went overland across a secondary chain of mountains. They went in the spring to a beautiful rolling plain along the upper river, where they planted tobacco, and they returned late summer to harvest their crop and dig bitterroots, the edible root of a wildflower that grew there.

Thompson chose to take the overland route back to Kootenay House. His canoe was damaged and leaky, and the river was rising daily and would continue to do so until the surrounding mountains were clear of snow. He and his men left on May 19 with a reluctant young Kootenay guide and three pack horses loaded with furs, but the trails were flooded, forcing them up the steep, forested sides of the mountains. Thompson's knee was still lame. Food was scarce and on the second night they went to bed hungry. The next day their guide deserted. Thompson captured the desperation of the moment in a journal entry: "Passed the evening reflecting on our forlorn situation (without a Guide, Path or Provisions in these rugged Mountains)."

Two of the men, Lussier and Mousseau, went back to the Kootenay camp and returned on May 24 with Ugly Head. Thompson paid him in advance. He opened his trade goods and laid on the ground before the guide a long hooded cape, a red blanket, a large knife, an axe, ten balls and a corresponding amount of powder. Ugly Head was satisfied and they set off. After a twelve-day journey, they reached the upper river. Two men, Lussier and Le Camble, had lost all their possessions crossing a raging creek. The horses' legs were laced with cuts and scrapes and coated in dried blood. Everyone was fatigued and sore, but safe. For this they thanked Ugly Head. "Here we bid adieu to our Humane Guide, without whose (manly exertions,) Perseverance & Attention we had certainly never have been able to have reached this Place," Thompson wrote.

When they arrived at Kootenay House on June 8, they found it empty. Finan McDonald, a six-foot-four Scot with red hair and a bushy beard of the same hue, had been left in charge that spring and started downriver with those at the post, including a pregnant Charlotte Thompson and her children. Thompson and his men soon caught up and learned that the others had been forced by a shortage of provisions to eat most of the dogs. They now slaughtered a horse as food for the start of the journey over the mountains.

After a successful crossing, Thompson dropped his family at a post called Boggy Hall, below Rocky Mountain House near the junction of the North Saskatchewan and Brazeau Rivers, where Charlotte's brother, Patrick Small, was posted with his wife, the daughter of Thompson's good friend James Hughes. Meanwhile, Thompson and five men continued in canoes laden with bales of fur. They went down the Saskatchewan to its mouth at Lake Winnipeg, cruised the length of the big lake, went up the Winnipeg River and across Lake of the Woods to Rainy River.

They travelled remarkably quickly. One night, shortly after crossing the Rockies, their Indian hunter, a Chippeway from Rainy Lake, was clearly distraught. He sat near the fire with his hands on his knees and his head in his hands. "Supposing him to be ill, I enquired what was the matter with him," Thompson wrote. "Looking at me he said: 'I cannot make myself believe that from where we embarked in the Mountains we have come here in one day; it must be two days, and I have not slept.' By my journals, I found we had come one hundred and thirty two miles."

They arrived July 22 at Rainy Lake House, an advance depot built to serve traders who could not, because of distance, reach Fort William and get back to their posts before winter set in. They loaded two canoes with goods packed in twenty pieces, each weighing ninety pounds, and began the trip back. Among the merchandise were two kegs of alcohol. Thompson objected, but was overruled by fellow partners Donald McTavish and John McDonald of Garth.

"I had made it a law to myself, that no alcohol should pass the Mountains in my company, and thus be clear of the sad sight of drunkenness, and its many evils: but these gentlemen insisted upon alcohol being the most profitable article that could be taken for the Indian trade. In this I knew they had miscalculated; accordingly when we came to the defiles of the Mountains, I placed the two Kegs of Alcohol on a vicious horse; and by noon the Kegs were empty, and in pieces, the Horse rubbing his load against the Rocks to get rid of it; I wrote to my partners what I had done; and that I would do the same to every Keg of Alcohol, and for the next six years I had charge of the furr trade on the west side of the Mountains, no further attempt was made to introduce spirituous Liquors."

Thompson and his crew of ten were back at Kootenay House on November 2. He sent Finan McDonald, one of his most trusted assistants, and four others south to establish a post below Kootenay Falls, the big cataract that divided the upper McGillivray from the lower, and he instructed McDonald to dispatch some of his men to the tribes even farther south to establish relations with them. In addition, Jaco Finlay, who had left the company several years earlier to work as a free trader, was camped with his wife and family and trapping less than a day's ride north of Kootenay House. There was only one woman at the post—Mrs. Lussier, who had just given birth to her fourth child. Charlotte Thompson, who was nursing her infant son John, born August 25, 1808, was wintering at Fort Augustus, located adjacent to the Hudson's Bay Co.'s Edmonton House. With his family east of the mountains, Thompson prepared for a quiet winter, having travelled more than 4,500 miles in just six months.

The trade went well that winter, better than expected, and one day in the spring of 1809 Thompson watched with a mix of relief and elation as his French-Canadian labourers worked the fur presses. They piled on pelt after pelt and pulled the lever that brought down the rough-hewn log press to create a tight, ninety-pound piece, which was then wrapped in canvas. They pressed five, ten, fifteen, twenty, twenty-two pieces, a great haul, and later Finan McDonald and his party returned from McGillivray's River leading a train of pack horses that swayed and sweated under the loads. Their furs, when pressed, produced thirty-two pieces.

Thompson and his ten-member crew, who constituted the Columbia Division of the North West Co., had accumulated more than five thousand pounds of furs in the winter of 1808–09—enough, they hoped, to silence the skeptical partners who had wanted to abandon the trade west of the mountains after one unprofitable season. The Columbia Division would survive and, with it, Thompson's ambitions to explore and map a navigable route to the Pacific.

But his most immediate concern that spring was Lussier's wife. She was sick. She had hardly stirred in days and could not get out of bed, and at 2 a.m. on April 25 she died, with Lussier at her side. "She has left four small children, the youngest only 6 months old, which distresses me much," Thompson wrote. "At 1 PM. we buried the poor woman and take the best care we can of her children."

They took the youngsters downriver to Jaco Finlay's camp and entrusted them to Finlay's wife. Then they began transporting the furs over the mountains and down the Saskatchewan. By late June, they had reached Fort Augustus. Thompson sent the furs to Superior with James McMillan, a trusted aide, and he stayed behind with Charlotte and the children, whom he hadn't seen since the fall.

It was here, in all likelihood, that Thompson learned of the results of Simon Fraser's exploration of the river Alexander Mackenzie had identified by its Indian name, the Tacouthe Tesse; how Fraser had set out from Fort George, his post on the river, in late May 1808 with twenty-four men, including two Indians; how they had encountered one extraordinary obstacle after another and faced great danger over and over again; how the portages were so excruciatingly difficult that his men almost preferred to risk their lives by staying in the canoes; how they had been pestered by hostile coastal natives near the mouth of the river; and, most important, how Fraser's surveyor, John Stuart, had determined that the river met the sea just above the forty-ninth parallel, or about 220 miles above the mouth of the Columbia.

After a three-week layover at Fort Augustus, Thompson and Finan McDonald rode west with five French Canadians, a Saulteaux hunter and a Kootenay guide named The Thunder. Near the Kootenay Plains they met a Hudson's Bay Co. clerk, Joseph Howse, returning from an exploratory expedition—the first indication that the Company of Adventurers was contemplating a move across the Rockies.

In the pass, they encountered Jaco Finlay, his wife, their children and Lussier's brood. They were ragged, hungry and exhausted. The Piegan had visited their camp two weeks earlier and stolen the horses, the guns and most of the food—everything they deemed to be useful. Thompson lent Finlay horses and assured him he would provide him with the necessities to start over. The entire party then continued west toward the big, north-flowing river that Thompson now knew to be the Columbia.

The men saddled and loaded the horses by lamplight. Across the valley, the peaks of the Rockies were just visible against the grey morning sky, but the forest around Kootenay House was hunched and black. They departed shortly before 5 a.m. on August 20, 1809, and headed south. They left nothing behind except refuse. The post had served them well, but Finan McDonald's big haul the previous winter on McGillivray's River had persuaded Thompson to move the entire division south to develop the trade with the Flat Bows and an affiliated group of tribes—the Kalispels, the Salish, the Coeur d'Alene and the Spokane, who spoke dialects of a common language.

The traders travelled slowly, their pace set by Jaco Finlay's extended family, but Finlay earned his keep as a hunter. That first day, he brought down a nice deer to supplement the mountain sheep and two lambs the Saulteaux had killed. They reached McGillivray's River and travelled till 6:30 p.m., and Thompson finished the day with his customary expression of gratitude to the Creator: "Thank God for the safety hereto & we hope for his goodness throughout."

They worked their way down the river, some by canoe, some on horses, always looking for birchbark to keep the vessels repaired and food to ensure that they survived. A week after setting out, they reached the falls, which in the spring of 1808 had been a bloated and thundering cataract but were now much reduced, and they portaged around them with relative ease. Two days later, they came to what Thompson referred to in his journal as "The Great Road of the Flat Heads," and here they stopped.

They intended to proceed south and pass the winter among the Flat Heads, but they needed additional horses to transport the goods. Thompson sent The Thunder and a voyageur named Beaulieu to advise the Salish of their situation and they returned six days later with sixteen men and twenty-five horses.

The road to Salish country passed through a forested mountain valley. It followed a tributary of McGillivray's river to its source, went over the height of land and down another river that drained into a large body of water, later named Pend Oreille Lake—forty-six miles long and six wide in places, and surrounded by mountains. The entire party reached the lake on September 9 and found eighty families, a mix of Salish, Coeur d'Alene and Kootenays, awaiting them.

With the exception of the Kootenays, all were clothed in animal skins and armed with stone-headed spears and flint-tipped arrows.

The traders began building a post, which they named Kullyspel House after the Kalispel Indians, who lived on the lake, but were interrupted almost daily for two weeks by various Indians arriving with furs, and Thompson made note of the activity in his journal: "Spent much of the Day in trading with the Indians who brought abt 120 or 130 Skins. . . . Traded abt 20 Skins & and looked for wood for a Horse Collar. . . . Indians traded a few things &c & promised to bring all they have presently—traded a canoe for fishing &c. . . . All the Indians arrived with what they have to Trade, abt 1 3/4 Packs & much berries—we spent the whole day in this Business &c. . . . Traded 3 Horses which now makes 7 for the company. . . . 15 strange Indians arrived from the west; they are quite poor in everything seemingly—they each made us a small present of dried Trout or Salmon."

On September 26, with construction of the post well advanced, Thompson left to explore the river flowing west from the lake. The Indians informed him that it drained into the Columbia, but he advanced only to a point where it narrowed. Here the current became exceedingly strong and swift, and he realized that a major obstacle—likely a waterfall—lay just ahead. He turned back and reached Kullyspel House on October 6. Four days later, he left to meet a brigade coming down McGillivray's River with more trading goods. Rather than take a familiar route, the Great Road of the Flat Heads, he explored the Clark Fork River, which flows into Pend Oreille Lake from the southeast. He finished the journey by travelling overland about one hundred miles to connect with his men on McGillivray's River.

Thompson's final expedition of the season began November 1. He and seven men left Kullyspel House and went about sixty miles up Clark Fork to establish a second post, which they named Salish House. They travelled for eight days, the last two without eating, before choosing a site. Food was their first priority and the men spent several days hunting.

*Thompson's sketch of the Salish Mountains,
south of the 49th parallel, winter 1809–1810.*

This led to more misfortune. On November 12, the clerk
James McMillan was loading his gun. It discharged unexpectedly
and the ball shattered the forefingers of both hands. Thompson
dressed the wounds as best he could and comforted his friend, but
after a week, the left finger showed no sign of healing and he was
forced to amputate.

———

During the winter of 1809, the Salish gave Thompson an Indian
name, Koo Koo Sint, the Man Who Looks at Stars. On clear, mild
nights—and there were many in the mountain valley where Salish
House stood—Thompson would climb to a plateau several hundred feet above the post and hoist his telescope heavenward. The
instrument was large and heavy—three feet long and four inches
in diameter with a wooden barrel, a brass eyepiece and the name
of the manufacturer, DOLLOND—LONDON, stamped in the brass.

He always observed with his good eye, the left one. His right eye had never recovered from his first observations and candlelit calculations as an overzealous novice at Cumberland House twenty years earlier. The disability in no way diminished the joy he felt while observing.

Often, as he gazed at the celestial canopy and trained his telescope on some tiny point of light, he could hear a soft murmur behind him, the voices of Salish men who had accompanied him. They relied on the naked eye for their observations and saw something quite different than he did. To them, the majestic night sky was a giant graveyard and the stars the final resting place of the most accomplished of their nation.

The Salish told Thompson many stories about their ancestors, their beliefs and their country. They were a friendly, hospitable people, and seven lodges of Salish camped near the post that winter. Most evenings, their chiefs—the Orator and another dubbed Cartier because he resembled a French-Canadian trader of that name— would visit to smoke and talk. Usually, the two leaders, and others who accompanied them, arrived in a jovial mood. But one night in February 1810, they sat quietly, forgoing the customary greetings and salutations. Cartier, as Thompson later wrote, broke the silence.

"You know that our law is that a man who seduces a woman must be killed."

"I have no objection to your law," Thompson replied. "To what purpose do you tell me this?"

Then the Orator spoke. "My daughter with her mother has always sat quietly in my Tent, until these few days past, when one of your men has been every day, while we are hunting, to my tent with beads and rings to seduce my daughter. He is not here. But wherever he is, we hope that you will give him to us that he may die by our law."

Thompson knew who the culprit was—he had seen him slip out of the room as the chiefs arrived—and he knew the man was in serious trouble. The Salish were an industrious people with a strict code of morality. Women were to be chaste at marriage; those who broke this rule were put to death.

*The Salish Mountains: Thompson named them after the local
Indians and they named him Koo Koo Sint,
the Man Who Looks at Stars.*

"I have no inclination to protect the man," he said. "But as you are much in want of guns and ammunition for hunting and to protect yourselves from your enemies, if you wish me to return with these articles, and various others, you must give me a Man to take his place, otherwise I cannot return."

The chiefs considered this, and then one replied: "We cannot find a man capable, besides his going among strange people where he may be killed."

"Very well, then," said Thompson. "If you kill my man I cannot return to you, but shall stay with the Piegans, your enemies."

"Then what is to be done," exclaimed the Orator.

"Let him live this time, and as you are a noted gelder of Horses; if this man ever again enters your Tent, geld him, but let him live."

At that, everyone laughed, and when the laughter had subsided, one of the chiefs said: "Well let him live, but so sure as he comes to seduce our women, we shall geld him."

Thompson was relieved that he had avoided a confrontation, but angry at the assistant whose indifference to the values of the

Salish had nearly cost him his life. He chastised the man, whom he did not name, and advised him that when he was living among the Indians he ought to learn their laws and live by them.

Thompson left Salish House on April 19, sending a train of fur-laden pack horses ahead, and paddled downriver to Kullyspel House. For him, spring was always a time of anticipation and excitement, this year more so than most. He was planning to go all the way down to Fort William and from there to Montreal on a long-awaited leave of absence, but before commencing that marathon journey he made a short exploratory trip on the river that flowed west from Pend Oreille Lake. He wanted to ascertain whether this waterway would provide a navigable link to the Columbia.

Thompson left with one of his men and an Indian guide. They entered the river and descended until the speed and strength of the current forced them ashore. They were approaching a major waterfall and tried walking the last three miles, but were stopped by waist-deep snow. The guide informed Thompson that the river plummeted eighty to one hundred feet into a long, deep and narrow canyon and there began its final descent to the Columbia. Indians rarely ventured beyond the falls, and those who did encountered a tough, dangerous two-and-a-half-day march, frequently scrambling over steep rocks on their hands and knees.

This river, Thompson concluded, could not serve as a navigable trade route, and he returned to Kullyspel House. The men assembled a train of sixteen pack horses, loaded with more than four thousand pounds of fur, and they headed north on the first leg of a two -thousand-mile journey to Fort William. They went up McGillivray's River, down the Columbia and over the mountains. From there, he left James McMillan in charge of transporting the furs and embarked in a canoe with three other voyageurs, following the Saskatchewan River to Lake Winnipeg. Along the way, Thompson picked up his family at a post on the Saskatchewan and left them at another company house on Lake Winnipeg where Charlotte's sister-in-law was residing. Next, they went up the Winnipeg River, across Lake of the Woods and paddled to the headwaters of Rainy River, reaching the company's advance depot on July 22 after a long but otherwise routine trip.

Thompson had left Finan McDonald at Salish House for the summer, along with two French Canadians, Michel Bourdeaux and Bapteste Buché, and they enjoyed a season that was quiet and uneventful in all ways but one. In July, the Salish formed a large party of about a hundred and fifty men to travel to the plains to hunt buffalo. Formerly, they had pursued the great herds by stealth to avoid their old enemies, the Piegan. This year was different. Over the winter, they had acquired upward of twenty firearms and several hundred iron arrowheads from Thompson and now had no fear of the Piegan.

One morning, the scouts sent ahead to survey the country raced back shouting: "The enemy is on us!" The Salish immediately dropped their teepees and piled the baggage on top to form a simple barrier. They had no sooner done so than a hundred and seventy Piegan warriors charged on horseback. The Piegan raced at the Salish three times without breaking their line. With that, they dismounted about four hundred yards away, and the fight began.

It lasted all day. The Salish and their three white allies kept themselves concealed. The Piegan repeatedly sent men forth to taunt their adversaries. They danced so furiously they were hard to hit. Nevertheless, by evening, seven Piegan were dead and thirteen wounded. The Salish lost five men and had nine injured. Finan McDonald had fired forty-five shots. He killed two men and hit another. The French Canadians each fired forty-three balls and wounded one enemy apiece.

The Piegan had suffered a humiliating defeat. Furious, they blamed the white traders. They had given these interlopers free passage through their country and, in return, they had not only armed the enemy but joined the fight. The Piegan were a proud people. They resolved that white men would no longer pass unmolested through their lands.

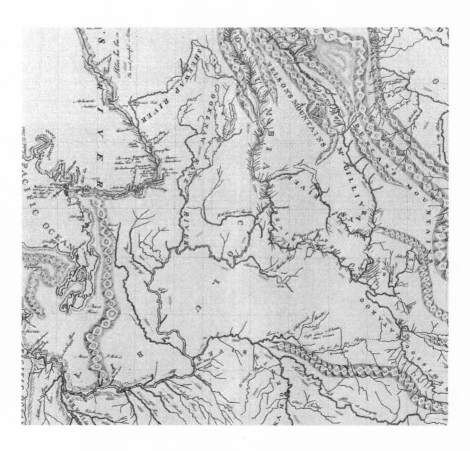

*Thompson's travels, 1810–1812: His journey down the Columbia
was the culmination of 28 years spent in the northwest
and the realization of his dream.*

To the Pacific

(1810)

THE FUNNY THING WAS THAT, FOR THE PREVIOUS THREE SEASONS —when Thompson had been eager to tackle the Columbia, to unravel its complex geography, to determine once and for all whether the great river of the west would provide the Montreal-based merchants of Canada with a navigable route to the Pacific— the merchants had been indifferent, had even stood in his way by giving him only enough men and resources to trade, but now that he was ready for a well-deserved and long-promised furlough—ten months in Montreal, his first taste of civilization in twenty-six years, some time with his wife and family, who no longer travelled with him—now they had postponed his leave and ordered him to travel down the Columbia all the way to the Pacific.

Things had changed for the merchants when word arrived from New York that John Jacob Astor was preparing to send two expeditions—one by sea, the other by land—to the mouth of the Columbia. Astor was a German immigrant. Born in the village of Waldorf in 1763, he sailed for America at the age of twenty and set-tled in New York, then a city of a little over twenty thousand inhab-itants. A man of limitless energy and ambition, Astor quickly made good in his chosen field—the fur trade—despite the dominance of the Hudson's Bay Co. and North West Co.

By 1800, Astor had amassed a small fortune—said to be worth $250,000—while trading only as far west as the valley of the Ohio River. But his horizons soon expanded. He began sending his best furs to Canton, the most lucrative market in the world, and bringing back tea, silk, spices and other exotic goods, which he sold in the United States or Europe for dazzling profits. He was thus positioned to take advantage of America's westward expansion, made possible through the acquisition in 1803 of the Louisiana Territory.

Astor envisioned a string of trading posts that would extend up the Missouri River, over the Rockies and down the lower Columbia, following the route of Lewis and Clark on their epic journey of discovery from 1804 to 1806. This enterprise would establish an American presence on the newly acquired lands and would compete with the Hudson's Bay Co. and the North West Co., who controlled the trade west of the Mississippi. But his scheme differed in one fundamental way from the operations of his rivals. Where they brought their furs east, the one to Hudson Bay, the other to Montreal, transported them across the Atlantic and sold them in London, Astor's traders would send theirs west to a terminal at the mouth of the Columbia and from there they would be shipped to China.

In February of 1808, he outlined his plan in a letter to President Thomas Jefferson, who endorsed it warmly and promised whatever support the government could provide. In April, Astor began organizing the American Fur Co. to bring his dream to life. He intended to retain control, but needed partners. The first place he looked was Montreal, the fur capital of North America.

Astor was well known there. He had, early in his career, made yearly trips to Montreal to purchase furs and trade goods. Now, he offered the agents of the North West Co., William McGillivray, John Ogilvy, Thomas Thain and a few others, a one-third interest in his new venture.

The agents of the North West Co. may have been skeptical about Astor's chances of success but they knew better than to be complacent. They had to respond. Their first move was to look for support from the British government, cleverly couching their appeals in political terms. The merchants of Canada, according to their correspondence, were thinking only of Britain's territorial claims, not the company's commercial advantage.

In September 1809, the committee of trade at Montreal, a body made up largely of businessmen involved in the fur trade, wrote to the British ambassador in Washington. They argued that the Americans had no claims to the Columbia River or any territory west of the Rockies. "The right in both cases clearly belongs to Great Britain by the discoveries of Cook, Vancouver and Mackenzie," they wrote. "No establishment of the States on that River or on the Coast of the Pacific should therefore be sanctioned."

More correspondence followed. On January 23, 1810, McGillivray, Ogilvy and Thain wrote to their London representatives to impress upon them the case for a government response. They stated that Britain had first claim on the basis of occupation, as well as discovery. "With respect to possession," they wrote, "that is also in our favor, for the posts of the North West Company are, and have been for several years, established on the Waters which fall into the Columbia, or on Branches of that River."

They made two proposals. First, they suggested that the government lift the East India Co.'s monopoly on trade with China and open the market to them as well so they might ship furs to Canton from the west coast of North America. Alternatively, they hoped to be compensated for expenses related to expanding their Columbia Division, either through direct financial payments or by being granted an exclusive right to trade on the river and adjacent coasts, and they justified this on the grounds that they would be serving the national interest of Great Britain.

In March of that year, William McGillivray's brother Simon, who was based in London, joined members of the Committee of

British North American Merchants for a meeting with Lord Liverpool, the secretary of state for war and colonies. The delegation
informed the minister of Astor's expedition and the potential
threat to England's claims on the Pacific coast. Lord Liverpool
referred the matter to his cabinet colleague the Marquis of Welles-
ley, secretary of state for foreign affairs.

And there the matter died. Nathaniel Atcheson, secretary of
the merchants' committee, wrote to the marquis on April 2, provided him with copies of the earlier correspondence and requested
an interview. The minister did not respond. Nor did he acknowledge a second letter from Atcheson asking for a meeting.

While they were trying to stir the British government into
action, the agents of the North West Co. were also negotiating with
Astor. A partnership would confer benefits on both. It would
relieve the New Yorker of formidable competition and it would free
the Nor'Westers of the onerous and financially draining task of
transporting furs all the way back to Montreal. It would also give
the latter access to Canton, which was off limits to all but the East
India Co. under the monopoly granted by the Crown.

As attractive as Astor's offer was, the Montreal-based partners had reservations. They resented the idea of being cast as
minority partners in the Columbia trade, which they had pio-
neered. Furthermore, they could not enter such a venture without consulting the wintering partners—the shareholders based at
the western posts—and so they deferred a decision until the
annual rendez-vous. There, in the Great Hall at Fort William, on
Superior's shore, a vigorous debate occurred. The wintering partners were all for Astor's offer and gave the Montreal agents a
mandate to commit up to ten thousand pounds for a one-third
share of his project.

The partners knew that negotiations with Astor might fail.
They also knew he would proceed with or without them, and they
needed to protect themselves against such a turn of events. This led
to another important decision. They would send David Thompson

down the Columbia to establish their presence on the river and to lay the basis for future territorial claims.

News of the decision awaited Thompson when he arrived at Rainy Lake on July 22, 1810, on his way to Montreal. At first, he was dismayed. He was expecting to continue to Montreal on his leave of absence, which had already been delayed two years. But upon reflection he realized that he had been given an opportunity to complete a survey of the great river of the west. He would soon have the last piece he needed to create a map stretching from Hudson Bay to Lake Superior to the Pacific. A few days later, he embarked on a historic journey with six canoes, twenty-four men and more than six thousand pounds of trade goods.

True to form, Astor had not waited for the partners of the North West Co. to reach a decision on his offer. On June 23, 1810, he incorporated the Pacific Fur Co. as a subsidiary of his American Fur Co. and began looking for other partners. He found three clerks of the North West Co.—Alexander McKay, who had accompanied Sir Alexander Mackenzie on his historic journeys of 1789 and 1793, Duncan McDougall and Donald McKenzie—as well as two other Canadians, David Stuart and his nephew Robert, who were willing to invest. He also lined up several American investors.

In early July, Donald McKenzie and one of the Americans left New York for Montreal, hired a crew of voyageurs and purchased ammunition, supplies and trade goods. They set off via the St. Lawrence and Ottawa Rivers for Michilimackinac, an island in the straits between Lakes Huron and Michigan and a gathering place for trappers and traders working on the Mississippi, the Missouri and the lands of the southern fur trade. They planned to paddle south on Lake Michigan to Green Bay, travel upriver and overland to the Mississippi and down that river to the confluence with the Missouri, where they would turn west.

The sea expedition to the west coast had to leave in the fall, sailing away from the northern winter and into the southern summer. It would round Cape Horn at the tip of South America and reach the mouth of the Columbia early in the spring of 1811. Astor spent the summer preparing.

He fitted out a ship, the *Tonquin,* capable of carrying 290 tons of cargo and armed with ten guns. He retained an American naval officer, Lt. Jonathan Thorn, to command the vessel and hired a crew of seventeen to maintain and sail it. He procured trade goods, provisions, ammunition and building supplies as well as the frame of a schooner to be assembled upon arrival and used to cruise up and down the coast trading with the Indians nations that inhabited the region. He lined up his personnel: McKay, McDougall and the Stuarts; eleven clerks, eight of whom were from Canada; and thirteen French-Canadian voyageurs, who paddled down the Hudson River from Lake Champlain. They arrived on a lovely morning and startled the inhabitants of New York with their precise paddling, exuberant singing, lively attire and hats decorated with feathers and gaily coloured ribbons.

On September 11, 1810, Astor shook hands with his partners. He bade them farewell and watched from the docks as the sails of the *Tonquin* were unfurled and trimmed and the ship slipped past Manhattan and out to sea.

Alexander Henry had never known a situation like it, not in all his years in the trade. He had just arrived at Rocky Mountain House, which had been unoccupied for several years. It was the first week of October 1810, late in the season to be getting established for the winter, and here were Thompson's men—the Columbia brigade—but where was Thompson? His concern only deepened as the days passed.

Henry had come upriver to trade with the Piegan, the Blackfoot and the Bloods. He had spent the previous winter at Fort Vermilion, three hundred miles downstream at the mouth of the

Vermilion River, and the Indians had tormented him and his men. Henry, one of the few Nor'Westers besides Thompson to keep a daily journal, made note of all the incidents. In early November 1809, an old woman informed him that the Cree and Assiniboine had declared war on the fur traders and were advancing up the river to clear it of whites and steal their horses, though the report proved to be unfounded. Several times, he heard from friendly Indians that some of their brethren wanted to kill him, though Henry did not disclose the reasons for their hostility in his journal.

On December 31, he received word from James Hughes, his counterpart at Fort Augustus, that the Blackfoot had accosted two of his men on the plains, had stolen all their goods and would have murdered them had a chief not intervened. Three weeks later, two men arrived from Augustus with news that the Blackfoot were threatening daily to attack the post.

Then the Indians, Blackfoot and Stoneys, began stealing horses. They stole thirty-seven belonging to Henry and his men on January 27. A few days later, three went missing from the nearby Hudson's Bay Co. post. On February 6, they hit the Nor'Westers again, this time taking five horses, and four days later they made off with another thirty-two. There were more thefts throughout the winter. Traders were threatened or harassed. Reports circulated that the Cree and Assiniboine were gathering to make war on the Blackfoot.

Henry and Hughes responded to the trouble by abandoning their posts in the spring and building a new one, Terre Blanche House, about midway between Forts Augustus and Vermilion, at the mouth of White Earth River. They reasoned that one establishment would be cheaper than two and, by joining forces, they could better defend themselves, if necessary. The Hudson's Bay Co. men at the Vermilion River also pulled out and built right next to the Nor'Westers, although a range of stockades separated the two posts.

The summer was peaceful, convincing Henry and Hughes that they could again maintain separate posts. They decided to reopen

Rocky Mountain House, the most westerly settlement on the Saskatchewan. It would serve the Piegan, Blackfoot and Bloods. They hoped the Cree and Assiniboine would patronize Terre Blanche House, thereby reducing contact between these warring tribes.

Three canoes left Terre Blanche House on September 24. A fourth followed the next day. Henry departed September 26 on horseback with three men. He reached Rocky Mountain House on October 5, ahead of his four canoes, and was startled to see smoke rising from the chimneys and men loitering around the gates of what was supposed to be a deserted post. Initially, he assumed they were Indians, but as he approached, he saw that they were Thompson's men, and they told him a troubling story.

They had come up the river in canoes. Thompson, Henry's cousin William and two Iroquois hunters were travelling ahead of them on horseback, shooting deer and buffalo and supplying the canoe brigade with meat, which they dropped at designated places along the river. Their last contact with Thompson occurred on September 15 at an abandoned post about a hundred and twenty miles up the river from the newly established Terre Blanche.

The two parties, one travelling by land, the other by water, planned to meet at Rocky Mountain House. There, Thompson and his three companions would board the canoes for the run up the river to the Kootenay Plains, where the voyageur Bercier was waiting with horses to carry the cargo over the mountains. The canoe brigade reached Rocky Mountain House on September 24, but Thompson wasn't there, so the men continued upriver for a day, until they encountered a Piegan camp of four tents. The Piegan— still smouldering over their defeat at the hands of the Salish three months earlier—had set up a blockade on the Saskatchewan. One of their chiefs, Black Bear, told the traders they would not be permitted to go any farther.

Hearing all this, Henry was "sorely perplexed," as he put it in his journal. He had to find Thompson, but didn't know whether he was upriver or down. Henry wanted to send the Columbia brigade on its way, but small parties of Piegan, including a group led by Black Bear, kept coming in to trade. The Indians appeared friendly, but watched the traders closely and talked quietly among themselves in a language the nervous Henry did not understand. They also dug up a burial site where the remains of two Cree and a young white girl were interred and they scattered the bones—a bad omen, in Henry's opinion. "This open grave, with the remnants of the deceased's dress and her bones half-eaten by wolves, was a melancholy sight," he wrote.

On October 7, the Piegan left, and Henry sent Thompson's men toward the mountains. They returned two days later, telling him they had had to tow the canoes because the river was so low. Their footprints were plainly visible on the beach, and several Piegan had followed the trail to their camp and ordered them to return to Rocky Mountain House. The men stayed overnight but were watched continuously, which convinced them it would be foolish to proceed any farther.

Another band of Piegan arrived to trade. They came from the west—upriver—and Thompson's men recognized his horse among those the Piegan brought with them. One of the Indians produced a pair of blue cloth leggings, which he said he had found at a campsite. These belonged to Henry's cousin. Henry was now convinced that Thompson was upriver, probably waiting for his men at the Kootenay Plain. As soon as the Piegan departed, he suggested that the men of the Columbia brigade head west to meet Thompson, but they refused to leave unless accompanied by Henry or his assistant Angus Bethune.

After a lengthy discussion, Henry agreed to stay at Rocky Mountain House while Bethune went with Thompson's men. Henry also concocted a plan to elude the Piegan blockade. He sent the men downstream at mid-afternoon October 11 with orders to turn around and begin the journey upstream toward the mountains once darkness fell. In the meantime, if any Piegan arrived, Henry would get them drunk enough to pass out.

As it turned out, three Bloods and a Sarcee came to trade, and Henry plied them with liquor. Around 11 p.m., he went down to the river. It was a clear, moonlit night and soon he discerned the shadowy forms of the men towing the canoes. They stopped and took on more freight and by 2 a.m. resumed their journey.

Henry thought he was finished with the Columbia brigade, but another surprise awaited him. The following evening at sunset three of his four canoes arrived at Rocky Mountain House, and there, seated in one of them, was his cousin William, who had astonishing news to report: Thompson was fifty miles downstream near the confluence of the Brazeau and North Saskatchewan Rivers. Furthermore, Thompson had sent orders: the Columbia brigade was to join him there because he had decided to take a different route across the mountains.

The next day—October 13—Henry sent a man upstream to stop the Columbia canoes. Then he, his cousin and several others left to meet Thompson. "At noon we embarked," Henry wrote in his journal, "and at 4 p.m. reached Mr. Thompson's camp, on the N. side, on top of a hill 300 feet above the water, where tall pines stood so thickly that I could not see his tent until I came within 10 yards of it. He was starving and waiting for his people—both his own canoes and those men who were coming down with his horses."

Thompson's four-week absence has become one of the most controversial episodes in his long career as a trader and traveller. The mystery surrounding those days has been heightened by Thompson's silence about them. He began keeping a daily record of his activities in October 1789, while posted at the Hudson's Bay Co.'s Cumberland House and, for the next twenty-one years, seldom missed an entry. To the chagrin of all who have studied his life, there is an uncharacteristic gap of fourteen weeks—from July 22 to October 29, 1810—in his journals. His silence has invited speculation, and most of it has been negative.

Two prominent historians, Arthur Silver Morton and Richard Glover, the first writing in the 1920s and 1930s, the latter in the 1950s, concluded that Thompson had cowered in the face of the Piegan threat, retreated in a cowardly fashion and hidden from the world for almost a month. According to these historians, to hide his shame, Thompson either destroyed or discarded that part of his journals. Others, most notably Peter C. Newman in his three-volume history of the Hudson's Bay Co., have repeated and even amplified this interpretation of events.

But there is another explanation, and it comes from Thompson's contemporary William Henry, as recorded in the journals of his cousin Alexander, a prolific diarist. This version casts an entirely different light on Thompson's character.

In all his years in the trade, in all the wilderness journeys he'd made and all the miles he'd travelled, Thompson had never lost his way, nor had anyone perished while following him. But a curious thing happened after he and his companions—Henry and the two Iroquois—left Upper Terre Blanche House on September 15. Thompson had, in fact, got lost.

They had left the Saskatchewan and set off in a southwesterly direction, following an old Indian trail through thick, tangled forest. He assumed the trail would deposit them at Rocky Mountain House or close to it. Instead, they reached the river again many miles west of the post, near the first range of mountains. The natural thing to do would have been to wait for the canoes to arrive and travel with his men to the Kootenay Plain to meet Bercier. But the Piegan blockade made that impossible. Thompson did not make direct contact with them, but he saw their horses and the camp and he suspected the Piegan were watching them. He understood what was happening. The Piegan were there to prevent him from crossing the mountains because he had been supplying their enemies with firearms. Thompson was now cut off from the canoe brigade and, at that moment, he acted wisely and decisively. He knew that the only safe course of action was to avoid a confrontation with the Piegan.

They were unlike other Indian nations on these northern plains. They had been a nuisance and a menace to him from the time he first crossed the Rockies, in June 1807. They were quite willing to harass, steal from and even murder traders who crossed them. Now, they were after him. If there were a confrontation between the Piegan and Thompson's canoe brigade, it may well have resulted in bloodshed and lives lost on both sides. That could have led to a broader conflict, a war in which the Piegan, the Bloods and the Blackfoot aligned themselves against the Nor'Westers and the British traders. That would have served no one's interest.

So Thompson turned around. He and his men retraced their steps along the overland route that had brought them to the edge of the mountains. And even as they were doing that, he had already made a crucial decision. He had had enough of the Piegan. It was time to find an alternative route across the Rockies, and he had one in mind.

The fire had burned low and by then most of the men and the three women in the party were stretched out under blankets or buffalo robes. They were in wooded country, a few miles from the North Saskatchewan, where they had started the day. It was a cool, cloudy night, but no snow had fallen yet. Thompson lit a candle, rummaged through his personal belongings and retrieved his journal, a bottle of ink and a pen. He turned to a clean page and, for the first time in three and a half months, entered the date—October 29, 1810—and began recording the highlights of the day.

"Early began collecting the Horses: 24 in Number belonging to the NW Company, each loaded with the weight of 180 to 240 lbs of Goods for Trade, Provisions & Necessaries. We in all 24 Men including myself . . . We have 2 professed Hunters in Bap[tiste] Bruneau & the Yellow Bird; and Thomas the Iroquois for our Guide across the Mountains when we have ascended the Athabasca River, for which we now bend our Course." He concluded by noting that they had halted for the day at 2:30 p.m. because the horses were tired and that they had gone to bed without dinner.

Thompson and his party were travelling along an old Assiniboine trail that went west from the Saskatchewan River toward the more northerly Athabasca River, a distance of about a hundred and ten miles as the crow flies. From there, he would lead his men up the Athabasca and over the Rocky Mountains. He knew this route was feasible because some adventurous Nipissing and Iroquois free hunters from Canada had already used it.

Yet the plan provoked heated debate between Thompson and Henry, who thought they should stick to the proven route up the Saskatchewan. Thompson held his ground. He used as his base an old post called Boggy Hall, where one of his children had been born. He had the horses brought down from Kootenay Plain and sent men downstream to another post for sled dogs and leather for boots and snowshoes.

When the preparations were complete, he led a large party west from Boggy Hall. There were twenty-four men, including three who had brought their wives, and twenty-four pack horses loaded with six thousand pounds of goods. It was late in the season, the country unfamiliar, and Thompson began with his customary appeal to providence, which he recorded in his journal: "At 10 Am we were all ready and set off—pray Heaven to send us a good Journey."

The journey to the Athabasca River took a month. They travelled through rough, wooded country, advancing only five to ten miles a day. They had to cross rivers, detour around bogs and hack their way through brush and forest. Game was scarce and hard to find. The ground was frozen but there was no snow, and so no tracks for the hunters to follow. Food was a problem from the beginning, and Thompson's men, mostly French Canadians, were hearty eaters. "A French Canadian has the appetite of a Wolf and glories in it," he would later write. "Each man requires eight pounds of meat pr day, or more: upon my reproaching some of

*Thompson in the Athabasca Pass, January, 1811: His men believed
they had entered the domain of the woolly mammoth.*

them with their gluttony, the reply I got was: 'What pleasure have
we in Life but eating.'"

Some days, they were denied even that. From the first to the
third of November, they got a dram, or about half an ounce, of
rum daily, nothing more, and on the fourth a helping of pemmican when two men arrived from the Saskatchewan with provisions.
Two days later, they received a double handful of pemmican and a
helping of buffalo fat.

Feast followed famine when the hunters brought down a buffalo or a moose. All work stopped. A fire was built and kettles of
meat and water brought to a boil. The men devoured pound after

pound and then quarrelled over their portions. Thompson came up with a solution after two of his men had killed a buffalo cow. "Weighed the Meat," he wrote, "& found 1400 pounds which I seperated among the Men, each to carry his Share to prevent waste & dispute."

When they reached the Athabasca, they were about fifty miles from the Rockies. They pitched their tents and spent nearly four weeks building sleds and snowshoes and rearranging the goods. During that time, the snow piled up and was soon knee deep, and it was bitter cold. Thompson noted that the temperature was minus thirty-two on the morning of December 24, and each night for the next week it was minus thirty or below.

Some of the men became surly and uncooperative. Their hearts were not in this venture, and Thompson's spirits sank too. He could share his misgivings with no one, not with the prevailing mood in the camp. Instead, he recorded his feelings in a letter to an old friend, Alexander Fraser, who had helped persuade him to leave the Hudson's Bay Co. fourteen years earlier and who was now retired and living near Montreal.

Thompson wrote that he yearned for a taste of civilization, something he hadn't experienced since leaving London in 1784 at age fourteen, but he stuck with this life of trade and travel because of his children. The eldest, Fanny, then nine, was already attending school in Montreal and he had three others to think of, though they were living at a company post with their mother. "It is my wish to give all my children an equal and good education," he told Fraser. "My conscience obliges me to it, and it is for this I am now working in this country.

"If all goes well," he continued, "and it pleases good Providence to take care of me I hope to see you and a civilized world in the autumn of 1812. I am getting tired of such constant hard journeys; for the last 20 months I have spent only barely two months under the shelter of a hut, all the rest has been in my tent, and there is little likelihood the next 12 months will be much otherwise."

Thompson's reservations were unquestionably genuine. He had endured long separations from his wife and family. He hardly knew what it was like to sleep in a bed. And here he was, camped on a frigid, snowbound river, preparing for a mid-winter trek over the Rockies with reluctant, apprehensive men. Who could avoid misgivings under such circumstances? But Thompson did not surrender to his doubts or fears. His apprehensions could not subdue his desire to finish the work of exploring the Columbia and reaching the Pacific.

On December 28, 1810, Thompson and his men prepared to leave their camp on the Athabasca. The expedition had been reduced to twelve, the others having returned to Rocky Mountain House. They had stored most of the goods in roughly constructed huts from which they could be retrieved later. The men loaded eight sleds, strapping seventy pounds of luggage and trade goods on those to be towed by one dog, a hundred and twenty on the ones to be hauled by two. They had four pack horses to carry the provisions—two hundred and eight pounds of pemmican, thirty-five pounds of grease, sixty pounds of flour, eighty pounds of partly dried meat and a load of fresh meat.

The next morning, with the temperature resting at minus thirty-two, they set off. They wore woollen clothing under leather coats, hats and heavy mitts, and loped along on snowshoes; Thomas the Iroquois guide out front, Thompson behind him and the French Canadians following with the dogs and the horses; a little caravan of men and beasts proceeding up the broad, icebound Athabasca toward the immense and intimidating wastes of the Rocky Mountains.

Several of the French Canadians had been recruited from the Fort des Prairies department of the North West Co., which was responsible for the trade on the upper Saskatchewan. They were accustomed to living at trading posts on the northern fringe of the prairie. A few of them may have seen the mountains, but none had crossed them, and they were unnerved by the prospect. They

*Fort Astoria: A canoe, a British flag and a crew of
Canadian boatmen led by a well-dressed gentleman
who introduced himself as David Thompson.*

quickly turned into a troublesome minority, and Thompson
became exasperated with them.

The expedition had no sooner entered the mountains than
some of the men convinced themselves that there were mammoth
lurking about—huge, woolly elephant-like creatures that could
gore them with long curved tusks, or crush them beneath their
hooves. Thompson tried to reason with the men. If such creatures
dwelt here, he asked, where were the tracks? The believers conceded
that there were none to be seen, but this did not dissuade them.

As they began their ascent to the pass, they had to abandon
the horses and use the dogs to haul everything. By then, the Fort
des Prairies men had become despondent, even rebellious. The
most defiant was a man named Du Nord, whom Thompson
described as "a showy fellow before the women but a coward in

heart." He beat a dog to death on January 8 and two days later refused to handle a sled. Thompson ordered him to leave for Rocky Mountain House, but let him stay after he expressed remorse.

They reached the height of land—the divide between Atlantic and Pacific—and the view was magnificent. To one side, less than half a mile away, there was a glacier, about two thousand feet in height and a striking green colour. On the other, there was a steep wall of rock hundreds of feet high. Thompson was elated. "It was to me a most exhilarating sight," he wrote, "but to my uneducated men a dreadful sight."

Energized by this, Thompson went off to explore after they stopped for the day. He returned to find his men boring into the snow with a pole twenty feet long. They could not reach the bottom, but all were intrigued when they looked into the hole. The snow beneath the surface was blue, light near the top and darkening to a deep indigo. That night they slept on beds of pine boughs and built a small fire, which soon sunk into the snow and went out. The men were restless and nervous, but struck by the brilliance of the stars, and one said they seemed close enough to touch.

They began their descent in the morning—January 11—and within three days had reached a valley at the foot of the mountains and begun following a river to the Columbia. The west side of the Rockies bore no resemblance to the east, and this, too, upset some of the men and to such a degree that Thompson named the river the Flat Heart. The temperature hovered around freezing. It could snow one day and rain the next. The snow was wet and heavy and the trees enormous—fifteen to twenty feet around and two hundred feet high or more.

The dogs could not haul the sleds through the deep, sticky snow, and Thompson ordered the men to remove all but the bare essentials and to hang the goods in a tree to be retrieved later. "The Courage of part of my Men (those from FDP) is sinking fast," he noted. "They see nothing in its proper Colour—the soft Weather is a thing; it seems they never felt before. The Snow, now reduced to 3 & 3 1/2 feet is

Thompson's sketch of Nelson's Mountains,
west of Kootenay House, winter 1808–09.

beyond all thought, yet they talk of 6 & 7 feet Snow in Montreal. I told them it was no matter the Snow was 20 ft deep, provided we went well over it, & had they been with me last Spring they would have carried Packs & Canoes over much deeper—but when Men arrive in a strange Country, fear gathers on them from every object."

They reached the Columbia on January 18 and began walking on the beaches and along the banks. They were travelling south and moving upstream, but the conditions were so difficult that they advanced only twelve miles in five days. At noon on January 23, they found their path blocked by a steep, rocky and heavily wooded point that jutted into the river. Thompson proposed that they build a raft to get around it. The men refused.

"Du Nord with the FDP men, having long been dispirited & useless as old Women, told me he would return, & as I was heartily tired of such worthless fellows & but poorly equipped for such a long Journey as still remained before me, & the Season so far advanced, I determined to return to the Junction of the Rivers Flat

Heart & Canoe River . . . & there wait for more Goods, Provisions &c, & build Canoes for the Journey."

The Columbia begins its journey to the sea a little above the forty-ninth parallel in a valley between the Rockies and the first range to the west, which Thompson named Nelson's Mountains in honour of the British commander who defeated Napoleon. From there the river flows north for two hundred miles before turning abruptly and travelling the opposite way through another mountain trench toward the forty-ninth. Thompson and the three men who remained loyal to him—Pierre Pareil, Joseph Coté and René Valade—spent the rest of the winter at the big bend in a hastily constructed twelve-by-twelve-foot cedar hut that stood on a three-foot-thick foundation of hard-packed snow.

Here, two other rivers join the Columbia. The Canoe comes in from the northwest and Thompson's Flat Heart, later renamed the Wood, flows from the northeast and Athabasca Pass. Thompson had planned to begin his journey at the turn, to proceed downriver to the forty-ninth and to continue all the way to the mouth of the Columbia at the forty-sixth degree of latitude. But he knew better than to travel with just three men through a vast extent of unknown country and the lands of many Indian nations, some of whom would be meeting white men for the first time. He expected most would be friendly, but what could a party of four do against a hostile tribe?

Thompson decided to proceed upriver rather than down. He would pass through familiar country, first to the source of the river and then farther south to the Columbia Division posts—Salish House, Kullyspel House and the newly established Spokane House—where he would hire additional crew and begin his journey. He and his men had built a twenty-five-foot canoe of cedar planks—the milder climate west of the Rockies made the birch rind too thin—and on April 17 they embarked, carrying with them about 300 pounds of trade goods and 235 pounds of provisions.

Nelson's Mountains.

The river was still frozen, except where a series of fifteen rapids had churned and thrashed all winter, and they travelled nine days before reaching water that was navigable. Most of the time, they towed the canoe over the ice. Their days were short and hard, as Thompson noted in his journal on April 19: "We were obliged to camp at 1 PM quite harassed & benumbed & swelled with cold Water & Snow—we searched for a place of encampment but could not find less than 5 1/2 to 6 ft of Snow & put up in the Snow as we were too fatigued to do anything—the Road we have come is always bordered by high Snowy Mountains, that almost touch each other."

Thompson and his companions portaged from the Columbia to McGillivray's River and paddled 270 miles before storing the canoe and trading for horses. They then rode seventy-five miles overland to Salish House on the Clark Fork River. The post was deserted, so they built another canoe and proceeded down the Clark Fork to Kullyspel House on Pend Oreille Lake, but it had been vacated as well. Thompson sent two Indian messengers to Spokane House, about sixty-five miles southwest of Kullyspel

House, to alert his men of his whereabouts, and two days later Finan McDonald and several others arrived at Kullyspel House with thirteen horses.

On the journey south from his winter camp, Thompson had added two more men to the party he planned to take down the Columbia. He had met a small group of Nipissings and Iroquois travelling north toward the Canoe River to trap beaver for the summer and had hired one of the Iroquois, a man named Charles, who was known as a highly skilled canoeman. He hired another Iroquois with a reputation for being good in a canoe, a fellow called Ignace, whom he met in a large camp of Salish.

Thompson also took time one evening to sit by the fire with an old Salish man who told the story of his youth and how he had once joined a large war party going to fight the Piegan. He carried a large club and felt confident going into battle. But he and his brethren had returned home frightened and dispirited.

"[Our] enemies had two Guns and every shot killed a Man. We could not stand this and thought they had brought bad spirits with them. We all fled and hid ourselves in the Mountains. We were not allowed to remain quiet. War parties now harassed us, destroyed the Men, Women and Children of our Camps and took away our Horses and Mules, for we had no defence until you crossed the Mountains and brought us firearms. Now we no longer hide ourselves but have regained much of our country, hunt the Bisons for food and clothing, and have good leather Tents."

Having heard this story, which he would come to record, Thompson was dismayed to learn when he reached Spokane House that the Indians there, a mix of Coeur d'Alene and Spokane—some of whom had dreaded the Piegan all their lives— had formed a war party to try their newly acquired guns against the Okanagans, a defenceless tribe to the southwest. The assembly of warriors had already departed, but Thompson dispatched two respected Spokane Indians with gifts of tobacco and vermilion for the chiefs and a speech for their followers.

Nelson's Mountains: Thomspon and his men were
"harassed & benumbed & swelled with cold,"
as they passed these mountians in the spring of 1811.

He reminded them that until his arrival three years earlier they had lived meagrely on fish and roots and in perpetual fear. He advised them that he would soon be trading with the Okanagans and supplying them with guns and iron arrowheads. And he challenged them to show real courage and go to war against the Piegan.

Thompson's words found their mark. About fifty warriors left to join a war party of Salish and Kootenay who were marching against the Piegan and their allies, and the remainder gave up all thought of combat to join the salmon fishery on the Columbia. Having helped prevent a massacre of Okanagans, Thompson turned his attention to his principal objective: the journey down the great river.

Thompson had decided, before putting paddle in water, that he would stop to meet people on his way down the Columbia. He would explain his purpose and lay the groundwork for future trade, and he would ensure safe passage on the return trip, when he and his men would be paddling into stiff, unrelenting currents and would be unable to flee if attacked.

Nine men made the journey: the French Canadians Michel Bourdeaux, Pierre Pareil, Joseph Coté, Michel Boulard and François Gregoire; the two Iroquois, Charles and Ignace; and two Salish-speaking Sanpoil interpreters. They left Spokane House and rode northwest for two days over a well-established trail to a set of waterfalls on the Columbia about forty miles below the forty-ninth parallel.

The waterfalls, which came to be known as Kettle Falls, were some three hundred yards wide but only about ten feet high. There were two falls within half a mile of each other and they had a spectacular appearance. The water sped through channels, spilled over ledges and roared through gaps carved in enormous, upturned slabs of rock. Here, bands of Indians who spoke Salish, or dialects of the language, converged each summer to fish for salmon with nets and spears. There was a gathering, more than a thousand strong, at the falls when Thompson's party arrived on June 19.

Now, their biggest challenge was to build a canoe. The country around the falls was mountainous, but dry and sparsely wooded. His men and some of the Indians searched the countryside for cedar and birch, but in two days found none. They finally sought out a grove of cedars they had passed on the trail. It was seven miles back from the river. The wood was inferior, some of it damaged by fire, but they it cut anyway and hauled it to the Indian camp.

The canoe was completed on July 2, and the next day Thompson and his crew embarked on a historic journey "to explore this River in order to open out a Passage for the Interiour Trade with Pacific Ocean," as he put it in his journal that day. They carried with them the flesh of half a horse and enough trade goods to barter for additional food.

The river below was wholly new to them and most of it unexplored by white men. The Americans Lewis and Clark had travelled and mapped the lower Columbia and Thompson had read published accounts of their work. But he had discovered the source of the river. He was the first to explore and chart the upper Columbia and its major tributaries. Now he would complete that work and, with this journey, become the first white man to travel from the headwaters to the mouth.

The Columbia's powerful current swept them along at a brisk pace. They covered ninety miles that first day, travelling south and stopping for the evening near a Sanpoil camp. Thompson invited the leading men to come and smoke with him. Once all were seated, the chief greeted the visitors and offered them food: two partially dried salmon and half a bushel of root vegetables. Thompson and his men sampled the food and afterward filled four pipes and everyone enjoyed a smoke.

Then they got down to business. The chief stood. Everyone fell silent. He said he had learned from Indians who had come from the fishery at the big falls up the river that white men would visit his country. He hoped they would stay and trade with his people, who were eager to acquire guns, axes, knives, awls and any other things that would improve their lives. At present, they had nothing to trade because they lived in a poor, barren country bereft of game and forests, but they were willing to work and would pay for whatever was advanced to them. Thompson's response pleased them greatly. He said he was travelling to the sea and, if the river were navigable to its mouth, traders would return in large canoes laden with goods.

The two Sanpoil interpreters stood and broadcast the news they had picked up about the various bands at Kettle Falls and elsewhere, and afterward the women and children were invited to come down from the camp to meet these wondrous strangers. The pipes were passed around once more—the women being allowed one puff while the men took three or four—and to conclude the meeting the Indians performed a dance.

Over the next five days, Thompson visited four villages. The inhabitants spoke Salish, or versions of it, but were distinct peoples. These were the Nespalem, the Methows, the Wennatchees and the Yakimas. Each time, a similar scene unfolded. Thompson landed unarmed but was accompanied by the interpreters and five well-armed men. Two others remained in the canoe in case a hasty exit was necessary. Thompson offered tobacco, his hosts food. Both sides spoke and the Indians entertained with songs and a dance.

Most of these people could provide no information about the river beyond the next village. None had ever seen a white man. At one stop, Thompson wrote, "a fine looking man came and sat close to me with strong curiosity in his face; after eyeing me all over, he felt my feet and legs to be sure that I was something like themselves, but did not appear sure that I was so."

These bands were scattered along a stretch of the Columbia that resembled a crude S and flowed three hundred miles across a high, arid plateau and down to a plain. The land in most places was parched and brown. Trees were sparse and stunted, and rattlesnakes lurked in the sagebrush and the short, patchy tufts of grass. It was a hard country that provided the bare necessities of life. The only wood the natives had was that which drifted down the river. Deer and other large animals were scarce so the people were poorly clothed. They lived on roots, berries and salmon and were too impoverished to wage war, Thompson concluded, since they carried no shields, clubs or lances, only weak bows and stone-tipped arrows.

Thompson's party left the last of the Salish-speaking bands where the Columbia begins its descent from the plateau. The winds were strong and they erected a sail to take advantage of them. They travelled a hundred and forty miles southeast across a dry, open plain until the river made a big turn and curled west toward the Pacific. A major tributary, later named the Snake River, flows in at this point. Its mouth was five hundred yards across, according to Thompson's estimate, and the Columbia eight to nine hundred yards wide. Here dwelt a band of Shawpatin, about twenty men and their families who lived much the same way as the tribes upstream, though they were not quite so poor.

At this village they met Yellepit, chief of all the Shawpatins, who made a strong impression on them. He appeared to be about forty years of age, was nearly six feet tall, well dressed, handsome and inquisitive. He had around him couriers who carried his messages to other bands and warriors who ensured that the people followed his orders. Yellepit dispensed with the customary formal greeting and speeches and addressed his visitors directly.

He urged Thompson to build a post at the confluence of the rivers and assured him his people would welcome such an establishment. "Under our present circumstances," he said, "we can never hope to be better. We must continue in the state of our fathers and our children will be the same unless you white men bring us arms, arrows shod of iron, axes, knives and many other things you have and we very much want."

Thompson was struck by the medal that hung from a chain around Yellepit's neck and examined it closely. It was bronze, round and about three inches across. The chief had received it from the American explorer Meriwether Lewis six years earlier. On one side there was an image of Thomas Jefferson, and on the other there were two hands, one white, the other native, clasped in friendship.

Before departing, Thompson erected a sign. It was nothing more than a stick with a sheet of paper attached to attest to his visit and his intentions. "Know hereby," he wrote, "that this Country is claimed by Great Britain as part of it's Territories and that the NW Company of Merchants from Canada, finding the Factory for this People inconvenient for them, do hereby intend to erect a Factory in this Place for the Commerce of the Country around. D. Thompson, Junction of the Shawpatin River with the Columbia, July 8th, 1811."

They left at dawn on July 10 and paddled eight miles before going ashore for breakfast. Thompson observed for latitude and longitude but doubted the accuracy of his sextant, which had been shaken for days by the river's powerful current. Likewise, the needle of his compass had vibrated constantly, making it difficult to plot the course of the river. The Columbia surged along at a rate of ten miles an hour. Rapids frequently broke its flow, currents jostled and clashed, creating dangerous whirlpools, and they now encountered ferocious headwinds that blew spray in their faces like drifting snow.

Thompson concluded his journal entry for the day by noting: "Heard news of the American ship's arrival." Word of this remarkable event had spread quickly. At that time of year, there were bands camped every few miles along the lower Columbia. He knew the Americans were Astor's men, but his informants had not yet met the newcomers, and could provide no information about them.

Thompson and his men paddled west with keen anticipation. The land rose and the profile of a range of coastal mountains appeared on the western horizon. One snow-shrouded peak stood alone and majestic above the others. The Columbia flowed through a gorge several miles wide and hundreds of feet deep. Travelling on the water, the men of Thompson's party saw only cliffs of black rock towering above them on each side. Much of the river was about a thousand yards wide, but there was a two-mile section that was only sixty yards across. "Imagination," Thompson would later write, "can hardly form an idea of the working of this immense body of water under such a compression, raging and hissing as if alive."

They carried their canoe and goods around this frightening place and upon embarking saw seals bobbing in the river. Soon the country changed. The arid interior gave way to lushly forested mountains and the inhabitants seemed to be a race separate from those just a few miles upstream. They were shorter and stockier, and spoke a language that bore no resemblance to any Thompson had heard coming down. Most went about naked. Some of the women made advances to the French Canadians, but as Thompson recalled later: "They were so devoid of temptation that not one pretended to understand them."

On July 15, Thompson and his companions washed, shaved and put on their best clothing before departing, later than usual, at 6:25 a.m. By midday, they sighted the mouth of the Columbia, where its turbulent and powerful waters collided with the incoming surge of the Pacific. Thompson was elated and ordered the canoe ashore at a prominent point to gaze at this wondrous sight, but the men complained that the ocean lacked the grandeur and wildness of the Great Lakes. After a brief stop, they paddled a final two miles until a clearing on the south shore and a cluster of buildings with the flag of the United States flying overhead came into view. This was Fort Astoria, a small, drab, insignificant settlement standing amid the enormous trees of a coastal forest.

All hands at Fort Astoria had been puzzled by the arrival, a month earlier, of two strange Indians who travelled as man and wife. Local natives had met them a short distance upriver and escorted them to the post, but they seemed to have come from a great distance. They wore long garments, leggings and moccasins, all of dressed leather, and spoke the language of some unknown tribe.

Their appearance raised a host of questions. Who were they? Where had they come from? And who had sent them? The traders, most of them French Canadians from Montreal, put these queries to them in languages they had learned while employed with the North West Co. Cree proved to be the one both sides understood. The visitors were not fluent, but could manage a simple conversation.

They explained that they were there to deliver a letter, which they promptly produced. Written by Finan McDonald, Thompson's clerk, who was then residing at a post on the Spokane River, the missive was addressed to Mr. John Stuart, Fort Estékatadene, New Caledonia. Stuart had accompanied Simon Fraser on his journey of discovery three years earlier. New Caledonia was the name Fraser had given to the country that he had opened north of the forty-ninth parallel and west of the Rockies. The message bearers had lost their way, but heard that there were white men at the mouth of the Columbia and assumed they would find John Stuart among them.

Astor's men received from the couple favourable reports of the interior, and the prospects for trade, and decided to send an expedition. They set July 15 as the date of departure and were busy bundling their cargo when someone observed a canoe, paddled by white men, coming down the river. The work stopped and everyone gathered by the shore. Among the crowd was a young French Canadian, Gabriel Franchère, who recorded the incident in his daily journal and later recounted it in a book of his adventures.

"We saw a large canoe with a flag displayed at her stern rounding the point which we called Tongue Point. We knew not who it could be . . . We were soon relieved of our uncertainty by the arrival of the canoe, which touched shore at a little wharf that we had built to facilitate the landing of goods. . . . The flag she bore was British, and her crew was composed of eight Canadian boatmen or voyageurs. A well-dressed man, who appeared to be the commander, was the first to leap ashore, and addressing us without ceremony, said that his name was David Thompson and that he was one of the partners in the North West Company."

Duncan McDougall, a Scot from Montreal and the Pacific Fur Co. partner in charge of Fort Astoria, welcomed Thompson and opened the post to him and his men. They spent the day exchanging stories. Thompson described his travels of the previous year and McDougall provided an account of the voyage from New York under the despotic and erratic Lieutenant Thorn.

The naval officer and Astor's partners had quickly come to hate one another, and the ill will spread to the men under them. Thorn imposed military discipline and spared no one, not his officers, the crew or the fur company partners and employees. He abandoned several passengers who had gone ashore during a stop at the Falkland Islands and failed to return on time. Thorn turned back only when Robert Stuart, a partner, held a pistol to his head and threatened to blow his brains out. Five sailors deserted while the *Tonquin* was docked at Hawaii, but three were caught and brought back to be flogged. Thorn had two sailors whipped for returning late and banished a third even though the man wept and pleaded to be allowed aboard.

Tragedy befell the expedition at the Columbia. They arrived March 22 and found the mouth of the river to be four and a half miles wide, with a rocky five-hundred-foot-high cape on the north shore and a low, sandy point on the opposite side. Sandbars, as well as turbulence caused by the meeting of river current and ocean breakers, made navigation dangerous. The weather that day—high seas and squalls of wind—made things even worse.

Nevertheless, Thorn lowered a boat and ordered five men— his first mate, Ebenezer Fox; an old French sailor; and three young French Canadians, two brothers and a Montreal barber—to search for a channel into the river. Their craft capsized and they were never seen again, nor were their bodies recovered. A few days later, three more men drowned after being sent out on a similar mission.

The deaths shook everyone, including Thorn, but the work of the expedition continued. Their first task was to find a site for a trading post. They settled on a prominent piece of land twelve miles from the mouth of the river, and on April 12 thirty-three men went ashore to start building.

The Nor'Westers listened to all this with interest, and afterward Thompson cleared up the mystery of the two strange letter carriers who had arrived at Fort Astoria in mid-June and were still there. He recognized them immediately.

They were both women, he told the astonished Astorians, though the one posed as a man. She had been married briefly, three years earlier, to one of his employees, a French Canadian named Boisverd, but her conduct was so loose that Thompson had expelled her from his post. The woman, a Kootenay, had wandered from camp to camp making a nuisance of herself. She eventually claimed to be a prophet, declared that she had been transformed into a man and took a wife.

At some point during his first day at Fort Astoria, Thompson took time to write a letter formally introducing himself and out-lining the relationship between the two companies. "Gentlemen," he began. "Permit me to congratulate you on your safe arrival & building in the mouth of the Columbia River: Your situation is such as to enable you with the aid of good Providence to command an extensive commerce & humanize numerous Indians in which I wish you success.

"With pleasure I acquaint you that the Wintering Partners have acceded to the offer of Mr. Astor, accepting one third share of the business you are engaged in, their share of Capital not to exceed 10,000 [pounds] without further permission—I have only to hope that the respective parties at Montreal may finally settle arrangements between the two Companies which in my opinion will be to our mutual Interest."

Thompson based his letter on information he had received at Rainy Lake in July 1810, when he was told to return to the Colum-bia and travel to the mouth. He had undoubtedly heard the same from some of the wintering partners who resided at posts in the west while travelling up the Saskatchewan River. But his assertion of a partnership took Astor's men by surprise. To the best of their knowledge, no such agreement had been reached prior to their departure from New York in September.

The Astor partners, Duncan McDougall, David Stuart and Robert Stuart, responded in writing the following day. They, too, welcomed a joint undertaking, but could not proceed until seeing the final terms. In the meantime, they offered to assist the Nor'Westers if they wanted to establish a post at the mouth of the Columbia or decided to return inland.

The visitors stayed a week and were treated more like old friends than competitors. Indeed, one Astor employee, the Mon-trealer Alexander Ross, thought the partners were too open with

Thompson. Ross, like Franchère, kept a journal, which he later turned into a book. He noted that "M'Dougall received him like a brother; nothing was too good for Mr. Thompson; he had access everywhere; saw and examined everything; and whatever he asked for he got, as if he had been one of ourselves."

On July 18, one of the Stuarts took the guests across the river to visit a Chinook village and from there they climbed to the summit of a large hill where, as Thompson noted in his journal, "we gratified ourselves with an extensive view of the Ocean & the Coast Southd."

Three days later, they embarked on the return trip. "I pray kind Providence to send us a good Journey to my Family & Friends," Thompson wrote that day. "At 1:24 Pm set off in company with Mr David Stuart & 8 of his men; they are to build a Factory somewhere below the Falls of the Columbia at the lower Tribe of the Shawpatin Nation."

Thompson spent the winter of 1811–12 west of the Rockies, managing the affairs of the Columbia Division. He was forty-one years old and had worked for twenty-eight years in the fur trade. He was a wilderness traveller without equal. Only two of his peers, Alexander Mackenzie and Simon Fraser, and the Americans Meriwether Lewis and William Clark, had led expeditions to the Pacific. But he had travelled farther—some fifty thousand miles—and more extensively than any of them.

That winter Thompson had reached a crossroads in his life. The previous summer, the partners of the North West Co. had appointed a new director of the Columbia Division, his brother-in-law and old friend John McDonald of Garth. They intended, as they put it in a resolution, "by this arrangement that Mr. David Thompson should be left to prosecute his plans of discovery on the west side of the Rocky Mountains toward the Pacific."

But discovery was all but behind him. He had one section of

the Columbia left to explore, a two-hundred-mile stretch from the big bend to Kettle Falls, and he charted that section in late October, thereby becoming the first person to travel the river from its source to its mouth. On April 22, 1812, he left Kettle Falls at the head of a brigade of six canoes, loaded with a hundred and twenty-two packs of furs, each weighing ninety pounds. He was destined for Montreal, where he would be reunited with his wife and family. And he would settle nearby, in the village of Terre-bonne, and there begin one of the major works of his life: the map of the North West Territory of the Province of Canada.

PART THREE

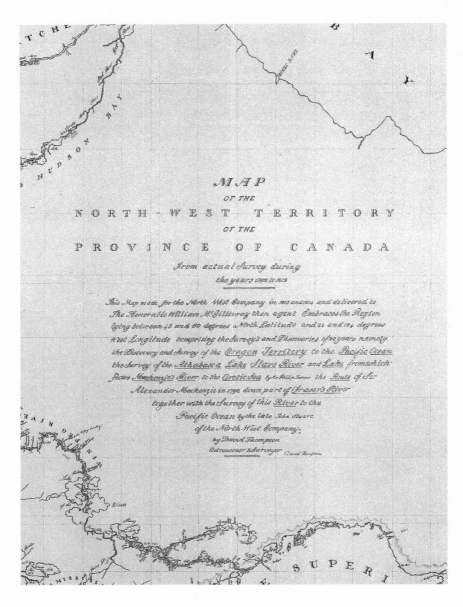

Map of the North-West Territory: McGillivrary had never seen such a thing. Half the continent lay on the table before him.

The Great Map

(1812)

ENGLAND AND AMERICA WERE WELL DOWN THE ROAD TO WAR AT the dawn of 1812 and the prospect filled the citizens of Upper and Lower Canada with dread. This war would be fought on their frontiers or within their borders. Their farms and villages would be at risk of plunder and destruction at the hands of an enemy far more numerous than they. The Canadas numbered fewer than four hundred thousand souls; America had a population of eight million, and the boisterous republic would have one of two things in mind. It would endeavour to drive the British from North America or it would seize the Canadas in order to force England to address its grievances.

This conflict, which threatened the existence of Canada, was nothing more than a subplot in a much larger drama: England's desperate struggle to defeat Napoleon. America took no part in the Napoleonic Wars, but had maintained commercial relations with France. England was determined to strangle the French economy, in part by disrupting its trade with other nations. To that end, the British government enacted Orders-in-Council in November 1807 giving the Royal Navy the authority to seize any ship sailing for a port controlled by France. The navy captured nearly four hundred American vessels over the next five years, infuriating the people and the politicians of the United States. The second, and equally galling, irritant was the Royal Navy's practice of boarding American ships on the high seas and impressing British-born sailors to serve on its vessels. By the beginning of 1812, at least three thousand and perhaps as many seven thousand seamen had been forcibly removed, and by then the hawks in the U.S. Congress saw war as inevitable, even desirable, and they regarded Canada as a prize to be taken with minimal effort.

Canadians—those who could read—followed the escalating crisis through the colonial newspapers, weekly journals of six to eight pages that devoted their front pages to advertisements and commercial announcements. The news, culled largely from British and American publications, was tucked away inside, and it was full of foreboding.

On January 13, 1812, the *Montreal Gazette* filled two columns with a long letter to the editor of the *Quebec Mercury* signed by "A CANADIAN." "I set out with a thorough conviction in my own mind, that war is at no great distance," it read, "and that we shall soon be called upon to defend every thing dear to us . . . A division of the lands in the Canadas, amongst the soldiery of the conquering army, is held out as a bait to the enterprizing part of their community to induce them to embark on this wild crusade."

A week later, the *Gazette* informed its readers that "the hum of preparation has now succeeded to the din of war," this startling assertion occasioned by the news that Henry Clay, speaker of the House of Representatives and a vociferous hawk, had argued that an army of twenty-five thousand would not be adequate for the conquest of Canada. Another congressman, a Mr. Widgery, jeered at this. Why, the militia of New England could handle the job itself, he boasted.

Amid this clamour, one voice remained reasoned and pragmatic. It belonged to Maj.-Gen. Isaac Brock, commander of the military forces of Upper Canada and head of the colonial government. Opening a session of the legislature at York in mid-February, Brock advised the populace to brace for war. "Insulting threats are offered and hostile preparations actually commenced; and though not without hope that cool reflection and the dictates of justice may yet avert the calamities of war, I cannot, under every view of the relative situation of the Province, be too urgent in recommending to your early attention, the adoption of such measures as will best secure the internal peace of the country, and defeat every hostile aggression."

By May, the papers were able to provide readers with the broad outlines of the anticipated assault on Canada. According to the *Gazette,* Maj.-Gen. Henry Dearborn was said to be assembling five thousand troops at Albany on the Hudson River, and Montreal readers knew those soldiers would come from Lake Champlain down the valley of the Richelieu River to attack them. Six hundred troops of various New York militias had reportedly been ordered to gather at Niagara, where a second offensive would be launched. The third would come from Detroit on the western frontier, where William Hull, governor of the Michigan Territory and a newly appointed brigadier-general, was organizing an army of three thousand.

The newspaper said nothing about the strength of the forces that would defend against this three-pronged invasion; that would surely have alarmed readers. There were, at the time, a mere fifteen hundred British regulars posted at a string of garrisons stretching from Quebec City in the east to Amherstburg on the western frontier and up to St. Joseph Island in the river linking Lake Superior with Huron. These troops could count on support from about three thousand Canadian volunteers, organized into militias, and an indeterminate number of Indians of various nations.

All hopes for a reasoned and just solution were dashed on June 18, 1812. President James Madison that day declared war on Great Britain and its dependencies. The New York newspapers carried the story on June 20, and these reached William Gray, publisher of the *Montreal Herald,* six days later, just in time for the June 27 *Herald.* "The crisis is therefore undoubtedly arrived," Gray wrote, "and the *Conquest of the Canadas* is the main object. . . .

"Canadians and Fellow-subjects," he continued. "Arouse from your lethergies! Call forth all those energies of character that were so pre-eminent in your ancestors. . . . You have your wives, your children, your property, your liberty, your holy religion, your happy government and all that is dear in this world to preserve; and in comparison with which, life itself must be an inferior consideration."

The annual meeting of the North West Co. at Fort William was usually a raucous affair, a few days in mid-July when the wintering partners, the clerks and the voyageurs from the posts of the vast interior gathered to eat, drink and dance, to share news, rumours and stories and to enjoy the camaraderie and conviviality of a larger society after months of isolation. But the meeting of 1812 was different.

On July 15, an express canoe arrived from the British garrison on St. Joseph Island bearing news that England and America were at war. The couriers also brought a request from Capt. Charles Roberts, commander of the garrison, for voyageurs to support an attack on the American military post on the island of Michilimackinac, forty miles west of St. Joseph Island in the strait between Lakes Huron and Michigan.

The partners were alarmed by the news. They had a year's take in furs to transport to Montreal and the big maître canoes loaded with ninety-pound packs had to pass through the waters around St. Joseph Island, now a war zone, on their way to the North Channel of Georgian Bay and the French River.

The partners convened the meeting on July 18 and concluded their business the same day—an unusually quick disposition of the issues before them. They resolved to send as many men as possible west to the depot at Rainy Lake to bring the furs out with the utmost haste. Archibald McLennan and James Grant, who ran departments on Superior, were sent out to raise an escort of Ojibway to protect the brigades until they reached the French River. And the partners agreed to send a small contingent to Sault Ste. Marie aboard the schooner *Invincible* to support the attack on Michilimackinac.

There were several other, less pressing pieces of business on that year's agenda. One was David Thompson's future with the company. Thompson had arrived at Fort William on July 12. He had already sent Charlotte and most of his children to Montreal and he let it be known that his days as a wilderness trader and traveller were over. His fellow partners agreed to pay him a salary of one hundred pounds annually and his share of the profits for three years while he produced his map. After that, he would be considered a retired partner and would receive one one-hundredth of the profits for seven years to compensate him for the use of his instruments and materials.

On August 15, the Montreal-bound canoes left Fort William with Thompson aboard one of them. As he later recalled, everyone was uncertain what awaited them at Sault Ste. Marie. They were relieved to learn upon arriving that this part of the country remained securely in British hands.

One month earlier Captain Roberts had led a motley force west to Michilimackinac. His forty-four British regulars were backed by a hundred and eighty French-Canadian voyageurs and three hundred Sioux, Winnebagos, Menominees, Ottawas and Chippewas. They landed at 3 a.m. on July 17, climbed the steep hundred-and-fifty-foot cliffs that rose from the beach and crossed the tiny island, which was less than five miles long. By dawn, they had surrounded the American military post, which overlooked a village of settlers and fur traders at the water's edge. The commanding officer, Lt. Porter Hawks, and the sixty or so men under him were completely unprepared. Hawks had not even been informed by his superiors in Detroit, three hundred and fifty miles to the south, that a state of war existed. Seeing the hopelessness of his position, he surrendered without firing a shot.

The quick, bloodless victory gave the British control of the upper lakes, and the Nor'Westers travelled the wilderness waterways down to Montreal without fear of attack or loss of cargo and arrived in late August, leaving the tranquility of the forest for a town in the throes of war.

Thompson and his family spent two months in Montreal, though he left no record of what they did or where they stayed or how and when Charlotte had travelled from the Northwest to the town. He and Charlotte were undoubtedly absorbed in personal affairs. They had to find a place to live in Montreal or elsewhere, and had to adjust to their new surroundings. Montreal was a modest place of perhaps four thousand citizens and was surrounded by farms and villages carved out of towering forests. But after nearly three decades of wilderness life Thompson surely found it crowded and noisy, his wife and children even more so—they had never set foot in a town before. Everything to them was novel: the ships at anchor in the St. Lawrence, swayed by wind and current, the chime of church bells, the height of the spires, the clatter of hooves and wheels on cobblestone and the throngs on St. Paul Street where the merchants lived and worked in sturdy two- and three-storey buildings of stone.

The talk in the aisles and over the counters, between shopkeepers and customers, between all variety of Montrealer was dominated by the war. Militia units were drilling in every village. Detachments of British soldiers in red coats patrolled streets and waterfront. And the papers reported news of the glorious victory at Detroit. The fight had taken place August 16; an official report was written at Niagara six days later and was published in the *Gazette* of August 31.

"On the night of the 13 instant, General Brock arrived at Amherstburg with a reinforcement of 400 including militia and regulars, and immediately proceeded to make arrangements for advancing to Sandwich, which the enemy had evacuated a few days before. On the evening of the 15th, a fire was opened from our batteries and continued for an hour with great effect, and recommenced before day on the morning of the 16th, from 3 mortars, one 18 pounder, and two 12 pounders, at which time our troops crossed the river under cover of the Queen Charlotte and Hunter brig at a point called Spring Wells, about three miles below Detroit, preceded by a body of 600 Indians who were landed a mile lower down, and marched through some thick woods with the intention of covering the left flank.

"The landing was effected in good order without any opposition, the Gen. being among the first boats. Our army consisting of 700 men advanced in column; and took up a good position in line, about a mile and a half in front of Detroit, every preparation was instantly made for the assault of the Fort, at one of the salient angles, which would have taken place in a few minutes, had not a white flag been perceived coming from the garrison, the bearer bringing proposals from *the exterminating Gen. Hull,* offering to surrender upon conditions. . . . The fruits of this achievement have been the capture of 2,500 regulars and militia, and 25 piece of ordnance and other valuable stores, artillery &c. without the loss of one drop of British blood."

Two weeks later, on September 12, a Saturday, Montrealers were startled to see an escort of British regulars and Canadian militiamen arrive with the captured American general and three hundred and fifty of his soldiers. "That General Hull should have entered our city so soon at the head of his troops rather exceeded our expectations," the *Herald* reported. "We were, however, happy to see him and received him with all the honours due to his rank and importance as a public character.

"When they arrived at the governor's house the general was conducted in and presented to his Excellency, Sir George Prevost. He was received with the greatest politeness and invited to take up residence there during his stay in Montreal. The officers were quartered in Holmes Hotel and the soldiers were marched to Quebec Gate Barracks. The general appears to be about sixty years of age and bears his misfortune with a degree of resignation that but few men in similar circumstances are fitted with."

By the time these events occurred, Thompson had settled on a place to reside and was preparing to depart for the village of Terrebonne, thirty miles northeast of Montreal. Before doing so, however, there was one spiritual matter to address. On September 30, he had Charlotte and the children baptized at the St. Gabriel Street Church in Montreal, the Scotch church, so called because it was founded by fur traders of Scottish origin, although English, Irish and even a few French Canadians involved in the trade also attended services at this Presbyterian place of worship.

The Thompsons, dressed in their best attire, stood shoulder to shoulder around the baptismal fount: David, eleven-year-old Fanny, Samuel, Emma and John arranged according to age, and Charlotte with eighteen-month-old Joshua in her arms. They clasped their hands, bowed their heads and listened intently. The cleric read the baptismal rite. He sprinkled holy water over all but David and welcomed them into the community of Christian faithful.

Roderick Mackenzie lived in a grand house, the biggest by far in Terrebonne. The two-storey flat-roofed home was elegantly designed and had a stately entrance—a protruding podium that was six steps above the street, with four white columns supporting a second-floor balcony. It was a suitable dwelling for a man of his prominence. Mackenzie was a retired partner of the North West Co., he was the cousin of Sir Alexander Mackenzie and he was known to one and all as Le Seigneur—the proprietor of the Seigneury of Terrebonne—though he was, in fact, only managing the seigneury on behalf of the estate of the late Simon McTavish.

McTavish had acquired it in 1802 when he was fifty-two and the wealthiest person in Montreal. He paid twenty-five thousand pounds for the seigneury, which comprised five miles of waterfront on the Rivière des Mille-Îles and all the land for five miles back. Amid this domain of farms and forest stood the village of Terrebonne, a substantial community of about a hundred and fifty homes, some owned by their occupants, some by the seigneur. There were also shops, a sawmill, a grist mill and textile mills where wool was spun and dyed. McTavish invested in many of these enterprises. He repaired and refurbished buildings, purchased new equipment, made the mills more productive and used a three-storey bakery to produce biscuits for the fur trade.

McTavish's reign ended with his death in July 1804. He had been a dynamic owner, but never lived in Terrebonne and left day-to-day management to others. The seigneury had been an investment that enlarged his already extensive business interests. Mackenzie was different. He settled in Terrebonne and embraced the role of seigneur. He used part of the small fortune he had earned in the fur trade to acquire the house at 90, rue St-Louis from a local doctor while it was still under construction. McTavish had made Terrebonne into an important centre of the North West Co., and Mackenzie ensured that the village retained that role. He made it possible for retiring partners and clerks of the company to settle there by renting or selling them property and he provided the Thompson family with their first permanent residence—a two-storey brick townhouse.

Mackenzie felt a natural affinity toward Thompson. He was a learned individual who in the early 1790s had built a small library at Fort Chipewyan, on the western end of Lake Athabasca, then the remotest post in the western interior. After retiring as a wintering partner in 1801, he aspired to write a history of the fur trade and began collecting letters, journals and memoirs of retired and active employees of the North West Co. He was enthusiastic about Thompson's projected map and warmly supported the venture.

Thompson and his family took up residence in Terrebonne on October 20 and that day Thompson resumed his daily journal. One of the first entries noted that he had hired a housekeeper who was to earn ten dollars monthly and provide companionship to Mrs. Thompson. Another lists the household items he and his wife had purchased: twelve towels from a Mrs. Woolwich; a mattress and pine table four feet square from a Mrs. Park; a cask of brown lye and a box of candles.

On October 30, there was a brief entry on a totally different subject: "Married to Charlotte Small." He and Charlotte had wed fifteen years earlier, according to the customs of the Cree, which was perfectly acceptable in a wilderness beyond the reach of Christian influence or rule of law. But in their new home, such a union would be unacceptable in the eyes of man and God. So, Thompson had a notary draw up a marriage contract, according to the requirements of the colonial administration. Four days later, he summoned a member of the local clergy to their home. He and Charlotte stood before witnesses and their children, exchanged their vows and were declared man and wife.

Life in the riverside village was not as tranquil as usual that fall, not with a war unfolding on the frontiers of the Canadas and not with an American army assembled under Maj.-Gen. Henry Dearborn at Lake Champlain in preparation for an assault on Montreal. Thompson made note of all the news and rumours of enemy attacks, men killed and prisoners taken, and his journal entry of October 22 touched on one of the most important developments of the war up to that point: "Heard the sad news of Gen'l Brock's death . . . also of the Defeat of 2000 Americans all either killed or Prisoners."

Word of this event spread from friend to neighbour to total stranger. The dashing six-foot-two officer had been shot in the heart while trying to drive a contingent of Americans from the heights above the village of Queenston on the Niagara frontier. The newspapers carried voluminous accounts of the fight, of Brock's demise and of his funeral, right down to the inscribed silver plate on the coffin.

Terrebonne had its militia of local men ready to defend community and country. Mackenzie, the lieutenant-colonel, was responsible for raising and maintaining this battalion of volunteers, and he made Thompson an ensign-major on October 31. Less than a week later, Terrebonne's citizen soldiers marched off to reinforce Montreal's defences against an anticipated assault by Dearborn's army, but they returned before the end of the month without having fired a shot because unruly American soldiers had refused to march into Canada.

Thompson did not partake in this exercise. He was responsible for keeping the guns in working order and he recorded the repairs in his journal: "new stock . . . lock cleaned . . . hammer steeled . . . 2 small screws on pan mended . . . 1 new ramrod . . . hammer tempered." He also took on a more substantial defence assignment that winter. Lt.-Col. Ralph Bruyeres, commanding Royal engineer in the Canadas, commissioned Thompson to design a device that would reduce the recoil of cannons when fired from sleighs. This was a serious problem during winter campaigns, when cannons were known to lurch back up to five feet in deep snow and as much as thirty yards on ice.

In late November, he began designing a device, which he called the cannon frame, that could support a nine-pound gun and by December 20 had completed a scale model. Thompson arranged to present his work early in the new year, and on January 6, 1813, he set off for Montreal in his carriole, accompanied by his daughter Fanny, who was returning to her boarding school.

Lieutenant-Colonel Bruyeres was more than satisfied with Thompson's results. In a letter dated January 8 to the military secretary of the governor, Sir George Prevost, he commented: "I have seen Mr. Thompson's Model. . . . It is a most ingenious contrivance, and will in my opinion be very useful, and answer perfectly well on many occasions. I strongly recommend it to the notice of His Excellency."

Upon returning to Terrebonne, Thompson found his wife and younger children ill with measles and a week passed before they were, he wrote, "out of Danger." In the meantime, he was designing and building a model of the cannon frame that would support larger guns. By January 21, he had completed the work and mailed his drawings and the accompanying model to Edward Brenton, Prevost's civil secretary.

That was the end of the project for Thompson, who left no description or drawings of the device in his journals. The administration also lost interest. Everything was quiet on the frontiers and would remain so until spring.

"A very fine mild day," Thompson wrote on December 17, 1812. "Passed the day in arranging my accounts &c, &c and did nothing else." The break, a rare one, was well deserved and timely, coming as it did in the midst of the festive season with its roaring fires and blazing chandeliers, big meals and abundant drink. The first of the invitations, addressed to Mr. and Mrs. David Thompson, had arrived in late November and announced that Mr. Roderick Mackenzie would be giving a dance at his home on the evening of the thirtieth. A few days later, they attended a high mass celebrating the safe return of the Terrebonne militia and afterward dined with a party of sixteen at a local inn.

The tempo quickened around Christmas: dinner one night at the home of Peter Pangman, a retired partner and seigneur of Lachenaie, next door to Terrebonne; lunch two days later in Montreal with William McGillivray, a partner in McTavish, McGillivrays and Co., the firm that supplied and bankrolled operations in the northwest; a ball on the twenty-sixth given by the Robatailles that lasted till midnight. The swirl of activity ended with the funeral of Charles Chaboillez, a former partner, who was buried, as Thompson put it, "with all the Ceremonie of the Roman Church and Military Honours."

In the new year, after finishing the cannon frame, Thompson began work on a first draft of his map. He started slowly, but that changed as February turned to March, as the days grew longer and the sunlight stronger. He had a well-lit study, a desk with its surface tilted forty-five degrees—ideal for drawing—and in boxes on the floor, his journals, about three dozen of them. The dimensions and page counts varied, but most had covers of marbleized leather and were crammed with notes and calculations. They contained columns and columns of river courses, and page after page of trigonometry that produced coordinates of latitude and longitude.

All this data was a record of thousands of miles of wilderness travel that he would transform into images of rivers and lakes, hills and mountains. He worked on one sheet of linen paper at a time, started by drawing vertical and horizontal lines that represented degrees of longitude and latitude, and then added fixed points of latitude and longitude from his observations. Tracking surveys in which he recorded each change of direction and the estimated distance travelled allowed him to connect the points.

Many other fur traders, starting in the late 1600s, had produced maps of the rivers they travelled or the country around their posts. Most of these men—a few Nor'Westers and more than fifty employees of the Hudson's Bay Co.—had no experience at measuring distance, taking bearings or performing astronomical observations. Their maps were roughly rendered, were not drawn to scale and often contained glaring errors.

There were, however, two surveyors who produced a large body of work that rivalled Thompson's for technical competence. One was his mentor, Philip Turnor, the Hudson's Bay Co.'s first inland surveyor. The other was Peter Fidler, whom Turnor had chosen as his assistant instead of Thompson for the 1790 expedition to the Athabasca country.

Turnor worked in the northwest from 1778 until 1787, and again from the fall of 1789 till June 1792. He travelled extensively around Hudson Bay, inland as far as Lake Athabasca and north to

Great Slave Lake, above the sixtieth parallel. He produced eight maps, most of them charts of the rivers falling into Hudson Bay and the shore of the bay itself. But Turnor also drew two multi-sheet maps, one in 1792, the other in 1794, which were regional in scope and included the work of others. The second, a "Map of Hudson's Bay and the Rivers and Lakes Between the Atlantick and Pacifick Oceans," was his opus, a grand piece that measured five feet by eight and a half.

Fidler was far more prolific. Between 1789 and 1811, he produced 373 segmental sketches that included directions and estimates of distances. These were hastily drawn maps of lakes or short stretches of rivers and other features, often done as he travelled, and could be used as the basis of future cartography that was more polished and precise. Fidler also produced eighty-eight maps, the largest of them comprising twelve sheets and depicting the east end of Lake Athabasca and part of the Churchill River. However, most were limited in scope and covered small geographic areas.

The works of Turnor and Fidler, as well as all the others who produced maps for the Hudson's Bay Co., were never published. For more than a century, company officials viewed them as valuable commercial documents to be held confidentially at their headquarters in London. Toward the end of the 1700s, attitudes changed. The company began sharing its maps with cartographers and in the early 1790s established a business relationship with a talented and prominent London cartographer named Aaron Arrowsmith.

Arrowsmith was granted full access to the company's collection, which by then numbered several hundred manuscript maps. He incorporated the works of Turnor, Fidler and many others into his first major effort—*A Map Exhibiting all the New Discoveries in the Interior Parts of North America*—published in London on January 1, 1795. Arrowsmith depicted in considerable detail many of the principal trade routes between the western shore of Hudson Bay and what were then known as the Stony Mountains. He included the Hayes River, complete with lakes, islands and portages, from the

*Montreal, early 19th century: Charlotte and the children
were dazzled by the bustle and congestion of the town,
the first they had ever visited.*

bay to Lake Winnipeg, and the north branch of the Saskatchewan
almost to the mountains. He showed an "Asseneboyne River" joining the Red and flowing into Lake Winnipeg from the southwest.
He also included an image of the river that Alexander Mackenzie
had followed six years earlier to the polar sea.

There were huge gaps in the 1795 map. There was nothing
between the Rockies and the Pacific. The eastern flanks of the
mountains were blank, and Arrowsmith sketched in only fragments of the Churchill, Peace, Athabasca and South Saskatchewan
rivers. But he had published new editions in 1796, 1802 and 1811 and
each time incorporated more information, supplied mainly by
Fidler. He was working on yet another version as Thompson began
his own map.

Thompson was a keen student of the cartography of his day.
He had examined some and perhaps all of Arrowsmith's map. He

had studied the renderings of his fellow Nor'Westers, the maps that flowed out of the Lewis and Clark expedition and Vancouver's delineation of the west coast of North America. Beyond these sources, he was on his own, working in solitude and relying almost entirely on his own data.

He envisioned a map that would be grander than the work of his rivals. It would span the continent, it would contain more detail and it would be more accurate, and he recorded his progress, and occasional setbacks, in his daily journal: "Working at the Sheets for the English River Map but could do nothing for half the day for want of a ruler . . . the other 2 Rulers having warped obliged to get another made of wood . . . working at the Sheets and got them and the Table ready for Pasting . . . had very good Paste made by putting the infusion of Gum Arabic in it . . . pasted 2 Blank Sheets and nearly spoiled Them . . . lost all the Morning looking for my Nautical Almanac which I could not find . . . spent the Afternoon in planning the Scale of the Columbia Chart."

On April 4, Roderick Mackenzie visited Thompson at his home, accompanied by two Nor'Westers who had come out from Montreal on behalf of William McGillivray—Alexander Mackenzie, a nephew of the explorer, and McGillivray's nephew John. Thompson made a note in his journal and underlined it, and the next day he and Alexander Mackenzie dined together. Mackenzie asked Thompson to produce a map of the Columbia. It was spring—time for the Montreal-based agents of the North West Co. to plot their next moves in the ongoing battles against Astor and the Hudson's Bay Co. One logical step was to push their operations farther down the Columbia, and Mackenzie questioned Thompson about the river, its people and the potential for trade.

According to his journal entries for April 10 to 24, Thompson was "actively employed in drawing a rough Map of the Columbia." He sent it to Montreal on the twenty-fifth and devoted himself to other projects that might provide a livelihood once all his obligations to the company were met and his salary paid in full.

While he drew his map of the Columbia, Thompson was building a canoe, one he hoped would change conventional thinking. Canoes used in the fur trade and by most Canadians were still made of birch—as they had been three hundred years earlier when white men arrived in America—but Thompson's was built of cedar planks. He believed cedar was superior and had twice tested his belief.

He had built a cedar canoe while camped west of the Rockies with three French-Canadian voyageurs. After the extraordinary winter crossing of Athabasca Pass in January 1811, they were waiting for spring breakup to begin descending the Columbia. The birch rind was too thin and weak to be fashioned into a soup bowl, let alone a canoe, so they had used cedar, crafting planks with their axes, sewing them together with roots and sealing the seams with pine gum. It had taken six weeks, from March 1 to April 16, but they had constructed a canoe twenty-five feet long and fifty inches at the beam that was as light as birch but much stronger.

He had built a second in July 1812, during the rendez-vous at Fort William. This time, he and his assistants had sawed logs into planks and secured them with nails. They tested the craft on Lake Superior. It had been used by the brigade that took the south shore and had gained a hundred miles on the birchbark canoes during a five-hundred-mile journey to Sault Ste. Marie.

But the challenge now, as he and his men toiled in a shed behind his home, with all the best tools and latest materials, was to make it watertight, as one journal entry makes clear: "finished Sewing the Nails and upon watering her found her very leaky had her caulked . . . and again watered when she still leaked excessively   I had the rest of the day employed filling the Seams with Putty."

Despite this shortcoming, Thompson sent letters to potential buyers in Montreal offering his version of a north canoe at ten pounds and a Montreal canoe at twelve, exclusive of painting. He made no mention in his journal of having found any takers, but wrote to Lieutenant-Colonel Bruyeres on July 12 extolling the virtues of the cedar canoe and citing the surprising results of the test run on Superior the previous summer.

Canoes were not going to provide him with a livelihood, though, so he had taken up farming, first by planting a backyard garden and then by studying agriculture. By mid-June, everything was up: the potatoes and parsnips, the cabbage, lettuce and corn, the pumpkins, barley and buckwheat, and he began looking for a farm to buy. He inspected several before settling on one near the village of Mascouche, five miles north of Terrebonne, which he purchased from Roderick Mackenzie on July 20.

The farm kept him busy till late October. He and his men had harvested the corn, oats, buckwheat and other crops planted by Mackenzie's farmhands in the spring. They had put a new roof on the barn, ploughed several acres and sown some of next year's crops, including timothy, clover, potatoes and tobacco before the weather turned and put an end to farming for the year.

On November 8, 1813, Thompson paid a visit to Peter Pangman in Lachenaie. The two old friends were spending an amiable afternoon together when their conversation was interrupted by a hurried and incessant ringing of church bells. It was an alarm. Thompson hastened home and quickly learned the news. An American flotilla of three hundred and fifty small boats, five miles long and carrying eight thousand soldiers, was travelling down the St. Lawrence toward Montreal. The militias of Terrebonne and Lachenaie were being summoned to reinforce the town's defences.

They marched the following morning, citizen soldiers in work clothes, farmers, farmhands and craftsmen, French Canadian, Scotch and British who set aside their tools and their differences to defend the country. Thompson was among them.

Up till then, the war had been fought mostly on the distant, western frontiers of Upper Canada, first at Michilimackinac, next at Detroit, then at Queenston in Niagara. In each case, British regulars backed by Canadian militiamen and aboriginal warriors had prevailed over the badly organized, poorly led, but numerically superior American forces.

But in 1813, the tide had turned. The Americans captured and burned York, capital of Upper Canada, in late April. One month later, Fort George, at the mouth of the Niagara River, fell, though the British, Canadians and Indians kept the Americans pinned there throughout the summer. In mid-September, the American fleet on Lake Erie captured the British naval force. The British troops at Amherstburg, at the head of the lake, were now cut off from supplies and reinforcements from Niagara and were compelled to abandon Detroit.

These events had set the stage for a decisive strike at Montreal—the heart of British America. If the Americans could take the town, Upper Canada would fall like a branch severed from a tree. Two American armies were assembled, one at Lake Champlain commanded by Maj.-Gen. Wade Hampton and a second at Sackets Harbour, at the east end of Lake Ontario, under Maj.-Gen. James Wilkinson.

Hampton's army of four thousand men struck first. On October 21, they began advancing down the Châteauguay River, which flows from southwest to northeast and drains into the St. Lawrence about fifteen miles above Montreal. Five days later, they encountered the British and Canadian defenders, who, though only fifteen hundred strong, were so well entrenched on both sides of the river that the poorly trained, demoralized Americans retreated after a brief skirmish in which they suffered fifty casualties.

The militias of Terrebonne and Lachenaie had been called in to prepare defences against Wilkinson's army. Each volunteer carried a musket and ten pounds of ammunition, but upon arriving in Montreal they were told they wouldn't need their weapons.

Instead, they were given picks and shovels and sent to a piece of high ground two miles east of Lachine to dig trenches and batteries for cannon. They worked for five days, from November 14 to 19, before Montreal militiamen returning home from upriver informed them that the threat had passed. The invading army had been stopped during a battle on November 11 above the village of Cornwall. Upon receiving this news, the militiamen of Terrebonne and Lachenaie turned in their tools and marched home.

David and Charlotte Thompson began the new year by maintaining a vigil at the bedside of their five-year-old son John, the fourth of their six children. One or the other remained next to the youth night and day. They knelt and prayed when he slept, and did their best to comfort him when he woke. They administered calomel, a medicinal substance prescribed as a purgative, but nothing helped. The boy had been sick for several weeks and now was seriously ill. He was weak, suffering from severe headaches and unable to swallow. A slight improvement in the first few days of January proved temporary.

On January 10, Thompson noted that "my little John had a violent convulsive fit last night, he quieted towards morning." The next night he slept quietly, but had great difficulty breathing. "At 7 Am it pleased the Almighty God to take him from this World   had a Coffin of Oak made for him   he is 5 years 4 1/2 months old measures 3 ft 9 In and still appears a beautiful Boy   This loss has plunged us in deep affliction especially his poor Mother."

They buried their son on January 12 in the Protestant cemetery in Montreal. Thompson's journal entry for the thirteenth read: "Passed the day in consoling my poor wife."

But they could not grieve for long. Charlotte Thompson was nursing an infant, Henry, born July 30, 1813, at Terrebonne. She had four other children to look after and the home to maintain. Her husband was seeking a commission as a land surveyor from the colonial government and had written a letter to Joseph Bouchette, surveyor-general, but hadn't yet received an answer. He consulted with Roderick Mackenzie, who advised him that he should go to Quebec and appeal directly to Bouchette.

Thompson left February 5 aboard the Montreal–Quebec stagecoach, spent the night in Trois-Rivières and reached his destination at 8:15 the following evening. He took an exam under Bouchette, presented a letter of reference from Mackenzie, and by February 10 Sir George Prevost had signed the papers commissioning Thompson as a land surveyor.

He departed the capital early the next day and after a forty-eight-hour journey arrived home at 4:30 a.m. on February 13 to learn that his daughters, Fanny and Emma, were ill. Both had roundworms, a parasite common in children at the time, but Emma's condition was more serious. She was the third of the Thompson children, born in March 1806 at Reed Lake House, a North West Co. post, and was now a few weeks shy of her eighth birthday. "To my Sorrow," he wrote that day, "found my dear little Daughter Emma lying very ill of the Worms, 4 large round worms, she, poor thing, vommited up 3 days ago."

A physician from Montreal, Dr. Kennelly, was summoned and prescribed a cup of Carolina pink root every three hours, supplemented by calomel. Fanny began to recover, but not Emma. "At 11 am," Thompson wrote on the seventeenth, "poor Emma brought away 6 large round Worms all alive   seems to be relieved but very comatose and high fever every evening and all night with strong throbbing Pulse, high heaving of the Breast very hot skin."

The next day, she brought up another of these parasites, the largest Thompson had seen. He measured it and found it was ten inches long. Emma appeared to be recovering, but only briefly. Her strength lapsed, she couldn't swallow and she slipped into a coma; she died on the evening of February 22. "At 9 Am sent off the body of poor Emma," Thompson wrote two days later; "at 10 set off myself   at 1/2 Pm buried my poor little daughter close touching her little Brother John in the same Grave. God Almighty, the Saviour of the World, bless them both."

The map. William McGillivray wanted the map, and he wanted it that spring before he left Montreal for the annual rendez-vous at Fort William. Granted, he and his fellow partners had given Thompson three years to produce it, commencing with the meeting of July 1812, but circumstances had changed. The war, he was certain, would end soon. The Canadas would remain British. There was no reason to think the armies of the raucous republic would take British America this year, something they had failed to do in the summers of 1812 and 1813.

But elsewhere on the continent, the war had altered the status quo. The British navy had imposed a blockade on American ports. That had made it impossible for John Jacob Astor to send ships with supplies and provisions to Fort Astoria at the mouth of the Columbia. His links with the post had been severed and his trans-Pacific commercial enterprise had collapsed.

McGillivray had stepped into the breach. He had sent an expedition down the Columbia in the spring of 1813—two canoes and sixteen men under the command of his cousin John George McTavish, who was instructed to negotiate the purchase of Astoria with the Pacific Fur Co. partners based there. He had sent a second expedition by sea, this one led by John McDonald of Garth. In March 1813 the *Isaac Todd,* a North West Co. vessel, had left Portsmouth, England, destined for the Columbia and accompanied by a second ship, *The Raccoon,* as well as a naval escort, HMS *Phoebe.*

In the spring of 1814, sitting in the Montreal headquarters of the North West Co., McGillivray had no idea how these ventures had fared, but he was confident of their success and anticipated news at the rendez-vous in July. The acquisition of a post at the mouth of the Columbia would be a personal triumph for

McGillivray and a crowning achievement for the company.

His uncle, the bullish and powerful Simon McTavish, had pushed the trade into the Athabasca country and nearly to the foot of the Rocky Mountains. In the decade since McTavish's death, McGillivray had pushed it across the mountains and on to the Columbia. The Nor'Westers had left behind their old rivals—the Company of Adventurers—who were still stalled east of the Rockies. With Astoria, they would prevail over that ambitious upstart Astor, who thought he could achieve in an instant what had taken them decades. They would become unrivalled masters of a commercial enterprise stretching from Atlantic to Pacific.

McGillivray wanted the map to celebrate this triumph. He would hang it in the Great Hall at Fort William, the hallowed space where the proprietors of the company, both the Montreal agents and the wintering partners, met every summer to dine, to carouse and to plot their common future. The map would be informative and inspiring. The men of the North West Co. would be able to stand beneath it and discern in an instant the precise location of their posts and the routes they followed to reach them. But more importantly, they could behold the vast empire they had created by dint of hard work, perseverance and raw ambition.

McGillivray's demand for early delivery of the maps had put Thompson in a tight spot. He had planned to draw the map in 1814, but not by June. He was not even certain he would have his materials and supplies by then. These he had ordered from England the previous autumn—fifty sheets of Imperial paper, ten dozen black lead pencils for drawing, one dozen small camel-hair pencils, two cakes of the best India ink and one bottle of India rubber—and they would arrive at Montreal aboard a North West Co. supply ship as soon as the ice was out of the St. Lawrence.

Besides, Thompson had another obligation to meet that spring. The military had awarded him a contract for seven of his cedar-plank canoes. He hired three men and a boy and together they worked on the project from mid-March till late June.

Their progress and setbacks he recorded in his journal: "we began to clear away the Work Room to prepare the Bed for the Canoe &c. . . . began the Sides of the Canoe . . . put in three timbers toward each Stem and turned the bottom upward . . . finished the Bottom of the Canoe . . . Men rivetting the Nails . . . large canoe sent off with 3 Men by Noon for Montreal."

The big challenge, once again, was to make the canoes watertight. Three of the vessels were returned for additional caulking, and there were unexpected problems, which is evident from the journal entry of May 24: "I received a Letter from the Quarter Master General complaining that all the Pitch melted . . . we immediately set to work on the 4th Canoe   thought to be completely finished   took all the pitch out caulked it and repainted it in the best manner."

By late June, he and his helpers had completed the sixth canoe and were busy working on the seventh. He had also completed his map, though he devoted only a one-line entry to the subject, indicating he had delivered it on June 10: "done the Chart for Mr. Wm McGillivray and sent it him the 10th Inst." But he did not think it his best work. It had been produced on demand and he would later describe it as "a hasty, rough map."

The map arrived rolled and tied and McGillivray anxiously opened it. He and an assistant laid it flat on a table and placed books and other objects at the edges to hold it down. It was six feet, nine inches tall and ten feet, four inches wide and made of twenty-five sheets of paper glued together. McGillivray had never seen such a thing: a whole chunk of the continent lay on the table before him. His eyes roved from east to west, from the sweeping arc of Superior's north shore to Lake Winnipeg. From there he followed the Saskatchewan River to the squiggle of the Rocky Mountains. Here he paused to contemplate the drift of the Rockies, which pulled his eyes from top left to bottom right.

Beyond the Rockies were other ranges, of which he had known nothing till this very moment. The first was labelled DUNCAN'S MOUNTAINS. They began between the fiftieth and fifty-first parallel of longitude, continued southeast to the forty-ninth and straight south from there to the forty-eighth. Thompson had named these mountains after McGillivray's brother Duncan, who had died much too soon, in 1808 at age thirty-eight, and McGillivray, whose character had been hardened by a decade of leadership, was moved by this tribute to his sibling.

Immediately to the west, and commencing a little farther north, he saw NELSON'S MOUNTAINS. He saw his own name in MCGILLIVRAY'S RIVER, which flowed south from the valley between these two mountain ranges. McGillivray let his eyes wander back to the upper right-hand corner of the map, and here was a section of the Hudson Bay shoreline, complete with the coves and inlets that gave it an irregular shape, and just below it was Thompson's inscription in graceful handwriting:

MAP

of the

NORTH–WEST TERRITORY

of the

PROVINCE OF CANADA

From actual Survey during

the years 1792 to 1812

The Map made for the North West Company in 1813 and 1814 and delivered to The Honorable William McGillivray then Agent

Embraces the Region lying between 45 and 60 degrees North

Latitude and 84 and 124 degrees west Longitude comprising the

Surveys and Discoveries of 20 years namely The Discovery and

Survey of the Oregon Territory to the Pacific Ocean the survey of the

Athabasca Lake Slave River and Lake from which flows Mackenzies

River to the Arctic Sea by Mr. Philip Turnor the Route of Sir

Alexander Mackenzie in 1792 down part of Frasers River

together with the Survey of this River to the

Pacific Ocean by the late John Stewart

of the North West Company

by David Thompson

Astronomer and Surveyor

David Thompson

The map was filled with engaging detail. Each of the company's seventy-eight trading posts was accurately located and identified by the initials NWCo. Arrows indicated the direction in which the rivers flowed. All the major waterways that carried the company's men into and out of the country were represented and dozens of secondary streams were as well.

McGillivray was mesmerized. He could have spent the day there, but he had work to do. He was leaving soon for the rendez-vous. He had the map rolled and tied and placed with his luggage.

Fort William was a village, shut up behind sharpened palisades fifteen feet high. It was quiet most of the year, but came to life for about two months every summer when partners and voyageurs converged for the rendez-vous. There were dwellings for the partners, apartments for year-round residents, stores, warehouses and even a jail for wayward employees, and at the heart of the place a central square. Within the square there stood a large, impressive building with a grand entrance. There was a verandah, raised five feet, columns and a balcony. The front doors, centrally located, opened to the Great Hall, a space that would have seemed palatial to the clerks, the interpreters, the guides and the partners, who spent close to ten months each year in cramped, roughly constructed trading posts.

The hall was sixty feet long and thirty wide. Dinner for two hundred could be served at the long rows of narrow tables. The side walls were adorned with paintings: a full-length image of Horatio Nelson, a scene from the Battle of the Nile and portraits of Simon McTavish, McGillivray and others who had made the North West Co. the powerful enterprise that it was. The wall at the end of the hall, opposite McGillivray's seat at the head table, was empty, and it was there that he hung his magnificent map.

Wonder, curiosity, indifference: the map evoked all three in the hundreds of Nor'Westers who saw it. Nobody admired the map more than McGillivray. From his seat at the head table, he could glance at the other end of the hall and see the outlines of the grand natural features that defined the continent and his empire. After dinner, with a cluster of clerks and other underlings hovering behind him, he would examine the map in detail and those gathered around might point out their posts (Rocky Mountain House, Fort Augustus,

Spokane House, Kullyspel House) or relate adventures that had occurred in places like the Porcupine Hills, the Athabasca Pass and Pine Island Lake.

Only one person recorded his thoughts upon viewing the map and that was Ross Cox. He had served at Fort Astoria and joined the North West Co. after the sale of the post in 1813. Cox visited Fort William in August 1817 and described the map in his daily journal.

"At the upper end of the hall is a very large map of the Indian country, drawn with great accuracy by Mr. David Thompson, astronomer to the Company, and comprising all their trading posts, from Hudson's Bay to the Pacific Ocean, and from Lake Superior to Athabasca and Great Slave Lake," he wrote. "This immense territory is very little known, except to those connected with the Company; and if it did not interfere with their interests, the publication of Mr. Thompson's map would be a most valuable addition to our geographical knowledge of the interior of that great continent."

Cox was right. The map would have added much to the geographical knowledge of the day. It was the first comprehensive depiction of that territory. It contained more detail than any yet produced and it was more accurate. But McGillivray and the other Montreal-based agents had no interest in furthering the world's understanding of the western interior. That could only arouse interest in and curiosity about those lands and their economic potential and would ultimately lead to settlement.

The Nor'Westers had had their first brush with settlers—thanks to Thomas Douglas, the Earl of Selkirk, and his mad scheme to plant a colony of poor and displaced Scottish Highlanders at the forks of the Red and Assiniboine Rivers. The results were disastrous for both sides. Selkirk, a large shareholder in the Hudson's Bay Co., had been granted a territory of 116,000 square miles—five times the land mass of Scotland. Between 1811 and 1815, he settled about three hundred and twenty-five Scots and a few Irish in his wilderness colony.

The newcomers almost immediately found themselves besieged by an alliance of Nor'Westers and Metis who waged a campaign of harassment and intimidation to drive them from the country. The hostilities culminated in a wild gunfight on June 19, 1816, at a wooded area known as Seven Oaks, about a mile and a half west of the forks. When the shooting ceased, about twenty settlers and one Nor'Wester were dead. The Nor'Westers had carried the day, but they were then engaged in a larger, economic fight for survival against the Hudson's Bay Co.—a struggle they were destined to lose.

Thompson took no part in these disputes. His passion was science, not economics. His map was a product of the foremost science and the leading technology. It would enhance humanity's knowledge and understanding of the vast northwestern interior of North America, which had been mostly blank space on the maps of the world when he arrived there as a boy in 1784. He had not spent twenty years conducting surveys and making observations only to hang a map on a wall at Fort William. He wanted his work published.

He created two copies between 1814 and 1817, both improvements on the rough, hasty draft he had drawn for McGillivray, and he sent these to the British Foreign Office. In the summer of 1820, he tried to raise the money necessary to have the map published in England. He wrote a prospectus describing the work and the lands it would embrace and why his map was superior to those currently in circulation.

"Of these regions the map makers have no doubt given the best delineation they could acquire," he wrote, "but of what was known, so little was founded on astronomical observations; and their being obliged to fill up the vacant space with what information they could procure has led them into many errors.

"In this map now offered to the public, almost all the great Rivers on the above part of this continent, on both sides of the great Mountains are traced to their sources; the sources of the Mississippi, and several other great rivers, and the shores of Lake Superior have been examined and laid down by the Author only."

He also offered a chart—a map showing the broad outlines of the principal rivers, mountain ranges and hills, supplemented by an inventory of the natural resources of the region. It would include the position and limits of coal deposits, the various types of bedrock, the forests and plains and the habitat of bison, elk, red deer, wild sheep and other game.

Speaking in the third person, Thompson described how and why he had created these works. "Nothing less than an unremitting perseverance bordering on enthusiasm could have enabled him to have brought these maps to their present state; in early life he conceived the idea of this work, and Providence has given him to complete, amidst various dangers, all that one man could hope to perform."

But there were no takers. Thompson had no supporters or advocates in London, living and working as he did in a small and distant colony. Furthermore, decades would pass before those who wielded power in the world's capitals needed such a map. It would be twenty-five years before British and American diplomats began negotiating the division of territories west of the Rockies and required accurate maps. More than half a century would elapse before the newborn Dominion of Canada annexed the northwest territory from the Hudson's Bay Co. and sought out a detailed and reliable map to take stock of its new holdings.

In the meantime, Thompson's work did find its way into the cartography of Europe and America. His great map became the property of the Hudson's Bay Co. after the 1821 merger with the North West Co. and was made available to the Arrowsmith firm. Aaron Arrowsmith died in 1823, but his firm survived until 1874, first under sons Aaron and Samuel and later under his nephew John. They continued to publish Arrowsmith's *Map Exhibiting all the New Discoveries in the Interior Parts of North America* until after

1850 and enriched later editions by incorporating the work of David Thompson, but he remained an unnamed, uncompensated contributor, a mere colonial whose achievements were deemed unworthy of recognition.

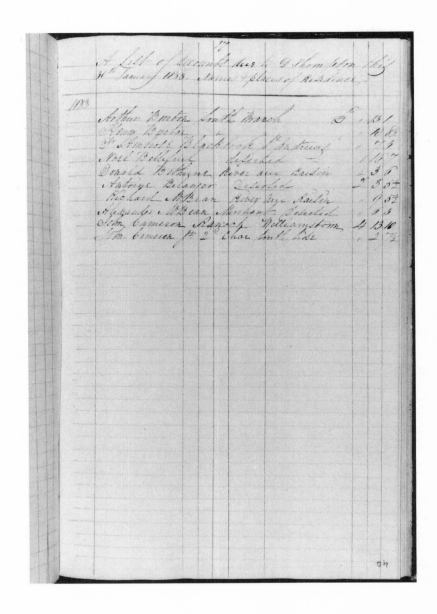

Journal entry, January, 1833, Thompson's creditors:
He was bewildered that neighbours would walk away from
their homes and their debts.

Williamstown Days

(1815–1836)

IT WAS STRANGE HOW THINGS HAD TURNED OUT, STRANGE AND at the same time maddening, so much so that many nights as he lay in bed, bedevilled by rheumatism, he would be hit by a rush of images—Charlotte's stricken look upon learning of the state of their affairs, the squeamishness of friends and neighbours during their last days in Williamstown, and that terrible notice posted all over the village and throughout the County of Glengarry:

AUCTION SALE

OF

REAL ESTATE

AT

WILLIAMSTOWN, U.C.

On THURSDAY, the 29th Sept.

At Noon, will be Sold,

BELONGING TO THE EST. OF MR. D. THOMPSON

and it had listed all his properties.

In years gone by, he had always tried to be cool and dispassionate, no matter how difficult or daunting the road ahead, but contemplating the future now, he was more often than not angry or dejected or perplexed. He was sixty-six, nearly penniless and needed work. Charlotte was fifty-one and they still had three young children at home: Thomas, Mary and Eliza, who were, respectively, thirteen, eight and six.

Time and again, he had asked himself how he had ended up in this position. No matter what line of reasoning he followed, no matter what chain of events he constructed, the answer was always the same, and always unsatisfactory. He had been undone by nebulous and incomprehensible forces—a calamitous crash in prices, demand and values that had rattled the economic underpinnings of Britain and America and wasted the economies of weaker entities like Upper Canada.

At the height of things, in the early 1830s, he had been a man of stature. He was the former astronomer and surveyor to the British commission under the Treaty of Ghent and had delineated, along with his assistants and the surveyors of the American commission, the border between British America and the United States from the village of St. Regis on the south shore of the St. Lawrence River, above Montreal, to the head of Lake Superior. He had been a justice of the peace in the Eastern District of Upper Canada and a large landowner in Glengarry County. The "EST. OF MR. D. THOMPSON" included: a house in Williamstown adapted for use as a store, with an excellent cellar and an acre of land; two-fifths of an acre in front of that plot; another village lot about one hundred yards from the Raisin River on which stood two potash houses and a boiling house with tubs, potash kettles and other equipment; lots containing ninety acres on the second concession back from the St. Lawrence River in the Township of Charlottenburgh; lots north of Raisin River containing forty-five acres on land commonly called the third concession; one acre at the crossroads known as Nutfield, on which stood a well-built house used as a dwelling and store, with a spacious cellar and garden, a blacksmith shop and a building rented as a tavern with a good stable; another lot of similar size and close by Nutfield, this one on a rivulet, containing two large potash houses, a boiling house and the utensils necessary for the manufacture of potash; and an island in the St. Lawrence, four miles above the mouth of the Raisin River, with a farmhouse, a stable and twenty cleared acres amid a hundred and sixty acres of forest.

But he had lost his properties, even the family home, and with them the prospect of a comfortable retirement.

The Thompsons had moved to Williamstown from Terrebonne in the fall of 1815. With the delivery of the map, he had fulfilled his obligations to the North West Co. and a new opportunity had arisen. The war between Britain and the United States was over and the two nations had concluded a treaty on Christmas Eve, 1814, in the Flemish city of Ghent. It provided for surveys in order to draw the boundary between British America and the United States. The diplomats who assembled at Ghent lifted their definition of the boundary from the Treaty of Paris, signed in 1783 at the end of the American War of Independence, and they agreed that the work would be done by joint commissions.

The first commission, guided by Articles IV and V, would start where the St. Croix River empties into Passamaquoddy Bay on the Bay of Fundy and would conclude at St. Regis, where, according to an earlier survey, the forty-fifth parallel of latitude struck the St. Lawrence. The second, operating under Articles VI and VII, would define the boundary for 1,700 miles, from St. Regis to Lake of the Woods. The line was to pass through the middle of the St. Lawrence, through the middle of Lakes Ontario, Erie and Huron and the waterways linking them, through Superior but north of two islands known as Isle Royale and Isle Phelipeaux to a body of water called Long Lake and from there to the most northwestern point of Lake of the Woods.

Thompson kept abreast of the treaty negotiations through the Montreal newspapers and eagerly pursued the position of astronomer and surveyor to the British commission under Articles VI and VII. His overtures were well received, both by colonial administrators who remembered his work during the War of 1812 and by John Ogilvy, whom the British government appointed commissioner in June 1816.

Ogilvy had immigrated to Canada from Scotland in 1790, when he was just out of his teens. For the next twenty-five years, he had been a leading member of the small coterie of Montreal merchants who controlled the Canadian fur trade. He was a partner in the firm Parker, Gerrard & Ogilvy. He had been a principal in the New North West, or XY, Co., formed around the turn of the century to compete with the Nor'Westers. He had participated in the negotiations that led to the November 1804 merger of the two firms and became a shareholder of the enlarged North West Co. He knew Thompson well enough to vouch for his character and capabilities and he supported his application.

Thompson left Terrebonne for Upper Canada in anticipation of his appointment. He was forty-five and Charlotte thirty and they had five surviving children. Fanny, their eldest, was fifteen. The youngest, named after her mother, was an infant of three months. Williamstown was a village of about four hundred people, five miles north of the St. Lawrence along the Raisin River, which French-Canadian voyageurs had called the Rivière aux Raisins because wild grapes grew profusely along its banks. The first settlers—about a thousand Gaelic-speaking Scots who arrived by canoe—called the stream Avon Dhu, or Dark River, because they had paddled beneath a thick canopy of vines that barely admitted sunlight but was teeming with feeding birds.

Those pioneers, Loyalists dispossessed by the American War of Independence, had begun to arrive in 1784. Most had resided in New York's Mohawk Valley. They had been tenants on lands granted by the king of England to Sir William Johnson, a wealthy businessman and the superintendent of northern Indians affairs at the time of his death in 1774. Some of the tenant families moved to

Canada early in the war with Sir William's son John, who inherited the estates, and the men served in John Johnson's Royal Regiment of New York. However, most left in 1783 at the end of the war and spent a miserable winter in camps around Montreal.

The following spring, the governor of Quebec, Sir Frederick Haldimand, sent them west to begin carving farms and settlements out of the primeval forests along the St. Lawrence and the Raisin River. Haldimand also granted John Johnson, Sir John by then, a large tract of land. Sir John built a manor house and a mill along the Raisin River, and these two structures formed the nucleus of a settlement that he named Williamstown, after his father.

Successive waves of settlers arrived from Scotland between 1786 and 1802 and took up farming on hundred-acre plots granted by the Crown in what had become Glengarry County. But many of their sons left for the fur trade, where they made ideal clerks in the remote western trading posts. They were reliable and honest and many of them were literate so they could keep books. And when they retired from the fur trade, many returned to Glengarry, or adjacent counties, and purchased farms with their savings.

The proximity of former Nor'Westers made Williamstown an attractive place to Thompson. His brother-in-law and close friend John McDonald of Garth retired at Gray's Creek in nearby Stormont County. Simon Fraser lived on a farm near the village of St. Andrews, about nine miles west of Williamstown. Hugh McGillis, whom Thompson knew from his first days with the North West Co., purchased Johnson's manor house—a stately one-and-a-half-storey clapboard country home with full-length verandahs front and back and along one side.

There was only one property in the village that was as large and costly as the manor house. It was the home of the Reverend John Bethune, his wife and their nine children and it was located right across the river from the manor. Bethune moved to the village from Montreal in May 1787 and established Upper Canada's first Presbyterian congregations in Williamstown and the nearby communities of Lancaster, Martintown and Cornwall. The Bethunes initially lived in a one-room log cabin with a half attic that served as the bedroom, but in 1805 a prosperous friend from Montreal, the retired fur trader Alexander McLeod, built the family a spacious and comfortable home that cost nearly $350, a hefty sum at the time.

The log cabin was retained and the exterior walls plastered over. A one-and-a-half-storey main dwelling was added as well as another wing to give the home a symmetrical look. The walls of the two new sections were built of brick, brought to Canada as ship's ballast, and covered with plaster. The original wing, with its big stone hearth that occupied nearly an entire end wall, became the kitchen, while the newly constructed sections included a parlour, a large dining room, a family room, a cozy study and three upstairs bedrooms. The family resided there until the death of John Bethune in September 1815. Two weeks later his widow sold the house and surrounding hundred-acre farm to Thompson, and he and Charlotte made this their home for the next twenty years.

In November 1816, John Ogilvy travelled from Montreal to Albany for his first meeting with Gen. Peter Porter, the American commissioner under Articles VI and VII. Porter, a forty-three-year-old lawyer and politician and owner of a large estate in Black Rock, New York, a community that would one day be part of the city of Buffalo, had served in Congress from 1809 to 1813 and had been a leading proponent of going to war against British America. He had led a contingent of volunteers and Indians that fought on the Niagara frontier, and his home had been burned by British forces. Nonetheless Porter quickly established cordial relations with Ogilvy.

At their initial session, the commissioners exchanged credentials, discussed procedure and settled on the necessary personnel. They would share a secretary and an assistant secretary. Each would have an agent who would manage day-to-day affairs but

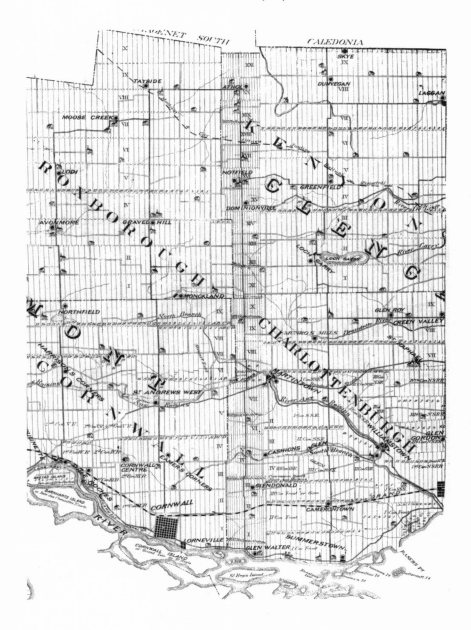

*Map of Glengarry, late 19th century: Thompson found
a home here among pioneering Scots who had sent
so many of their sons to the North West Co.*

take direction from them and each country's party would include a surveyor, assistant surveyor and trigonometric surveyor, as well as support staff such as cooks, waiters and boatmen. Salaries were generous and would range from $4,444 annually for commissioners and agents to $2,000 for the chief surveyors to $96 for the cooks. Finally, Ogilvy and Porter agreed to meet again on May 10, 1817, at St. Regis.

The Canadians went to work ahead of schedule. Ogilvy summoned Thompson to Montreal in mid-January 1817 and instructed him to determine where the forty-fifth struck the St. Lawrence. He was to begin at Fort Wellington, the British military establishment on the north shore next to the village of Prescott, and was authorized to hire an assistant.

Over the next two months, Thompson and his helper, a Glengarry resident named William Mackenzie, travelled by horse-drawn sleigh between Williamstown, Prescott and St. Regis. Apart from the extreme cold, their biggest challenge was finding adequate accommodations. Taverns did not suit Thompson's tastes and the commander at Fort Wellington had no room for them so they looked for private lodgings. A Prescott merchant offered them a vacant house and a supply of wood, but the place was so cold that they could not remove their greatcoats.

Thompson sent a message to Ogilvy requesting bedding and, in the interim, they spent days at the house and nights at an establishment called Wilson's Tavern. After eight nights, this arrangement proved unsatisfactory to the owner, as Thompson noted in his journal. "The Tavern keeper informed us that since we did not board there he would not spare us beds. With much ado, we got 2 Beds in a public House in a miserable Room full of broken Glass Windows stopped with Rags &c, &c and only thin Blankets on the Beds."

Thompson worked despite the discomfort and inconvenience. He took observations in and around Prescott as well as St. Regis and by late March concluded that the forty-fifth met the

Journal entries, January, 1817: Thompson notes the beginning of his work for the International Boundary Commission.

St. Lawrence about twelve hundred feet south of where an earlier survey had placed it. "By the few Observations I have had in this variable and cloudy season the line of 45° will not be found to correspond to the supposed Place and seemingly places a much larger portion of the Shores of the St. Lawrence in the British Dominions than expected," he stated. This meant the Americans would lose valuable river frontage and other features. "They will be keenly contested," he predicted, "especially as the Americans reckon Them as their own to a certainty and will not easily bear both loss and disappointment."

By late April, he was back in Williamstown, just in time for the birth of his daughter Elizabeth, who arrived at 8 p.m. on the twenty-fifth. "Pray God to bless her and give her to lead a happy virtuous Life," he wrote. One week later, Ogilvy summoned him to Montreal. The surveying season was about to begin and Thompson would not see his wife and children again until early November.

The St. Lawrence was a busy waterway during the spring and summer. Loyalists, soldiers, fur traders and Mohawks went up and down the river. Boatloads of immigrants from England, Ireland and Scotland, many of them ragged and impoverished, travelled upstream, disembarked at various settlements and marched up crudely cut trails and roads to start new lives in the forests of Upper Canada. The surveyors worked their way upriver as well, although at a much slower pace, the Canadians on the north shore, the Americans on the south.

Spring had come late that year. Snowdrifts and heaps of ice littered the shoreline as the two parties travelled separately out from Montreal on roads that were barely passable. Both were late. Ogilvy and most of his staff arrived May 13 at St. Regis, a Mohawk village located on a point that jutted into the river, and the Americans got there one week later. The two parties made their camps on the Isle of St. Regis, and the Canadians watched in wonder as the Americans erected a large, impressive marquee, or field tent, that would served as Porter's office and accommodation.

On May 23, Ogilvy and Porter, the two-member board of commissioners, met to inaugurate the work of the season. Papers were filed. Various officials took their oaths of office. A secretary and assistant secretary were chosen. Ogilvy reported the results of Thompson's observations for the forty-fifth parallel of latitude. The American surveyor, David Adams, was ordered to take fresh sightings and showed that Thompson had erred. The surveying parties were dispatched to their respective sides of the river, and so began a project that would take a decade to complete.

It would create friendships among some of the participants. It would be dogged by bureaucratic infighting and personnel changes. It would lead to the loss of life. It would be criticized as extravagantly expensive by politicians in London and Washington and attacked by British and American citizens when they were forced to cede territory. But for all that, the joint commission produced the first detailed and accurate maps of the Great Lakes and the rivers connecting them. It led to the peaceful creation of a boundary line from St. Regis to the head of Superior, though not all the way to Lake of the Woods because beyond Superior the two sides could not reach agreement. And it became a model for the resolution of contentious issues that arose along the border.

The surveyors used two techniques: theodolite triangulation and celestial observation. The first relied on the creation of imaginary triangles, which was done by driving two stakes, or pickets, into a stretch of shoreline. This became the baseline and was measured by running a surveyor's chain between the pickets. The surveyors trained the eyepiece of a theodolite at a fixed point on the opposite shore and did so from both ends of the baseline to create a triangle and then relied on the instrument to measure the angles. Knowing the angles and the length of the baseline, they could calculate the length of the other two sides, or the distance from shore to shore. Finally, they took celestial observations to determine geographical position, which was later used to plot the course of a river or the shape of a shoreline.

The cool spring gave way to a hot summer, hordes of mosquitoes, and a slow, difficult work. The surveyors moved upriver by canoe and camped in tents. They had to scramble up and down muddy banks and hack away underbrush before driving in the pickets and laying the surveyor's chain. The highlight of the season was a visit on August 1 by U.S. President James Monroe, who was on a tour of the northern states.

Work continued until the cold weather set in. "In the night heavy Snow with a Gale of NNE Wind came in and continued without intermission all day," Thompson wrote on November 2. "In the evening the Snow was about 6–8 Inches deep on the Ground   very uncomfortable in the Tents &c, &c." A day later, the commissioners declared the season finished and instructed the surveyors to prepare maps over the winter.

They had advanced only about thirty miles in 1817, but the work progressed much more quickly the next year. They reached the head of the St. Lawrence at the end of August 1818, charting some fifteen hundred islands in the process, and completed the north and south shores of Lake Ontario through the autumn. The surveying teams had become much more proficient and, once they reached the Great Lakes, were able to travel by steamboat, introduced after the war.

In the spring of 1819, the survey resumed at the mouth of the Niagara River. Things went so well that the two parties were approaching the west end of Lake Erie by late July. The commissioners, along with their secretaries and chief surveyors, met to plan their operations on the Detroit River and Lake St. Clair. A question arose about the vast marshes at the head of Lake Erie, where decaying plant and animal matter created a horrible stench during the heat of the summer. Thompson proposed that he and Capt. David Douglass, who had replaced David Adams as the American surveyor, conduct hasty surveys to determine the size of the marshes. Porter sprang to his feet and said: "The man that will dare to do it is dead. Dead."

Silence followed. Then Captain Douglass said, "It is in the cause of science. I will undertake to row round the marshes on the south side if you [Thompson] will do the same on the north side and each of us will give the best estimate he can of the extent of these marshes."

"Gentlemen," Porter replied. "You may do as you please, but I should not give a cent for your lives."

The two surveyors went ahead anyway. The heat and humidity were oppressive and the sultry winds provided no relief. Thompson and his crew slept on the beaches. They lived wholly on salted food and were unable to quench their thirst because the lake water was almost too warm too drink. Swamp fever, which they also called ague, but was likely malaria, appeared among them. The sick shook from the chills one moment, writhed from a burning heat the next and were often delirious.

One by one his men succumbed and the same happened among the Americans. Soon, Thompson was feeling the effects. They were then on Mid Sister Isle, an island of five to six acres located fifteen miles from the mouth of the Detroit River. "Found myself so ill that I twice fainted away in attempting to stand up," he noted on September 14. Two days later, the crew of an American steamboat rescued the Canadians, laid them on the deck of the vessel and took them to Amherstburg, where they were given rooms in a tavern.

Thompson spent ten days in bed before he was able to sit up or walk with the aid of a stick. Others were not so fortunate. "At abt 1/2 past 7 Am," he wrote on September 28, "the Servant of Commissioner Ogilvy came to me with the sad news that his Master had just expired." Two others, including Thompson's assistant, Baptise Belanger, died as well. Their deaths brought the season to an end. The American commissioner, General Porter, ordered everyone to pack up their equipment and supplies, and on October 1 they boarded an eastbound steamboat.

———————

Over the next two years, Thompson was away from home for all but a few days. He spent most of the winter of 1819–20 in Montreal working on maps. He was home for Christmas and New Year's, duly noting the latter in his journal: "May God Almighty in his mercy give us all to pass this year and every other in the practise of Obedience and give Gratitude to him." He returned to Montreal and then travelled to Cornwall on January 24 to be sworn in as a justice of the peace for the Eastern District of Upper Canada. He was home in March just long enough to hire a Robert Turnbull to run his farm that year for half the profit and was back again in early May to pick up his son Samuel, age sixteen, who was accompanying him on that summer's survey.

Significant changes in personnel occurred within the British party over the winter. Anthony Barclay, a twenty-seven-year-old lawyer and son of Col. Thomas Barclay, commissioner under Articles IV and V, was appointed to replace Ogilvy. In light of the calamity of the previous year, Barclay hired a physician, twenty-eight-year-old John Bigsby, as assistant secretary and medical officer to the commission.

The survey crews spent the early part of the season working their way up the Detroit River, around the shores of Lake St. Clair and up the St. Clair River. Both parties travelled in sailing vessels, the Canadians in a small Royal Navy ship, the *Confiance,* and the Americans in the schooner *Red Jacket,* and they agreed to leave the swamps and marshy stretches of shoreline for later when the weather was cooler and the threat of disease reduced. The Americans, meanwhile, broke to observe the fourth of July and celebrated aboard the steamboat *Walk-in-the-Water,* which left Detroit at 10 a.m. with about a hundred and fifty people aboard.

"Sit down to an excellent dinner at four o'clock," wrote Maj. Joseph Delafield, an assistant to General Porter. "The military band enables the party to join in the dance. Cotillions are danced with the same ease and grace as in our own part of the country and for politeness and good conduct in every particular, this party could not be surpassed in the most polished parts of the States. Salutes were fired from the boat, and the toasts reechoed from the mouth of the cannon. The day was passed in great mirth, and with entire satisfaction to every person."

Most of the season was spent farther north on Lake Huron, where Commissioner Barclay described the surrounding countryside as "very rough, and wild, still being in its pristine state: consequently it presents every obstacle which can be encountered, with little means of subduing any."

The obstacles included poor food, mosquitoes and illness as well as fog, and smoke from forest fires, all of which led to discouragement and resignations, according to Dr. Bigsby. "Several of the surveyors, although in high spirits at first with their good salaries and new mode of life, soon left us, subdued by toil and exposure," he wrote in his journal. "I have in my eye one gentleman of considerable energy, sitting by the half hour on a bare rock in the sun, wiping his perspiring face, and in angry contention with a cloud of mosquitoes. He soon went away. Another resigned because work was begun at four o'clock in the morning, or, as he called it, in the middle of the night."

Nevertheless, the surveyors reached the mouth of the St. Mary's River, the waterway between Lakes Huron and Superior. They had covered a thousand miles since 1817 and were nearing the completion of the work under Article VI when they retired for the winter. Thompson and his son Samuel stopped at Black Rock, New York, for several weeks, where he produced three sets of maps, one for Commissioner Barclay, one for the British Foreign Office and one for the Americans.

Father and son left by stagecoach on December 6 and travelled along the south side of Lake Ontario. At Ogdensburg, opposite Prescott, Thompson sent his boy home and continued to Albany, stopping for three days to confer with the American surveyors, then took a steamboat to New York City to purchase equipment. He returned to Montreal on December 26. Two days later, he departed for Quebec in an open carriole and arrived "far from well, having a violent cold threatening pleurisy," the result of exposure to the elements. In Quebec, he settled various accounts with John Hale, the agent to the British commission, then set out for home, arriving January 9, 1821.

Thompson spent nine days in Williamstown before receiving instructions to leave for Amherstburg, on the western frontier of the province, to survey the swamps and marshes passed over the previous summer. "I pray God Almighty," he wrote, "to take myself and Family into his good keeping and return me in health to my Home and my Family to be all well my   son Samuel with me."

The 1821 season proceeded without any notable setbacks, other than a few cases of swamp fever. This time around, however, all the sick men recovered. The two parties spent the spring and summer surveying sections of shoreline left uncharted the previous two years. By September, they were done and sailing back to Niagara.

Thompson and his American counterpart, David Douglass, spent the fall completing their maps so the commissioners could get on with the job of drawing the boundary from St. Regis to the mouth of the St. Mary's River. Barclay and Porter met in New York City in November 1821 and decided to apply four principles. The boundary would be on water, not land. This meant it would go around rather than across islands. Where there were two or more channels, the boundary would follow the one most suited to navigation. If there were more than one navigable channel, the line would be drawn through the largest. Finally, the line would go through the centre of a navigable channel to ensure that both sides had access to usable waterways.

By Christmas, the commissioners had drawn all but one section of the line. They made numerous trade-offs along the way. Barclay conceded the Long Sault islands near Cornwall, and the Americans compensated by giving up the strategically important Grand Isle, later named Wolfe Island, at the head of the St. Lawrence.

The loss of the Long Sault islands angered a group of businessmen from the eastern district of Upper Canada who published a letter criticizing Barclay and Thompson. The commissioner responded by noting that the islands in question were notorious as "the principal depots for smuggling along the whole Frontier." Grand Isle, he wrote, lay "in full view of the Dock Yard, and Fortifications and Town of Kingston . . . His Majesty's Dock Yard at Kingston is the most important establishment in those provinces, and I deemed it an object of primary consideration, to secure every thing that might preserve or contribute to, its advantages."

The two-member board became deadlocked over four seemingly insignificant islands in the Detroit River: Fox, Sugar, Stoney and Bois Blanc. These tiny land masses were of little or no economic value, but Barclay and Porter believed they would be valuable assets in the event of a future military conflict. The commissioners were unable to reach a compromise and turned the matter over to their superiors, Stratford Canning, the British minister in Washington, and John Quincy Adams, the secretary of state, who exchanged several proposals before agreeing that the U.S. would get Fox, Sugar and Stoney Islands while Bois Blanc would go to British America. This settlement brought to a conclusion the work under Article VI of the Treaty of Ghent.

Barclay and Porter met at Utica, New York, on June 18, 1822, to sign a paper formalizing the division of islands in the Detroit River as well as copies of a comprehensive joint report summarizing the agreements reached on the rest of the boundary line. By then the survey crews were preparing to start work under Article VII, though they travelled separately and would not meet all summer.

Thompson left Williamstown on May 24, accompanied by his son Samuel. He offered his customary prayer—"We pray God Almighty for a prosperous voyage and safe return to all my family"—and joined his men on the St. Lawrence at the mouth of the Raisin River. One month later, they reached Sault Ste. Marie, a meagre settlement of fifteen log houses and a substantial trading post built by the North West Co. but now the property of the Hudson's Bay Co., after the two companies' merger the year before. They spent three chilly days there before putting their canoe into Superior's waters. Thompson, who was fifty-two and for the first time feeling his age, complained at one point: "I have put on two vest and 2 pr of Stockings and yet shiver."

He and his men travelled west along the south shore, and Thompson had every reason to be confident the surveys would proceed to a satisfactory conclusion. A similar optimism prevailed among the Americans, though there had been changes in their camp. Captain Douglass had left and was replaced by James Ferguson, who was only twenty-four and had never travelled beyond Detroit. His assistant, George Whistler, was three years younger and an army engineer. People had continually come and gone on both sides, but five summers of field work and an equal number of winters spent planning, conferring and mapmaking had produced a reservoir of goodwill that should have seen the parties through the work ahead, but didn't.

Surveys that were expected to be finished by 1823 stretched into 1825. Harmony was soon replaced by discord, compromise by stalemate. The surveyors were working hundreds of miles beyond the limits of settlement in a place unknown to all the participants except Thompson. Dr. Bigsby, who was travelling with the Canadians, called the country around Superior "sterility itself, an assemblage of rocky mounds with small intervals of marsh." And General Porter, relying on second-hand accounts since he, like Barclay, was not in the field, informed Secretary of State Adams that the country was "totally wild and uninhabited" and the climate "so cold and inhospitable that a small portion of the year only can be employed in active duties."

The survey crews were guided by Article VII of the Treaty of Ghent, which stipulated that the border should run from Sault Ste. Marie "through Lake Superior Northward of Isles Royal & Phelipeaux to the Long Lake; Thence through the Middle of said Long Lake, and the Water Communication between it & the Lake of the Woods . . . Thence through the said Lake to the most North-westernmost Point thereof."

This article was lifted verbatim from the 1783 Treaty of Paris. The British and American diplomats who had convened in the French capital after the War of Independence had relied on a map of North America created in 1755 by the American cartographer John Mitchell. The Mitchell map, as it came to be known, contained a distorted image of Lake Superior and several large islands, most of which did not exist. It also showed a long, unnamed river flowing east uninterrupted from Lake of the Woods to Superior and which approximated the old voyageurs' road to the interior.

Thompson knew from his earlier travels and surveys that Mitchell's work was rife with inaccuracies and errors. He was aware that the continuous water link between Lake of the Woods and Superior was a fiction. This section of the voyageurs' road, sometimes called the Pigeon River–Grand Portage route, actually followed several rivers, some flowing east, some west, and crossed many lakes.

The American surveyors discovered the truth of this in the summer of 1822. Ferguson led his party over the taxing nine-mile Grand Portage and up the east-flowing Pigeon River. Some fifty miles inland from Superior, they reached the headwaters of the Pigeon and crossed the height of land. They put their canoes into waters that flowed west and entered a bewildering morass of lakes and rivers and swamps.

Ferguson relayed his findings to his immediate superior, Maj. Joseph Delafield, agent to the American commission, who was not perturbed at all that the words of the treaty did not accord with the geography of the country. He was certain that the framers of the treaty had had in mind the Pigeon River–Grand Portage route and he conveyed this to Adams, along with assurances that the survey would soon be complete.

"There is no longer any serious question open as to the general course that the Line is intended to run," he wrote in late September 1822, "and because it is now more certain, that upon the return of the surveyors, the next season, the Board will be possessed of the necessary information to determine the doubts under the seventh article of the Treaty, and designate the Line."

Thompson had an alternative interpretation of Article VII and what was meant by "the Long Lake," as well as "the Water Communication between it & the Lake of the Woods." His ideas would precipitate the conflict that led to stalemate once the commissioners sat down to draw the boundary. But first the surveyors would spend the 1823 season searching for the most northwestern point of Lake of the Woods.

The commissioners ordered their field parties to follow different routes to the Lake of the Woods and to conduct surveys along the way. The Americans were instructed to go out from Fort William and up the Kaministiquia River, which the North West Co. had opened in 1804 after moving its inland terminal north from Grand Portage. The British party took the Pigeon River–Grand Portage route, and it proved to be a lively expedition, according to Dr. Bigsby, who was seeing the country for the first time.

At the Lake of the Cross, which was thirty-four miles long and eighteen wide and dotted with some two hundred and sixty islands, wild rice grew so thick they could barely paddle their canoes. A little farther west, Dr. Bigsby wrote, they encountered a large band of Ojibway led by a chief named Two-hearts who was disturbed by the intrusion of strange white men who looked at the sky through shiny metal instruments.

"What is your purpose," he asked Thompson, "in rambling over our waters and putting them in your books?"

Dr. Bigsby was impressed with the astronomer's answer. "Mr. Thompson replied . . . that our purpose was to find out how far north the shadow of the United States extended and how far south the shadow of their great father, King George. He added that the Indians would not be disturbed in any way. Two-hearts expressed content."

The medical officer was also struck by Thompson's insistence on observing the Sabbath even in the wilderness. "Our astronomer, Mr. Thompson, was a firm churchman; while most of our men were Roman Catholics," Dr. Bigsby wrote. "Many a time have I seen these uneducated Canadians most attentively and thankfully listen, as they sat upon some bank of shingle, to Mr. Thompson, while he read to them in the most extraordinarily pronounced French, three chapters out of the Old Testament, and as many out of the New, adding such explanations as seemed to him suitable."

The British party spent nine days in late July conducting an astronomical survey of fixed points, rather than using the trigono-metric method, because of the size and complexity of Lake of the Woods, which was really three distinct but connected bodies of water, according to Dr. Bigsby. They followed the low, sandy shore of the southern body, the largest of the three, which the Ojibway aptly called the Lake of the Sand Hills. They found the northern division, named Lake of the Woods by the Ojibway, to be a maze of islands and deep, narrow bays with a highly irregular shoreline. The third body, known as Whitefish Lake, they bypassed because it lay to the east. Thompson concluded his survey at Rat Portage, where the three bodies of water that made up Lake of the Woods drained into the Winnipeg River, and it was here that Thompson placed the most northwestern point.

By early August, they were on their way back to Fort William, but nearly ran out of food and arrived famished and stressed after a three-week journey. "All our provisions were gone, except the men's soup, and of that there was little," the medical officer noted. "We were then glad to share a hawk (shot by Mr. Thompson, junior) between four. We had had nothing but salt meat, cocoa, and a very little biscuit dust for nearly three weeks."

They left for home on September 1 and after a journey of two and a half months reached the St. Lawrence, but one more surprise awaited them: an Upper Canada customs agent and his assistants met them in midstream near a place called the Cedars and ordered them ashore for a search, a startling dictate to men accustomed to the unlimited freedom of wilderness travel.

The result, according to a report Bigsby wrote to the commissioner, was a brawl. "The three canoes drifted down to the lower end of the village and near shore, when a combat, with paddles, poles, etc., commenced between our Bark Canoe and five customs house officers, which ended in both parties being considerably hurt and in the seizure of our property—even to the daily provisions of the men."

The American party, under the youthful Ferguson, had spent the season on Lake of the Woods and carried its surveys to Rat Portage as well. They returned home confident that the work was complete, but General Porter foresaw trouble and conveyed his concerns to Secretary of State Adams in a letter dated October 20, 1823. The root of the problem was Thompson's interpretation of Article VII.

"Mr. Thompson, the principal British Surveyor, who has long been well acquainted with the interior of North America, has heretofore entertained a belief that a boundary best according with the description of the Treaty, and the supposed view of the parties at the time of making it, could be traced through the bay at the South West extremity of Lake Superior, called *Fond du Lac,* and thence up the River St. Louis, in a direction toward Lake of the Woods; and I find that, on some of the printed maps, the boundary is laid along this route; while others represent it (no doubt

correctly) as passing along the chain of land and water communication, on what is called the *Grand Portage* route."

American traders were by this time established on the St.
Louis, but the Nor'Westers had been there first. Thompson, in fact,
had travelled down the river and surveyed it in the spring of 1797
after his visit to the Mandan villages on the Missouri. Its waters
entered Superior about a hundred and twenty miles southwest of
the Pigeon, and between the two rivers lay several hundred square
miles of territory.

Thompson made the case for the St. Louis in a report that
Barclay presented at a meeting of the joint commission at Albany
in February 1824. He maintained that it was the most substantial
waterway that entered the lake from the west. Furthermore, Fond
du Lac, which was fifteen to seventeen miles long and part of the
St. Louis watershed, was the biggest lake immediately west of Superior and was, therefore, the mysterious Long Lake of the treaty.

Thompson's argument created a rift, one soon widened by
other points of contention. Barclay, acting upon advice from his
agent, John Hale, insisted that as many as thirteen sizable streams
flowed into Superior from the west and warranted investigation.
The Americans responded by asserting that the boundary line
should follow the Fort William–Kaministiquia River route to Lake
of the Woods, a move that would have cost the Hudson's Bay Co.
the fur trade of the Rainy Lake district. These issues were enough
to keep the surveyors in the field for the summers of 1824 and 1825.

Another perplexing problem soon arose on Lake of the
Woods. Thompson and Ferguson, working independently, had put
the most northwestern point at Rat Portage, where the lake's three
big bodies of water discharged into the Winnipeg River—the high-
way to the interior and the emerging district of Red River. If the
surveyors were correct, the boundary would run from the mouth
of Rainy River at the south end of the lake, through the tip of a
west-pointing peninsula and north to the meeting of the waters.
Anyone travelling from the Canadas to Red River via the lake

would be required to pass through American waters, making them subject to U.S. law and their goods liable to U.S. duties.

The British government went to extraordinary lengths to preserve an unfettered channel of communication. A surveyor was sent out from England in the spring of 1825 to find a point farther north and farther west than those of Thompson and Ferguson. He was the German-born, university-educated scientist Johann Tiarks, former chief surveyor to the British commission under Articles IV and V of the treaty.

Dr. Tiarks reached New York on May 12 and, travelling with Barclay, who was making his first trip beyond Sault Ste. Marie, arrived at Lake of the Woods on July 24. The surveyor determined that the northwesternmost point could be found at the tip of a small inlet—"a fraction of a mile" west of where Thompson had placed it, according to Barclay, but enough to allow British citizens free passage across the lake.

By late August, Dr. Tiarks and Barclay set out for home with the rest of the British party and in early October reached New York. Dr. Tiarks returned to England while Barclay retreated to his lodgings to prepare for the negotiation over the placement of the boundary line.

The board of commissioners met briefly at Albany in November 1825. Neither side was prepared and the meeting was adjourned to May, and when May arrived it was put off till October. Thompson spent those twelve months in Williamstown. He arose at four each morning and retired at midnight. He supervised the work of his sons Samuel, twenty-two, and Henry, thirteen, and an assistant, who produced twenty-five maps of the country to be partitioned. And he re-established himself in Williamstown and the surrounding County of Glengarry.

He took up his duties as a justice of the peace and in late February joined a group of prominent citizens to entertain the lieutenant-governor, Peregrine Maitland, who had come out from York, the capital, on a tour of the eastern end of the province. The spring and summer he devoted to farming and maintenance of his property and on September 12 he left Williamstown for New York City, accompanied by Samuel, for a meeting of the board of commissioners.

The proceedings began October 4. Thompson had brought along eighteen maps, and four copies of each, and most days he attended the meetings to advise Barclay. He quickly sensed what was becoming clear to all the participants and made note of it on October 14: "The Commissioners could not agree on the route of the Boundary Line."

Discussions continued until November 10, when the board adjourned to March 1, 1827. Barclay and General Porter had reached agreement on two parts of the boundary: the section beginning at the head of the St. Mary's River and running north-west across Lake Superior to Isle Royale; and the segment that ran across Lake of the Woods from the mouth of Rainy River to the northwest corner as identified by Dr. Tiarks. Despite the four principles that had guided them successfully elsewhere, they failed to agree on a line through the several channels of the St. Mary's River or the route from Superior to Lake of the Woods.

Ministers of the two governments spent the next year searching for acceptable compromises, but all their efforts failed. After ten years' work and an expenditure of $178,102.50, shared jointly by the two nations, Britain and America had settled on the boundary from St. Regis to the mouth of St. Mary's River. The work under Article VII had been a costly failure, and the line to Lake of the Woods would remain a piece of unfinished business. The commissioners convened for a final meeting in October 1827. Thompson again attended these sessions, presented a few maps and on October 27 noted: "The board was finally closed and all Accounts settled."

———

Thompson was then fifty-seven, too old, he had decided, for the rigours of wilderness surveying. His eyes occasionally became sore and inflamed and he suffered from painful bouts of rheumatism. Otherwise, he was healthy and robust and could have enjoyed a comfortable old age farming the hundred acres around the family home and living on the substantial savings he had accumulated during his years in the fur trade and the boundary survey.

But he was as ambitious as ever. Ready for fresh challenges, he threw his still extraordinary energy into business and land development. He had money to invest, and Upper Canada was booming. Thousands of immigrants were arriving each summer. The government was building roads and bridges, digging canals and dredging harbours. Lumber merchants were shipping unprecedented volumes of timber and sawed lumber to England each year and farmers were exporting as much wheat and flour as they could spare.

Thompson employed sons Samuel and Joshua, as well as several hired hands, year round on the properties he had acquired over the previous decade in the townships of Glengarry County. He kept a crew busy clearing forested lands, extracting stumps with the help of explosives and preparing the soil for cultivation. He sent Joshua and a team to the hundred-and-eighty-acre island he owned in the St. Lawrence to begin stripping away the forest and to erect a house. Others worked lands that had already been cleared. Thompson filled his journals of 1828 and 1829 with entries pertaining to these activities and the business of farming: threshing and cleaning oats; scrubbing potatoes; harvesting wheat; husking corn; slaughtering pigs; salting beef; cutting firewood and cleaning stovepipes and chimneys.

Thompson also set up two potash operations, a common enterprise at the time. One was in Williamstown and the other was east of the village on a main north–south road and near the headwaters of the Beaudette River, the natural divide between Upper and Lower Canada. Potash was a chemical compound used to make dyes for textiles, and potash production was hot, dirty work that usually went on round the clock.

The manufacturer began by purchasing barrels of ash from settlers who had felled and burned the hardwoods on their land. The ash was mixed with water, which produced a highly caustic solution laden with dissolved chemicals. Workers ran the solution through sieves to remove undissolved particles before pouring it into kettles five feet high and three feet in diameter. Thompson's operations had more than twenty-four of these kettles, which were suspended over fires and heated until the liquid had evaporated, leaving behind potash, a dirty grey substance that had to be scraped out of the pots and pressed into cakes. Thompson sent his to a Montreal commodity trader, Horatio Gates, an original partner of the Bank of Montreal, who exported it to textile manufacturers in England.

Thompson's fortunes began to unravel in the summer of 1830. The previous October he had signed a contract to supply the British garrison at Montreal with fourteen hundred cords of firewood, which were to be cut over the winter and transported down the St. Lawrence on rafts in the spring. Thompson guaranteed delivery, although he subcontracted with another man to produce half the wood.

The deal made good sense from Thompson's perspective. He had a supply of wood on his island in the St. Lawrence and he intended to have the land cleared for livestock production. (In the days before barbed wire, islands were ideal places to raise cattle and hogs because the farmer was spared the trouble and expense of erecting fences of stone or wood.)

Thompson's men had cut two hundred and sixty cords by the second of February and he had five teams of horses and one of oxen available to move the wood. But his men were not producing as quickly as anticipated and a mild, wet winter made it difficult for the animals to haul their loads to the shoreline. By the first of March, Thompson began searching for a second source of wood and persuaded the Mohawks of St. Regis to allow him to harvest the forests along the Salmon River on the south side of the St. Lawrence.

His men moved the first raft in late May and it arrived safely. The trouble began after that. Thompson noted on July 21 that a raft had broken up and 163 cords were lost. The same day, Joshua and five men left with two loads, but they went missing until August 10, when Thompson learned that the rafts were at anchor near the village of Coteau Landing. A day later, someone informed him that Joshua was in Montreal, but when he went looking he found that his son had left for home.

Thompson spent all of September and October travelling up and down the river trying to fulfill the terms of the contract. He had to lease scows to move wood, hire men to ferry rafts downstream, pay to unload rafts that had run aground and search for others that went missing. "This is a sad business and I pray God in his mercy that no more may happen," he wrote in mid-September. And after one particularly bad day, he wrote: "Late went to a petty public house and passed a sad night in sad reflections."

He finally concluded the business on November 4. By then, he had had to purchase two hundred cords. He had sold six of twelve shares he held in the Bank of Montreal and paid off a one-hundred-pound note, leaving him with only two hundred on deposit at the bank.

While all this was going on, he was trying to stock and open a new general store. In early June, he had hired a contractor to dig a cellar measuring twenty-four by twenty-four by six feet deep. Throughout the summer he acquired inventory during his extended stays in Montreal.

The losses on the firewood contract were not, in themselves, fatal to his fortunes, but they left him financially weakened and unable to withstand the economic calamity that was about to befall the province.

One night at the end of January 1833, amid a winter of knee-deep snow and hard northwest winds, Thompson sat in his study brooding about

*Journal entries, February, 1817: "we got 2 Beds in a public
House in a miserable Room full of broken Glass
Windows stopped with Rags . . ."*

the future. There was a notebook on his desk: journal No. 70, which contained the fieldnotes from his survey of February and March 1817, when his old friend Colonel Ogilvy had sent him to St. Regis to locate the place where the forty-fifth parallel of latitude struck the St. Lawrence. That had been a happy time. This was not.

Thompson was consumed by doubts and anxiety. Business conditions were bad everywhere, in England and America, according to the newspapers, and in Upper Canada, which he knew first hand. Demand was down. Exports were in a slump. Prices were falling. Businessmen were going bankrupt. Farmers were abandoning their land and leaving debts unpaid. He wasn't able to collect money owed, and was having trouble making the payments on all the land he had acquired, most of which was worth less than he'd paid for it. Now, he wondered: Do my assets exceed my liabilities; am I solvent?

That night, on an empty page at the back of notebook No. 70, the reckoning began. He compiled a list of the people to whom he had loaned money: Arthur Burton of South March; Henry Burton of South March; Dr. Ambrose Blacklock of St. Andrews; Noel Bellefeul, who had walked away from his property and his obligations; Donald Bethune, who lived along the Raisin River; Antoine Belanger, who had flown; Richard McBean, who dwelled on the river; Alexander McBean, a merchant who had fled; John Cameron of Williamstown; John Cameron Jr. of the Second Concession, Charlottenburgh. Collectively, they owed him nearly a hundred pounds. On another page, he noted that there were, in the accounts of his various businesses, a hundred and forty-eight people to whom he had advanced goods on credit.

Thompson had made more than sixty other loans to settlers in the area who needed money to acquire land. They, in turn, had issued notes promising to repay the funds. He made a record of these that ran over fifteen pages in journal No. 70. Where appropriate, he commented on the status of the loan. "Absent Up Canada," he noted under the entry for Edward Dickson Weaver. Under the name Ronald McDonell, he wrote one word: "bad."

Journal entries, September, 1830: A sad business, he wrote of the firewood contract, and prayed that nothing else would go wrong.

Beneath the name Daniel Barton were the words "Run away." A mere five of the loans had been settled. A few of the debtors had promised payments by certain dates. The remainder were outstanding and there was some chance of collecting.

He believed on that cold, January night that he was still solvent, but knew he was sinking and worked tenaciously to save himself. Over the next few months, many journal entries pertained to finances: "Busy on Accounts all day . . . Set off to Nutfield arrived at 2 Pm and began to copy the Accounts . . . Henry going to Debtors . . . The people do not wish to pay their Debts . . . Attended Court all day and tried these two days in vain to get 10 pounds due to Joshua from Angus McDonald . . . received a letter from Mr. Davis said to contain 60$ but nothing in it."

He was bewildered that his neighbours would walk away from their homes and their debt. He hadn't thought such things possible in a Christian and civilized community. And how different this was from the frontier. There, beyond the reach of Christianity, of civilization, of the law, he had advanced the Indians goods on credit every fall and, almost without fail, they returned in the spring with furs to make good on their debts.

Thompson had debts of his own and creditors clamouring for payment and he was now having trouble meeting those obligations. But he would not walk away. Instead, he went back to work as a surveyor. On May 9, 1833, he received a commission from the governments of Upper and Lower Canada to survey Lake St. Francis, a widening of the St. Lawrence that begins just below St. Regis and stretches nearly to the confluence of the Ottawa and the St. Lawrence Rivers just above Montreal.

That job lasted a month. Afterward, he returned to Williamstown to work on the maps and to try to collect outstanding debts. Thompson spent many days that summer in a Cornwall courtroom seeking judgments against those who owed him money. He also developed a plan to go to England in the fall to find a publisher for his map and arranged a loan from Samuel Gerrard, a Montreal businessman long associated with the North West Co. and a founding partner of the Bank of Montreal.

In mid-September, as he was preparing to leave, Thompson was hired yet again by the governments of Upper and Lower Canada, this time to survey the boundary between the provinces from the St. Lawrence north to the Ottawa River. That job kept him busy through the fall, and he spent most of 1834 surveying the Eastern Townships of Lower Canada on behalf of the British-American Land Co., which had purchased more than thirteen hundred square miles of land that it intended to sell off to settlers.

But these endeavours only postponed the catastrophe that was slowly overtaking him. The economic conditions in the country continued to deteriorate. He could not earn enough as a surveyor to support his family, to keep his faltering businesses afloat and to meet the demands of his creditors. He could not recover the money he had loaned and he could not sell his land and property. These assets were now worth less than the loans outstanding against them, and he was unable to service or pay off those debts. By the end of 1835, Thompson was insolvent and in a matter of months had been pushed into bankruptcy.

In late May 1836, Sheriff D. McDonell of the Eastern District of Upper Canada published in the *Cornwall Observer* a notice of three lawsuits against Thompson. The courts moved quickly, rendering judgments in favour of the plaintiffs, Neil McIntosh, Robertson McIntosh and David Smart, and ordering the seizure of Thompson's land, his businesses and the family home. On July 16, James Court, the Montreal-based trustee in bankruptcy, issued a notice listing the assets to be sold at auction. It appeared weekly in the *Observer* until the sale was held September 29 at Williamstown.

By then, Thompson had left the province with Charlotte and seven of their ten children: Fanny, thirty-five; Henry, twenty-three; Elizabeth, nineteen; William, sixteen; and the three youngest, Thomas, Mary and Eliza. Their destination was Montreal and their future uncertain.

Journal entries, September, 1830: "Late went to a petty public house and spent a sad night in sad reflections."

Hard Times

(1837–1857)

THE THOMPSONS LIVED QUIETLY DURING THE WINTER OF 1836–37 though the community around them seethed with sectional strife and tension. Montreal, where they had settled, and the rest of Lower Canada were torn by divisions. French were pitted against English, merchants against farmers, and the elected assembly against the appointed legislative council. The French Canadians and their representatives in the assembly demanded responsible government, but were thwarted by a political system that placed power in the hands of the governor and his council. The English and the council wanted to raise taxes to build public works and strengthen the economy, but were blocked by the assembly, which refused to levy taxes that would be paid largely by French Canadians. The assembly chamber and meeting halls and the columns of French and English newspapers reverberated with acrimony and invective. To complicate matters, a few reform-minded English speakers had sided with the French majority and some business-minded French Canadians had allied themselves with the English minority, and a new British governor, Lord Gosford, had been dispatched to the troublesome colony to unravel the conflict and to halt the slide toward armed conflict.

Thompson had no time for any of this. He had been stung by events in Upper Canada and had his own pressing challenges: earning a living, paying the rent and keeping his family fed and clothed. Sometimes, in darker moments during that first winter in Montreal, he wondered how he could have been so foolish. How could he have trusted people he barely knew?

He could see their faces, hear their voices and remember the conversations. Some had taken place in his home, some at the general store, some at the potash works. They had always been referred by someone, usually a fellow settler from this concession or that sideroad, someone else who had come to him for a loan.

He realized in retrospect that he had probably acquired a reputation as the man to see if you needed money. There was no denying that the settlers of Glengarry County needed credit. The whole country did. It took time and money to turn a plot of forest into a productive farm, but there were no banks except in Montreal, Kingston and Toronto. He had become, for all intents and purposes, Glengarry's banker, never anticipating that business conditions could go from hot to cold so suddenly.

Thompson had saved a few pounds for himself, which kept his household afloat till he found work, and he thanked God for that. The surveyor-general of Upper Canada, John Macaulay, commissioned him to produce a series of maps of the St. Lawrence and the Great Lakes, based on his work with the international boundary commission. He and his son Henry, then twenty-three, spent the winter of 1836–37 at the drafting table, producing detailed and accurate renderings of the waterways between Upper Canada and the United States.

Money was never far from his mind. "Went to the bank but no word of my draft from Toronto," he noted on November 9. "Paid the baker," he observed on the sixteenth, his funds having arrived a day earlier. In early December he wrote, "Borrowed 5$ of Mary the Maid and went to the Market   bought beef, pork, butter."

The new year brought more of the same. On February 9, he was obtaining a loan of ten dollars from a D. W. Ross. On March 28, he was at the bank presenting a letter from Macaulay in order to secure a loan of twenty-five pounds and later that day he paid the rent. In mid-April, he noted: "Thank God received my money at the Montreal Bank and paid several debts."

That spring, Thompson learned from Macaulay that the government of Upper Canada was planning a survey of the Muskoka District, which stretched from Georgian Bay to the Ottawa River, to determine whether it would be feasible to link these waters by a canal. Thompson resolved to apply in person. He took the stagecoach to Prescott and a steamboat to Toronto and arrived May 20. "Waited on the Governor at Noon," he noted on May 24. "He told me he had appointed commissioners tho not yet made Public and that my name with other applicants will be laid before them."

The governor, Sir Francis Bond Head, would do him no favours, but Macaulay was willing to assist. The surveyor-general shared the names of the commissioners, a Captain Baddeley of the Royal Engineers and John Cartwright, both of Kingston. Macaulay wrote a letter on Thompson's behalf and told him to present it personally as soon as possible. Thompson left immediately for Kingston and met Cartwright at 8 p.m. on June 1. "I saw him for a few minutes," he noted later that evening. "He kindly said there was no difficulty in my appointment and to wait upon him at 9 Am the Morrow."

By June 8, Thompson and his son Henry had left Kingston for Toronto aboard a steamboat laden with cargo and Irish immigrants. From the capital, where they stopped to hire a crew, they went north to Lake Simcoe and west to Penetanguishene and began looking for the mouth of the Muskoka River, where the survey was to begin.

The work commenced on August 7, in a country Thompson described as "very rude and without Soil," and lasted till mid-December. The Muskoka tumbled out of a rocky highland.

Thompson and his men travelled upriver and portaged forty-two times in the space of a hundred and fifty-three miles, but there were unexpected pleasures, like the body of water the Indians called Hun ge lowe nee goo mooks Lak a ha gan, or Lake of the Many Fingers because its shoreline was all bays, points and inlets. "The fineness of the country induced me to explore all the Coasts of this Lake," Thompson wrote.

At the end of the survey, he and his men went to Bytown—later renamed Ottawa—and spent nearly two weeks settling their accounts. They learned that armed rebellions had occurred in both Lower and Upper Canada that fall, and Thompson saw startling evidence of the battles on the journey back to Montreal. "Came to the Grand Brulé and stopped to feed the horse," he noted on December 30. "Here is a sad view of the effects of ancestral Rebellion. The Church and many Houses Burnt." Later that day, he passed through St. Eustache, northwest of Montreal, and thought: "Here is a sadder spectacle. The Church and 40 or more Houses burnt."

Thompson was bedridden much of the winter and housebound until late April with a stiff, swollen and painful left leg. Nevertheless, he drew maps of the Muskoka District and wrote a report on the country. The work alleviated his concerns over money, and on April 7 he noted: "My daughters had their shoes today."

He had regained full use of the leg by mid-May and at the end of the month travelled to the village of Chambly, on the Richelieu River, fifteen miles southeast of Montreal, to settle by survey a property dispute between two neighbours, a Mr. Slate and a William Wilson. Neither was pleased with the results. "Mr. Slate loses the east part of his House," Thompson wrote, "and B. Wm. Wilson almost all his garden and passage to it and his Stables."

That summer and for the next four, Thompson received substantial commissions from the provincial governments. He spent two seasons on Lake St. Peter, a widening of the St. Lawrence below

Montreal; surveyed Lake of the Two Mountains and Lac St-Louis, two bodies of water formed by the confluence of the Ottawa River and the St. Lawrence west of the island of Montreal; and surveyed a portion of the Ottawa.

The work ran out in the fall of 1842, and Thompson's troubles began in earnest. "We are without wood," he wrote on January 28, 1843, a clear, cold day. Two days later, he managed to buy a quarter of a cord, but concluded that day's journal entry with three words: "sad hard times."

There followed, over the next several months, a series of cheerless journal entries.

March 1: "Rheumatism in my Leg."

April 3: "My left Leg very painful   did very little   at a loss what to do."

April 21: "Drew up a rough Letter to Mr. Gerrard for a loan of 25 pounds."

April 24: "Waited on Mr. Gerrard for Loan of 25 pounds but refused. I am destitute. I do not know what to do."

April 27: "My Son Henry Thompson was married . . . to Barbara McDonald. . . . May the blessings of the Almighty be on them and their children. Received a Letter from the Board of Works   contained a Check of 25 pounds. Thank God."

April 29: "All day myself with Fanny and Nancy"—their name for Eliza—"walked about to find a house to rent in which we failed. I am the morrow 73 years old but so destitute that I have not where with to buy a Loaf of Bread. May the Pity of the Almighty be on us."

May 1: "Doing little else than getting ready to pack up to remove; my fine girls walking about to look for a house fit for us, without success."

May 2: "At length obliged to take Mr. Grey's house from Desautel, Packing etc."

May 4: "Got most of our things in the House but everything so very dirty and offensive we could not sleep; and the kitchen intolerable."

May 5: "Disgusted with the filthy House we are in   Thomas told us of a range of new rooms over a shop close to Mr. Black's church to be rented   went to Lionais and settled with him for 50 pounds per year."

The rooms were cramped, the walls smelled of fresh plaster, and they could not move Thompson's desk up the narrow staircase. These were minor problems. He was unable to find anything but small jobs surveying the lots of property owners in Montreal or farmlands outside the town. In mid-July, he sent Thomas, then twenty-one, to New York City aboard a steamboat to seek employment with Anthony Barclay, the former boundary commissioner who had been appointed British consul in that city. Still, his financial problems continued, and so did the grim journal entries.

July 10: "Called on Mr. Benny and showed him my situation   he kindly agreed to let me have bread a little longer   God only knows my distress and friendless situation."

August 11: "Busy going abt for a loan of 15 pounds."

August 18: "Went about for the Loan of Money to pay my Rent but nothing."

August 19: "From Mr. Eadie, Savings Bank, got the Loan of 12 pounds 10 pence and my Chronometer for security."

All the while that he was pleading for money and credit, Thompson was also meeting with and writing to people in high places, including Sir Robert Peel, the prime minister of England, and Lord Aberdeen, his foreign secretary. He wanted them to know about his maps of the Columbia River. These, he believed, would be of great value to the British government when it began negotiations with the United States to partition lands west of the Rockies, which included the Oregon Territory that he had explored and opened for the North West Co.

Thompson had good reason to think that the Oregon Territory— those lands drained by the Columbia—would soon command the

A page from Thompson's manuscript: Old and impoverished, angered by the British surrender of Oregon, he set out to tell the story of his remarkable travels.

attention of the political leaders of Britain and America. In 1842, they had signed a treaty that had settled all the outstanding boundary issues from the Bay of Fundy to the foot of the Rocky Mountains. The negotiations had been handled by Alexander Baring, who held the title Lord Ashburton, and Daniel Webster, the American secretary of state.

Ashburton, then sixty-seven, was the son of Francis Baring, founder of the British banking firm Baring Bros. In the early years of the century, he had represented the family firm in the United States and had worked on behalf of the American government during the Louisiana Purchase of 1803. Ashburton arrived in Washington on April 4, 1842, and the banker turned diplomat had a broad mandate.

Britain and America were at odds over sections of the eastern boundary, which stretched from Passamaquoddy Bay, at the head of the Bay of Fundy, to St. Regis on the St. Lawrence. It was the most pressing issue because armed conflicts had erupted in the late 1830s between settlers in contested areas of Maine and New Brunswick. The boundary up the St. Mary's River between Lakes Huron and Superior remained in dispute, and the two nations had not decided on the placement of the line from the west end of Superior to Lake of the Woods. From there to the Rockies, harmony prevailed. The Rush-Gallatin Convention of 1818, negotiated by American diplomat Richard Rush and his British counterpart Albert Gallatin, stipulated that the forty-ninth parallel would serve as the divide.

Beyond the Rockies, an unusual arrangement prevailed. The Rush-Gallatin Convention left those lands open to citizens of either country for ten years. In 1827, Britain and America tried to partition the territory and extend the boundary to the Pacific. The Americans argued for the forty-ninth parallel while the British held that the Columbia should form the border. The negotiations failed, and they settled on shared use for an indefinite period.

In 1842, the British foreign secretary, Lord Aberdeen, sent

Ashburton to Washington with instructions that the Peel government would accept one of two alternatives in Oregon. The boundary could follow the continental divide south from the forty-ninth to the Snake River and go down the Snake to the lower Columbia, and from there to the Pacific. This would align the border with the route Lewis and Clark had taken from the mountains to the sea. Or it could cross the Rockies to McGillivray's River, follow that river to its confluence with the Columbia and then proceed down the latter to the sea. The border, in this case, would reflect Thompson's path to the Pacific. Either way, almost all of Oregon would become British.

The negotiations between Ashburton and Webster had proceeded quickly, and by August 9 they were able to put their names to a treaty. They had resolved the thorny eastern boundary, though both were harshly criticized in their own countries for the concessions they made. They had settled on a line through the St. Mary's River and they chose the Pigeon River–Grand Portage route from Lake Superior to Lake of the Woods. And there they stopped.

Ashburton and Webster set aside the Oregon question because they feared that failure on that issue would undo the agreements achieved elsewhere. But the political leadership of both countries knew that the boundary from the Rockies to the Pacific would have to be settled. For thirty years, the territory had been the preserve of fur traders, first with the North West Co. and then with the Hudson's Bay Co. Those days were ending. American settlers were beginning to move in. Some form of government would soon be necessary, and that meant that either Britain or America would have to take control.

Oregon was coveted territory. It was a huge country and a fine one. The climate, inland and at the coast, was moderate, the forests enormous, and the land would support cattle or grain.

The American claim would rest, in part, on the travels of

Lewis and Clark and the ventures of John Jacob Astor's American Fur Co. Thompson, however, was convinced that his endeavours surpassed theirs and produced a stronger case. Lewis and Clark had explored the final three-hundred-mile stretch known as the lower Columbia, whereas he had travelled from the source of the river to its mouth, a full twelve hundred miles. Lewis and Clark had conducted cursory explorations of the tributaries in the middle section of the river. He had explored much more thoroughly several major tributaries of the upper Columbia and built four trading posts on those rivers. His posts had established a lasting British presence through the North West Co. and then the Hudson's Bay Co., which in the early 1840s remained the dominant commercial enterprise operating in the Oregon Territory. By comparison, the American Fur Co.'s Fort Astoria had survived a mere two years. Finally, he had surveyed the entire Columbia, and the proof of that could be found on his "Map of the North-West Territory of the Province of Canada," on which he had depicted the river from the headwaters to the Pacific, with its major tributaries.

He had done much of the exploration and all of the surveying on his own initiative. At the time, he had sought neither reward nor recognition. Now, in the spring of 1843, he believed that his work could be of use to the government, and his need was great. He began knocking on doors and writing letters, hoping to sell his maps to the British government and to obtain compensation for his long and loyal service to the Crown.

He started with the governor of the Hudson's Bay Co. in North America, the wealthy and forceful Sir George Simpson, who was based in Montreal and owned a luxurious home in Lachine, about ten miles west of the town. "Waited on Sir George Simpson who spoke to me on the maps of the Oregon Territory which I am to show him as soon as he has time," Thompson wrote on April 25, 1843, concluding his entry with the words: "No money."

Sir George invited him to dinner on the evening of the thirtieth, and Thompson eagerly made his way clutching a roll of maps.

The meal was splendid and he ate heartily in the governor's opu-
lent dining room, but left in low spirits. "I took the Maps of the
Boundary Line with me," he noted, "he did not wish to give any
thing for them   returned in a dark, rainy bad night."

Thompson hoped for more favourable treatment from the
government. He began drafting maps, including detailed depic-
tions of the Oregon Territory, and writing to officials in London as
well as Kingston, capital of the newly united Province of Canada
East and Canada West. The first letter, dated June 20, 1843, was to
Sir Charles Metcalfe, the governor, who deemed it worthy of being
forwarded to the Foreign Office. It drew his attention to a recent
statement to Congress by President John Tyler. "I strongly recommend . . . ," Tyler had told the senators and representatives assembled before him, "the establishment of a chain of military Posts
from Council Bluff [on the Missouri] to some point on the Pacific
Ocean within our limits."

The republic was on the move. It was looking to expand its
borders, as it had done so many times since Thompson was
young and new to the continent. The Americans wanted Oregon
this time, and he provided Metcalfe with a clear picture of what
Britain stood to lose: two hundred and ten miles of coastline if
the forty-ninth parallel were extended from the Rockies to the
Pacific and, by his estimate, 316,804 square miles of territory
drained by the Columbia. And not just any territory, but a place
both rich and resplendent.

"In the summer season the Columbia River, and it's branches,
are visited by myriads of fine Salmon, which are of five species,
weighing from five, to fifty five pounds, the Sturgeon are excellent,
weighing from three to five hundred and fifty pounds," he told Metcalfe. "Vegetation is on the same scale. I have measured Pines . . . of
42 and 48 feet girth, and 200 feet in height without a branch;
immense groves of finest Cedar of 18 to 36 feet girth; the Oak 18 feet
girth; even the Raspberry measured 18 to 21 feet in height. Whoever
settles in this fine country and climate has no wish to leave it."

Thompson completed his maps, slipped them into a round tin case and forwarded them on July 25 to J. M. Higginson, Metcalfe's private secretary, along with a second lengthy and detailed report on the Oregon Territory. One month later, he wrote a letter to the Crown seeking compensation for all his services. It was addressed to The Right Honourable, the Earl of Aberdeen, Her Majesty's Secretary of State for Foreign Affairs. "Your Memorialist, who is now in the seventy fourth year of his age," Thompson wrote, "most respectfully requests a pension of Two Hundred and Fifty Pounds sterling Pr Ann. May be granted to him, for the few years, if any, of his natural life; and after his decease, a pension of one hundred pounds sterling to my aged widow for her natural life."

This request was in addition to an earlier one for two hundred pounds for the maps themselves. The response to these overtures was disappointing. Metcalfe sent the report on Oregon to London, but held back the maps until he was sure the Foreign Office was interested. As it turned out, officials there were indifferent. "Received a letter from the Chief Secretary informing me that my Maps were not wanted by the Foreign Office," he noted on October 10. "The Labours of 4 months this Season are lost."

At that point, Thompson decided to circumvent the colonial government. He wrote to his friend Anthony Barclay, explaining what had occurred. Barclay recommended he send the maps but leave the issue of compensation to the discretion of the foreign secretary. Thompson concurred and, on December 9, 1843, forwarded to the New York consul a copy of the general map of the northwest, stretching from Superior to the Pacific, which Barclay promptly sent on to the Foreign Office.

In September 1843, Thompson had begun selling his possessions to keep his family afloat. Some of his maps went first. His surveying tools and instruments were next. The sale of his surveyor's chains and a compass fetched a little over twenty-six pounds, a great

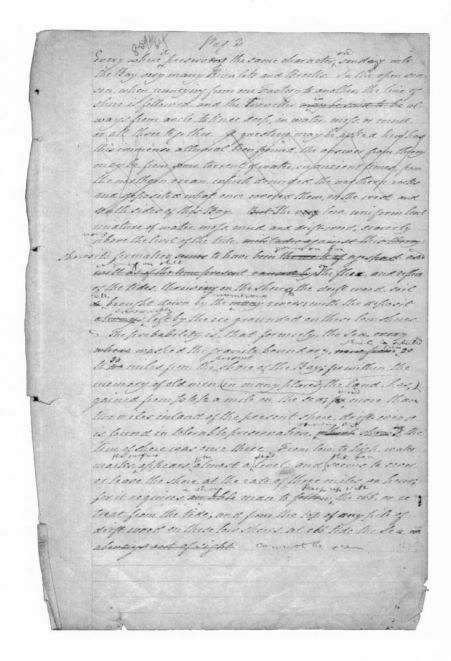

Thompson's manuscript: He worked in cold rooms, by the light of the sun and despite his mounting infirmities.

relief, Thompson noted in his journal. He pawned his theodolite twice for short-term loans, recovered it on both occasions and finally sold it privately in late November. "A hard bargain," he called it, "but necessity compels me to do it."

Misfortune followed him into the new year. "Cannot bear the cold," he wrote on January 9. "Too weak to do anything," he observed the next day. "I do not know what to do," he noted on February 2. "Times are dreadful." He visited a pawn shop again and parted with his only decent coat for a loan of five pounds, ten pence. Later in the winter, he sent a bed to an auction company and pawned the leggings of an Indian dress.

Next, he had to find families willing to take in two of his daughters, who were to perform domestic duties in return. Sixteen-year-old Mary left first. "My poor daughter Mary had to leave us to go to reside at Cornwall with Mr. Rolland McDonald," he wrote on February 6. "Mary went off at 4 p.m." In mid-March, he and Charlotte said goodbye to Eliza, who was then just fifteen.

Almost daily that winter, health and weather permitting, Thompson walked around Montreal looking for work. He found nothing and, as the weeks passed, his troubles mounted. On March 4, a letter arrived from a Mr. Moreau, the lawyer for his landlord Lionais, who demanded just over twenty-eight pounds in rent unpaid to February 1. He had no means of complying, and the lawyer promptly obtained a court order allowing him to seize all Thompson's furniture if he remained in arrears. A few days later, a bailiff delivered the notice and announced that he was taking possession of the furniture, though he gave Thompson time to settle with Moreau.

Thompson spent the next two months fighting to keep his household effects. He found a lawyer named Driscoll who was willing to represent him. The objective, he disclosed in his journal, was to delay the proceedings. In the meantime, he and his family vacated Lionais' apartment for what he called "our small low house." He was still waiting to hear, through Barclay, whether the Foreign Office would compensate him for his maps.

The dispute with Lionais was finally resolved on May 21, twenty minutes before the bailiff was due to confiscate his possessions. Thompson was saved by the generosity of two Montreal businessmen, including George Moffat, owner of an import-export company and president of the Board of Trade, who loaned him enough money to settle with the landlord.

Thompson was able to repay his benefactors. On June 26, he received a letter from Barclay informing him that the Foreign Office would be forwarding a hundred and fifty pounds for his maps—funds that would cover some but not all of his debts.

Whatever relief he gained from this news was immediately snatched from him by Henry, who had long caused him grief. His third son, now approaching his thirty-first birthday, was a talented mapmaker, but could not hold a job. Thompson had sent him to New York the previous autumn hoping he could find steady work with the help of Barclay and his brother Thomas, but he returned in late March. Henry had a drinking problem, and the news that his wife, Barbara, was pregnant with their first child sent him on a spree.

Thompson and his daughter, Eliza, who had returned from Cornwall, went looking for him. They were joined by William Scott, who was married to Elizabeth Thompson and was an engineer with the Montreal Board of Works. The search lasted four days and took them as far as Lachine. "At length," Thompson wrote on June 30, "in the afternoon Mr. Wm Scott met Henry and brought him here in a sad state."

Over the next fifteen months, Thompson made what amounted to a prolonged and desperate attempt to solve his financial problems. Everything he tried ended in failure. He appealed to the governor, Sir Charles Metcalfe, for a position as supervisor of a canal and then as a collector of customs duties on the east side of Lake Huron. He drafted a proposal for a government-sponsored survey of the roads from St. Regis to Stanstead in the Eastern Townships and tried to enlist the support of the Cornwall business community.

In the spring of 1845, he provided a memoir, along with samples of his maps and sketches of the Rocky Mountains, to Sir James Alexander, a British military officer stationed in Montreal and a member of the Royal Geographic Society. Alexander forwarded the material to London with a recommendation that the society consider publishing it.

In the meantime, he did something that must have troubled his conscience, given his dedication to British interests in North America. He offered his maps of the Oregon Territory to James Buchanan, the American secretary of state, who was preparing for negotiations with the British envoy Richard Pakenham.

Thompson wrote Sir Charles in early August 1845 requesting a small loan so he could travel to New York City to show his maps and sketches to publishers there. The governor advanced him ten pounds, and on September 15 Thompson set off. His son Thomas, who was still working in New York, arranged a meeting with a bookseller named Coleman, who was also a publisher.

"He showed me what he had to sell but paid no attention to what I had," Thompson wrote afterward. "He seemed to think there was too much in the market already but promised to direct me to where I can get my maps printed."

Thompson tried again that fall to have the maps published, this time in London. He could not afford to send them, but his friend George Moffat graciously shipped a roll of maps to the London publishers and booksellers Wiley and Putnam.

As he awaited a response from London, Thompson assessed his circumstances. He had no reason to think that Wiley and Putnam would publish his work. Nobody else had been interested in the maps. Nor had he been able to find a position with the provincial government. He had no choice but to try something else.

For several years, he had thought about publishing an account of his journeys in the northwest. Books of travels and adventure were popular. New works were frequently advertised in the newspapers. More than an eighth of the two thousand titles in the catalogue of the Montreal Library were classed as "Voyages and Travel." Thompson had read some of these works. His experiences compared with the best of them. He was confident of his ability with a story. And so his mind was made up.

The old man began writing in late October 1845. He wrote as legibly as possible given his advanced age and often unsteady hand. He used black ink and bluish grey foolscap and filled each line with tightly compressed script and every page with as many words as possible. He started with a description of Hudson Bay and life along its shores, and the first words he wrote were these: "Hudson's Bay extends from Latitude 52 degrees to 60 degrees north. It is in the shape of a horseshoe and covers an area of 192,777 square miles. On its west shore it receives Seal River, Churchill River (The Missinippe) Nelson's (The Saskatchewan), Hayes, Severn, Albany and Moose Rivers, besides many lakes and streams."

He produced rough and fair copies of most all he wrote, the rough ones being first drafts with words, lines and paragraphs crossed out. He wrote notes in the margins. He circled phrases and drew arrows across the page or to a line below to indicate where they belonged. He revised passages and pasted new versions on top of old ones.

The work went slowly that winter. His rooms were usually cold. On many dull, cloudy days he could not see well enough to produce anything. He did nothing at all after sunset because he could not afford to keep a lamp lit. He became ill with dysentery in early December. He devoted several days to producing maps for a Montreal printer named Stewart Derbyshire who was going to make prints of them. But this venture ended badly.

"At 8 Am by his appointment waited on Mr. Derbyshire who gave me much abuse and denied the accuracy of my Maps,"

Thompson wrote on March 25, 1846; "at length 10$ was got from him and I left him, an ignorant man and full of self-sufficiency."

He had produced twelve polished pages of his travels before another personal crisis interrupted his work. What happened is not entirely clear because there is a gap of a year in his daily journal. By August 1846, however, he and Charlotte were living in the home of William Scott and their daughter Elizabeth.

Thompson had resumed writing. Money remained a pressing concern, but he had a second motive. Britain had surrendered almost the entire Oregon Territory to the United States. On June 15, 1846, in a ceremony that took place in Washington, Pakenham and Buchanan signed a treaty that extended the border from the Rockies to the Pacific along the forty-ninth parallel. The country Thompson had explored, surveyed and opened was now lost, and he was determined to inform the public of Britain and the Canadas what a rich and bounteous land their government had ceded to America.

The old man worked at a fervid pace. In the space of a year, between mid-1846 and August 5, 1847, he produced a 272-page rough copy of his travels. He also prepared an index, and the entries provided a tidy summary of the diverse subject matter he had covered.

In one section of three pages, he had written about red deer, wolves, antelopes, hawks, foxes, badgers, squirrels and mice. The entries for page 228 contained a tidy summary of a journey and an encounter with the Piegan:

—228c Lake Winnipeg and Saskatchewan

—228d to the Rainy Lake, woman prophetess

—228e Goods for 4 Canoes, return, my men stopped

—228f Piegans pursue us

—228g Find my Men, send for Horses

—228h Commence the Journey for the Athabasca River.

While he wrote, Thompson wrestled with two questions. Who would publish his work? There were no book publishers in Montreal or elsewhere in the province of Canada at the time. And

Index to my travels: In the space of a few pages, Thomspon wrote of hunting seals, Esquimeaux snow houses and his journey to York Factory.

how could he realize a return on the work before it appeared as a book? His solution to the latter was to prepare a prospectus that would attract supporters. It appeared for the first time in the *Montreal Gazette* of October 16, 1846.

"To be Published," the prospectus began, "the Travels of David Thompson, being of twenty-eight consecutive years in the northern part of the continent of which twenty-two were employed on the discovery of countries not known or examination of countries known to the fur traders."

Much was promised: descriptions of mountains, rivers and lakes and of the forests, beasts, birds, fishes and insects of various regions; accounts of the native peoples, their languages, religious beliefs, manners, modes of life, their territories and their wars. "This will not be a dry detail, many curious facts will be for the first time given . . . which will interest the reader."

With assistance from the public, the author would publish the first of three volumes in January 1847, the price not to exceed five shillings. "The proposition now is that in order to enable him to devote his whole time to the publication of his travels, a few gentlemen should form a company to allow him one dollar per day for the maintenance of himself and his family, say 30 dollars per month. That this company shall be entitled to and in recompense for the support afforded to him shall have half the net profits of the publication of his travels and himself the other half out of which shall first be paid the money advanced to him."

The proposition was generous, but by late March 1847 no gentlemen had come forward and he pulled the prospectus. Still, he continued to write. He was completely reliant on the generosity of his daughter and her husband, a situation he found intolerable, and this led to one last appeal for support.

"I have no other claim on you, than common humanity," the old man wrote on a day—August 17, 1847—when his hand was free of tremors and his script clear and strong. He was sitting at his table in the rooms he and Charlotte now occupied and writing a good copy of a letter to Sir George Simpson of the Hudson's Bay Co. "For the last three years I have been endeavouring by every means in my power to obtain something like a livelihood, and a chance survey gave me, now and then, a few dollars: but for the last year there is no employment . . . I am for this year past, and am now, living on the charity of Mr. Wm. Scott in whose house I lodge, and board, but this can last no longer, and hunger is before me. Some compassion, perhaps, may be shown to the oldest servant alive who has been in the service of the Hudson's Bay Co."

He had for Sir George two proposals. The first pertained to the book he was writing. "My hope, and request is that you will be so good as to patronise the work, of which I shall make honourable mention and that by your influence a small subscription may be made for me Pr month, till I have got it corrected for the press, which may take me near three months, but not more . . . And permit me to add, that in case this may not be agreeable to you, to be so good as allow me some place of retreat, I do not care where it is, even to the coast of Labrador; but could wish it to be in some other place where I can be useful under the orders of the Person in charge: I am a good fisherman, a maker of nets and canoes, and therefore at a fishing Post, can be useful, especially in the curing and smoking of salmon. Be so good as to take my sad case into your consideration, and afford me some relief."

These appeals, like all the others of recent years, came to nothing. Nevertheless, he continued to write. Almost every day that fall, and into the winter of 1847–48, he worked on the fair copy of the manuscript. He also produced a hundred and two pages of new work, which included an account of his journeys on the Columbia in 1811 and 1812 and a fresh twelve-page version of life along the shores of Hudson Bay. He did all this even though it was often a struggle to take up the pen. "2 pages only," he noted one day, "my wretched poverty and desponding mind prevented more."

On January 1, 1848, his first New Year's entry in nearly a decade contained a hint of hope and optimism. "I pray the Almighty to be kind to us, and that so far as Life is granted to us it may be prosperous and happy and that we may all live in pious gratitude and obedience to the Supreme and great Redeemer."

But life proved to be just as hard in January as it had been in December. "Too cold to write," he noted on the ninth, and on the eleventh he observed: "Live in dark and cold rooms." The arrival of Fanny on January 26 and Eliza ten days later cheered him up temporarily. But after they departed, his miserable circumstances again weighed upon him. "No fire," he observed on February 10. "Could do nothing." The next day, he noted: "Very cold day   could not write."

And then on February 14, something truly frightening occurred: he lost his sight. "This morning," he wrote several months after the fact, "I arose blind in the left eye, the only eye with which I saw. The right has been blind now 50 years with a cataract. The left eye is now afflicted with a cataract."

Fortunately, his son-in-law William Scott was willing to pay for treatment. Two Montreal physicians examined Thompson and concluded that nothing could be done. A third, a noted eye doctor named Dr. Henry Howard, thought otherwise. He treated Thompson over a three-month period and wrote an account of it in a book of his case histories.

"David Thompson of Montreal, aged 78, was led by his daughter to my surgery on the 24th of February 1848," Dr. Howard noted. "He stated that he had been blind in his right eye since February 1789 and did not expect I could do anything for it, but that the sight in his left eye had always been good up to the past three months when it became a little cloudy, which cloudiness gradually increased up to ten days previous to his coming to me on which morning he awoke so perfectly blind as to not know it was daylight."

The doctor determined that cataracts had caused the problem. Thompson visited him almost daily for three weeks and was soon able to make his way to the physician's office without assistance.

"The treatment in this case was exactly alike for both eyes," Dr. Howard wrote. "Everyday that he came his eyes were fumigated with hydrocyanic acid and his eye brows lids and temples brushed with a solution of veratria; sparks of electricity were drawn from round the orbit about three times a week and occasionally I dropped on the conjectura the two grain solution of atropins. For the first two weeks every morning, he took a wine glass full of the infusion of gentiam, containing a small quantity of the sulphate of magnesia and sulfuric acid."

This unusual mix of treatments worked. "After attending me for three months he was able to read and write at all hours during day light. I prohibited him from reading or writing by artificial light; some time past he told me that on the previous evening he had seen a particular star with his right eye for the first time since he was 19. I then examined his eyes and found scarcely a vestige of cataract remaining in the left eye and the right cornea so clear that the whole of the iris and pupil were visible."

On May 4, 1848, the old man was back at his desk with pen in hand and paper before him. That his sight had been restored seemed miraculous and he would take full advantage of it. He worked almost daily, reviewing the manuscript of his travels, now nearly four hundred pages long. He found many parts to be unsatisfactory, especially those he had written while his vision was failing. He would not send such work to a publisher. Instead, he set it aside and started over.

He was blessed that spring by good health and, for the first time in a decade, something like peace of mind. His debts had been repaid or forgiven. He and Charlotte enjoyed satisfactory accommodations thanks to the Scotts and no longer had to worry about paying the rent or where their next meal was coming from.

Thompson was free to concentrate on his work, and the result was extraordinary. He wrote letters to his children and to public officials, turned out six articles for the *Montreal Gazette,* mostly having to do with his adventures in the northwest, and he produced a fresh draft of 344 pages, which included 278 pages of new material.

He accomplished all this in the space of twelve months. Then, in the spring of 1849, uncertainty re-entered his life. He and Charlotte had to leave the Scotts' (Thompson did not disclose the reasons) and move in with Joshua and his wife.

The disruption precluded work. Thompson felt uncomfortable, less than completely welcome at Joshua's, and did not unpack his journals or papers. A cool, wet spring added to his unsettled frame of mind, though he soon discerned what had made this normally pleasant season so unpleasant.

"By the Papers of Yesterday," he noted on June 10, "the Island of Newfoundland for a short time and at present is surrounded by Ice to the depth of 50 miles and the inhabitants requesting to be taken from it, if this is the case it accounts for our dark hazy weather."

Summer was, as usual in Montreal, hot, humid and oppressive, ideal for the spread of disease, and by late June, the *Gazette* was carrying a daily advertisement on its front page for DWIGHT'S CHOLERA MIXTURE. "The formula for this preparation," the ad read, "was communicated to the American public, in anticipation of the Asiatic Cholera by the Rev. Dr. DWIGHT, American Missionary at Constantinople, where it was found extremely useful.... The same remedy has recently been used with success in New Orleans. No family should be without the remedy during the summer months as it is equally efficacious in the treatment of Diarrhea and Dysentery."

By mid-July, cholera had, in fact, appeared in Montreal. "Much sickness," Thompson noted on the eleventh. There was another entry four days later: "At 4 Am I was attacked by the cholera, which did not leave me until 5 1/2 PM and then very weak. Dr. McCulloch attended me. Once there was very little between me and death, but, Thank God, I live."

A page from the index: Thompson drafted a prospectus to find patrons for his book and published it in the Montreal Gazette, *but there were no takers.*

That day, the outbreak was reported for the first time in the *Gazette*, which informed its readers: "There have been a few cases since Saturday but we are unable to give a correct report of them as the Local Board of Health has not made its return." On July 19, the newspapers began publishing a daily report on the number of deaths from cholera and other maladies, and distinguishing between Catholic and Protestant victims of disease. By July 31, fully 754 people had died, including 398 of cholera.

Thompson made a full recovery. The remainder of the summer was uneventful and the fall as well, until October 24, when he noted: "My fate not yet settled nor where I am to go." The next day, he wrote: "Joshua packing up but I can do nothing." His son was leaving for Toronto, and by the end of the month, he and Charlotte were back at the Scotts'.

For the next two weeks the siblings sent letters back and forth attempting to reach a consensus on what was to be done. William and Elizabeth Scott wanted to send the elderly couple to Gray's Creek, a small settlement on the St. Lawrence near Williamstown where Fanny lived with Charlotte's widowed sister, Nancy. Thompson had no desire to go and was relieved when Elizabeth and her husband decided on November 12 that he and Charlotte would stay with them at least until May.

Spring arrived and there were more changes in their lives. William Scott had taken a position as a station manager with the partly completed St. Lawrence and Atlantic Railroad, which was conceived to provide Montreal, Sherbrooke and other Quebec towns with year-round access to an ocean port, in this case Portland, Maine. Construction started in 1846 at Longueuil, on the south shore opposite Montreal, because there were no bridges across the St. Lawrence at the time. The railroad ran east to the Richelieu River, south to Sherbrooke and east again to connect with a line being built west from Portland.

Scott was posted to a station forty-six miles east of Longueuil and moved to the south shore village to be closer to his work. He and his wife agreed to take her elderly parents with them, and on April 27, 1850, David and Charlotte Thompson, along with their daughter Eliza, left Montreal. They hired a cab, which crossed the river by steamer and deposited them at their new home.

Three days later, Thompson turned eighty. "Thank God," he wrote, "through my Redeemer for his goodness to me hitherto and pray the few days I have to live may be spent in piety and gratitude to him."

He was soon arranging his papers and intended to resume work on his travels. He had hardly touched the manuscript in a year. The writing was complete, but the pages had to be corrected. He worked occasionally, editing a few pages here and there, but a sustained effort was no longer possible. His eyesight was poor, his energy failing, and his hand shaky.

As the months passed, he turned to the work less and less. He no longer made any effort to have his travels published. In late November, he sorted some of his papers, bundled them up and put them away. One day early in December, he noted that he was reading the manuscript. He made his last reference to the work on January 15, 1851: "Looking over the Pages of my Travels."

He continued his habit of keeping a daily journal after the move to Longueuil, but the entries were brief and revealed a preoccupation with his children and grandchildren. "I thought I saw my two absent sons William and Thomas," he wrote on June 24. "They both appeared in good health and were well dressed."

On July 31, he received a letter from George Shaw, a banker who had married his daughter Mary amid the cholera epidemic of 1849. They were living in Cobourg, Canada West, and she had given birth, three weeks earlier, to a baby boy. He noted the birthday of a grandson on August 29: "Little William Scott seven years of age. The blessing of the Almighty be on him."

In late September, he recorded the departure of Eliza, who was off to live with her sister Mary, and in early October he observed the birthday of his son-in-law William Scott, who was now thirty-two. Henry's wife, Barbara, and her father, William, a former British military officer, visited on January 21, 1851, and informed Thompson that Mary's infant son had died. Three days later, he received a letter from Joshua. It contained two dollars.

There was nothing in these entries about Samuel, the eldest of his five sons. The two had become estranged, likely over quarrels and disputes that took place while the family lived at Williamstown. Samuel had last visited in 1838, shortly after the move to Montreal. For the next twelve years, no correspondence flowed between father and son, nor was there any contact.

By the winter of 1850–51, the old man's once prodigious energy was nearly spent. That was evident from the journal he was keeping. "A mild overcast day but too dark to read old writing," he noted in early February, and he continued in this vein. "Could barely see to read. . . . Can do nothing. . . . Tried but could do nothing, too dark. . . . Ill all night with a cough and this Morn less severe." He made a short entry in a shaky hand on February 28— "steady Snow with ENE wind and drift   bad weather"—set down his pen, closed his journal and did not return to it.

David Thompson left no record of his last years. William Scott later recalled that his hair had turned white and he let his beard grow. He talked little, read the newspapers and his Bible, and received few visitors other than the pastor of his church. Charlotte was his steady companion, and the two would often stay out most of the night observing the stars.

William David Scott, named for his father and grandfather, once described his grandmother Charlotte Thompson as slightly built, active and wiry, with coppery complexion. She dressed plainly but neatly, loved her home and was an excellent housekeeper. In her ways and manners, she was extremely reserved except when among family. As for his grandfather, the younger Scott said: "He cared nothing for society and showed a preference for the companionship of his wife rather than anybody else."

The Thompsons lived with the Scotts until William accepted a position as an engineer on a canal project in Elkhart, Indiana, and the young couple left for America. David and Charlotte remained in Longueuil with their daughter Eliza, who had married Dalhousie Landel, the cargomaster of the Grand Trunk Railway, which in 1853 had acquired the St. Lawrence and Atlantic.

David Thompson died on February 10, 1857. His estate consisted of a few personal possessions, more than eighty journals, a few unpublished maps and a handwritten manuscript of some seven hundred pages. Outside of family and friends, his death was unlamented and scarcely noticed. Montreal's English-language newspapers published a brief obituary, but nothing else: "Longueuil—10 inst., at the residence of Mr. D. Landel, (his son-in-law), David Thompson, Esq., Surveyor and Astronomer, and for many years a partner in the North West Co., aged 87 years. The remains will be moved this day, Sat., the 14th inst, at ten AM, to Mount Royal Cemetery."

Charlotte Thompson outlived her husband by three months. She died at age seventy-one on May 4, 1857, and was buried next to him in the Landel family plot.

The Return of David Thompson

OTTAWA, LATE MAY 1883. A WESTBOUND TRAIN PULLS OUT OF THE capital of the Dominion, the whistle blowing and clouds of dark, heavy smoke spewing overhead. It speeds across eastern Ontario toward Toronto and then turns north to begin the long, slow climb toward the Canadian Shield and the upper Great Lakes. Passengers embark and depart at the numerous stops, but not the men from the Geological Survey of Canada: the distinguished scientist Dr. George Mercer Dawson and his promising clerk, Joseph Burr Tyrrell, who is twenty-five and spending his first summer in the field. These two ride as far west as the rails will carry them—to the newborn settlement of Maple Creek, two hundred miles beyond Regina, in the Assiniboia District of the Northwest Territory of Canada.

There, they encounter a hurled-together community of wooden buildings and canvas tents housing an army of labourers nearly a thousand strong employed by the Canadian Pacific Railway to raise a roadbed, lay wooden ties and hammer iron spikes into the ribbons of steel, all at a pace that will push the transcontinental through Calgary to the foot of the Rockies by season's end.

Mercer and Tyrrell stay long enough to hire horses, wagons and men, then set out for Fort Macleod, a foothills cattle town eighty miles south of Calgary. Over the next five months, they explore the Crows Nest, Kicking Horse, Athabasca and Yellowhead passes. Mercer and the hired hands ride, but Tyrrell walks. He conducts pace surveys, counting each step, stopping at regular intervals to take his bearings with a compass, studying rock formations and collecting specimens of flora and fauna.

Tyrrell returns to the West in 1884 and each summer until 1891 on assignments with the Geological Survey. He travels thousands of miles by canoe, on horseback and on foot. In the Red Deer River valley, he finds coal deposits that will lead to the establishment of the town of Drumheller. He uncovers a bed of dinosaur bones that will eventually prove to be a bonanza to the emerging science of paleontology.

At each stop, Tyrrell determines his position in degrees of latitude and longitude. During the winter months in Ottawa he weaves the data into maps, which he submits to his superiors. In his free time, he compares his work with the government's existing map of the Northwest Territory. He is surprised by its accuracy, so much so that he begins to wonder who conducted the surveys. Who created the map of a country so vast and untamed, and so recently the domain of the Indian?

His superiors can tell him little except that both surveys and map appear to be the work of one man, a fur trader named David Thompson who has been dead now thirty years and about whom almost nothing is known. But someone remembers that the trader's journals are in the possession of the Ontario Department of Crown Lands, and Tyrrell resolves to examine them.

Toronto, December 1887. Tyrrell spends Christmas with his parents at their home in the nearby community of Weston. Over the holiday, he meets with Andrew Russell, Ontario's assistant commissioner of Crown lands, who informs him that the Province of Canada acquired the journals in 1859 from one of its employees, Thompson's son Joshua, for six hundred pounds. Joshua Thompson also had in his possession a manuscript of his father's travels though the government declined an offer to purchase it. Tyrrell is intrigued, but Russell has no idea what happened to the manuscript.

Over the next two months, Tyrrell studies the journals. He writes a twenty-five-page paper, "A Brief Narrative of the Journeyings of David Thompson," which he reads to the Canadian Institute on March 3, 1888, and which the city's leading newspaper, the *Daily Mail*, describes as "very interesting and valuable."

Meanwhile, Tyrrell's father tells an acquaintance and fellow Weston resident, Charles Lindsey, of his son's interest in David Thompson. Lindsey, editor of the *Toronto Leader* and son-in-law of William Lyon Mackenzie, is eager to meet the younger Tyrrell. He has something in his possession that will interest him greatly: the manuscript of David Thompson's "Travels."

Lindsey acquired the 670-page handwritten work from Joshua Thompson in 1868. He recognized that it contained a remarkable story and should be published, but found Thompson's writing to be "neither good nor clear," as he put it in an 1888 letter. Lindsey had rewritten parts of the manuscript and paraphrased others, producing a handwritten work that ran to 760 pages.

Tyrrell leaves Lindsey a copy of his Canadian Institute paper and suggests it would be a useful conclusion to the "Travels." In November 1888, the newspaperman sends Tyrrell a chunk of his manuscript and suggests they collaborate, that the geologist should rewrite it yet again, employing his first-hand knowledge of the country and that they should split the profits.

Tyrrell turns down the offer and returns Lindsey's work in June 1891. Soon after, Lindsey abandons the project and tries to sell Thompson's manuscript. He places it with Albert Britnell, a Toronto bookseller, in June 1894 and asks £1,700, but Britnell is unable to sell it. The following March, he turns the material over to C. F. Libbie and Co., a Boston auctioneer. Again, it does not sell. Two months later, Lindsey finds a buyer—Joseph Burr Tyrrell— who agrees to pay four hundred dollars.

The geologist is eager to publish. He has, in fact, approached several American firms even before acquiring the manuscript. Macmillan Publishers of New York expressed interest, and Tyrrell sends them the work once it is in his possession. By mid-June, George Platt Brett, a partner, writes back suggesting changes.

"There is altogether too much matter," Brett writes, "the style in a number of instances requires correction and altogether the book should be thoroughly worked over before being submitted to a publisher."

Toronto, January 1909. Tyrrell has done nothing with David Thompson's manuscript for almost fourteen years. From 1895 to 1899, he was immersed in northern and Arctic exploration on behalf of the Geological Survey. Afterward, he resigned and went to the Klondike to look for gold. Now financially comfortable, and working as an advisor to mining companies, he again turns his attention to Thompson's work.

Tyrrell sends a letter of inquiry to Macmillan on January 30, 1909, and receives a prompt response. The New York publisher asks for a copy of the manuscript. But Tyrrell does not submit it. He is busy editing a similar work, Samuel Hearne's *Journey from Prince of Wales's Fort in Hudson's Bay to the Northern Ocean*. It will be issued by the Champlain Society, which was founded in 1905 to publish first-hand accounts of Canadian history.

In April 1910, Tyrrell again approaches Macmillan about publishing Thompson's "Travels" and sends a draft of his introduction. The publisher requests the manuscript and this time Tyrrell complies. After reading the whole package, an editor suggests cuts, mainly to Tyrrell's introduction and other supporting material, and in late July 1810 the publisher forwards a contract for "The Autobiography of David Thompson." Tyrrell signs and sends it back, but rejects the proposed changes.

Macmillan withdraws its offer, and the manuscript sits another eighteen months, until March 1911, when Sir Edmund Walker, president of both the Canadian Bank of Commerce and the Champlain Society, expresses interest. By June, the two men have agreed to the terms and Tyrrell turns over the heavily revised version of Thompson's work that he had prepared for Macmillan.

Sir Edmund doesn't like it and asks William Stewart Wallace for help. A historian by training, the twenty-eight-year-old Wallace is working at the University of Toronto library. He begins editing the work in the summer of 1912, restores Thompson's spelling, grammar and punctuation and produces a manuscript that is much closer to the original. Sir Edmund gives his blessing and the work is sent to a publisher in Edinburgh to be typeset. By November 7, page proofs have been printed and later that month the Champlain Society announces in *Saturday Night* magazine the imminent publication of *David Thompson's Journal*.

Toronto, early 1916. After another three-year delay, caused by disagreements between Tyrrell and Wallace, and Tyrrell's prolonged absences due to business, the Champlain Society publishes *David Thompson's Narrative of his Exploration in Western America*.

It is a hefty volume. Thompson's story runs to 502 pages. There is a substantial introduction by Tyrrell, a year-by-year summary of the explorer's travel to guide the reader, and an index.

The publication of *David Thompson's Narrative* hardly registers with the public. The print run is small—only 520 copies—and the work is distributed privately to members of the Champlain Society. It seems most Canadians are preoccupied with the present rather than the past. Their new and youthful nation is engaged in a global conflict and suffering enormous casualties on the battlefields of Europe. Nevertheless, Tyrrell and all those who contributed to the publication of the *Narrative* have done their country a service by rescuing David Thompson from obscurity.

In his introduction, Tyrrell rendered two judgments, one personal, the other professional. Of Thompson's character, he declared: "There were few white men in the West in those early days who bore so consistently as he did the white flower of a blameless life." The surveys and maps made Thompson "the greatest land geographer the world has produced."

In the decade that followed, journalists and popular historians brought the story to a wider audience, and Tyrrell's pronouncements shaped their portrayals. Professional historians also examined Thompson's life. They began by questioning Tyrrell and concluded by knocking Thompson off his pedestal.

The leading voices in the anti-Thompson camp were Arthur Silver Morton and Richard Glover. Morton argued that in 1810–11 Astor's men beat Thompson to the mouth of the Columbia and that shortcomings in Thompson's character determined the outcome. "No Alexander Mackenzie or Simon Fraser this, but a scholarly surveyor; not without an element of timidity in him," Morton wrote.

Glover, a federal government historian, edited a second edition of the *Narrative* in the early 1960s on behalf of the Champlain Society. He set out, as he put it in his introduction, "to recognize facts that are damaging to the hagiographical myth that has long hidden the real man." He portrayed Thompson as cantankerous and obstinate, dishonest in his portrayal of others and, in all likelihood, sliding into senility when he wrote his manuscript.

It was left to Peter C. Newman to complete the demolition, which he did in the short profile of Thompson included in his 1987 book *Caesars of the Wilderness*.

Such a prolonged and damaging attack is a curious thing. A reading of his journals in the 1840s reveals a man in clear control of his faculties and one of enormous strength and courage. He had no way out, yet fought like a bear and emerged from the ordeal with his character enhanced rather than diminished.

Thompson's failings were, by any measure, ordinary for the time. He had a temper and could be rough with those who crossed him. It is said that once he nearly broke his hand beating a recalcitrant Kootenay. As a young man he succumbed to the same temptations as many of his peers in the fur trade. There is evidence, albeit slim, that before he met Charlotte Small, Thompson fathered a child, but abandoned the infant and his native mother. He was generous to a fault, which cost him most of his substantial savings after he had settled in Williamstown. He may well have been cantankerous and obstinate—he did, after all, refuse to transport liquor across the mountains for the trade with the Indians—yet a loyal and respectful following of English-speaking clerks and French-speaking voyageurs stuck with him through many years and thousands of miles.

There is much to admire about the man and much in his story that remains relevant.

He took a country wife of aboriginal descent, a common practice among fur traders, but defied convention and settled with her and their children in a pioneer society where bigotry and prejudice were prevalent.

He was an enormously resourceful individual who could build a house, make a canoe of birch or cedar and repair a gun, yet mastered the complex science and sophisticated technology required to gaze at the heavens and determine from the motion of the stars co-ordinates of latitude and longitude.

He spent decades observing celestial bodies through the eyepiece of a sextant, always using the left eye because a cataract had made the right useless.

He became fluent in French, Cree and likely Blackfoot and acquired a working knowledge of several other native languages.

He led many wilderness voyages yet never lost a man.

As for accomplishments, David Thompson enjoyed many and should be remembered for them.

Like Mackenzie and Fraser before him, he explored a long, mighty river. Along with them, he extended the reach of the North West Co. to the Pacific and made the fur barons of Montreal masters of North America's first transcontinental enterprise.

The object of the merchants was profit. Thompson had another purpose: to extend British influence and territorial claims in the northwest. This placed him in opposition to American expansionism—one of the most powerful political impulses of his era. Twice, he tried to resist the growth of the United States. Had his positions prevailed, the Canada–U.S. boundary between Lake Superior and Lake of the Woods would be farther south and the Oregon Territory would have been British and later Canadian.

His "Map of the North-West Territory of the Province of Canada" surpassed in detail, scope and accuracy the best that London's top mapmakers could produce. But it was more than mere representation. There was an idea embedded in the map, an idea found in the title: the North-West Territory of the Province of Canada.

Thompson created his map between 1812 and 1814. At the time, the Province of Canada extended as far as Lake Superior and included the rivers draining into it. In reality, the province was sparsely populated and settlement had hardly advanced beyond the shores of Lakes Ontario and Erie. There was no north-west territory. The lands that stretched from Superior to Hudson Bay and west to the Pacific were subject to a patchwork of claims: those of the aboriginal inhabitants, the Hudson's Bay Co., the North West Co., America and Russia. Nobody, save for David Thompson, saw them as part of the Province of Canada.

Thompson's vision of a Canada stretching from the mouth of the St. Lawrence to the shores of the Pacific was half a century ahead of its time. It had no appeal to his colonial contemporaries, but a similar dream resided at the heart of Confederation.

The motto of the new Dominion—*A Mari usque ad Mare*, from sea unto sea—was a broader version of the idea expressed in Thompson's map.

The first major project of Confederation, begun in the summer of 1867 and completed in late 1869, was the acquisition of the northwest from the Hudson's Bay Co. Canada had taken control of an empire, a near empty one that none of its leading politicians had visited. Fortunately for them, they had the map, and it proved immensely useful in the endeavours that followed: planning the transcontinental railway, suppressing the Metis uprising of 1885 and opening the West to homesteaders. The map not only served the interests of Canada's leaders, it spoke to their ambitions. More importantly, it was the first movement in a symphonic series of events that culminated in Canadian control of the west and the extension of the Dominion from Atlantic to Pacific.

A list of the major figures of nineteenth-century Canada would include many names: Sir John A. Macdonald and Sir George Étienne Cartier, the brokers of Confederation; their predecessors Robert Baldwin and Louis-Hippolyte LaFontaine; the rebels William Lyon Mackenzie and Louis-Joseph Papineau and Louis Riel; the general Isaac Brock and the railway builder Cornelius Van Horne.

To these, we should add David Thompson. He was a foundational figure in the creation of the country, and his map was one of the great individual achievements of the nineteenth century.

BIBLIOGRAPHY

DAVID THOMPSON MANUSCRIPTS

Journals. Toronto, Archives of Ontario, F443.
Letters, 1839–43. Ottawa, National Archives of Canada, Mg 19 A8.
Letters, 1843–45. London, Public Record Office, 5/415, 5/418, 5/441.

MANUSCRIPT SOURCES

Hudson's Bay Company Archives, Ottawa, National Archives of Canada.

OTHER SOURCES: PUBLISHED

Atherton, William Henry. *Montreal: 1535–1914*. Montreal: The S. J. Clarke
      Publishing Company, 1914.
Belyea, Barbara. "The 'Columbia Enterprise' and A. S. Morton: A Historical
      Exemplum." *BC Studies* 86 (1990): 3–27.
———, ed. *Columbia Journals: David Thompson*. Montreal and Kingston:
      McGill-Queen's University Press, 1994.
Bigsby, John J. *The Shoe and Canoe: Pictures of Travel in the Canadas*. Lon-
      don: Chapman and Hall, 1850.

Bond, Rowland. *The Original Northwester: David Thompson and the Native Tribes of North America*. Nine Mile Falls, WA: Spokane House Enterprises, 1970.

Carroll, Francis M. *A Good and Wise Measure: The Search for the Canadian-American Boundary, 1783–1842*. Toronto: University of Toronto Press, 2001.

Clark, Robert. *River of the West: Stories from the Columbia*. New York: HarperCollins West, 1995.

Classen, George H. *Thrust and Counterthrust: The Genesis of the Canada–United States Boundary*. Toronto: Longmans Canada, 1965.

Cochrane, Charles Norris. *David Thompson the Explorer*. Toronto: The Macmillan Company of Canada, 1924.

Coues, Elliott, ed. *New Light on the Early History of the Greater Northwest: The Manuscript Journals of Alexander Henry and David Thompson*. Minneapolis: Ross & Haines, 1965.

Cox, Ross. *The Columbia River: Or scenes and adventures during a residence of six years on the western side of the Rocky Mountains*. Norman, OK: University of Oklahoma Press, 1957.

Delafield, Joseph. *The Unfortified Boundary: A Diary of the first survey of the Canadian Boundary Line from St. Regis to the Lake of the Woods*. New York: 1943.

Franchère, Gabriel. *A Voyage to the Northwest Coast of America*. New York: The Citadel Press, 1968.

Glover, Richard. "The Witness of David Thompson." *Canadian Historical Review* 31 (1950): 1–25.

————, ed. *David Thompson's Narrative*. Toronto: Champlain Society, 1962.

Harmon, Daniel. *Sixteen Years in the Indian Country: The Journal of Daniel Williams Harmon 1800–1816*. Toronto: The Macmillan Company of Canada, 1957.

Hayes, Derek. *First Crossing: Alexander Mackenzie, His Expedition Across North America and the Opening of the Continent*. Vancouver: Douglas & McIntyre, 2001.

Hearne, Samuel. *A Journey From Prince of Wales's Fort in Hudson's Bay to the Northern Ocean*. Edmonton: Hurtig, 1971.

Hopwood, Victor G. *David Thompson: Travels in Western North America, 1784–1812*. Toronto: Macmillan of Canada, 1971.

Innis, H. A. *The Fur Trade in Canada: An Introduction to Canadian Economic History*. Toronto: University of Toronto Press, 1999.

————. *Peter Pond: Fur Trader and Adventurer*. Toronto: Irwin & Gordon, 1930.

Irving, Washington. *Astoria: Adventures in the Pacific Northwest*. London: KPI, 1987.

Jones, Landon Y., ed. *The Essential Lewis and Clark*. New York: The Ecco Press, 2000.

Lamb, W. Kaye, ed. *The Letters and Journals of Simon Fraser: 1806–1808*. Toronto: The Macmillan Company of Canada, 1960.

Laut, Agnes. *The "Adventurers of England" on Hudson Bay: A Chronicle of the Fur Trade in the North*. Toronto: Glasgow, Brook & Co., 1914.

Lavender, David. *Land of the Giants: The Drive to the Pacific Northwest: 1750–1950*. Garden City, NY: Doubleday & Company, 1956.

MacGillivray, Royce, and Ewan Ross. *A History of Glengarry*. Belleville, Ont.: Mika Publishing, 1979.

MacGregor, J. G. *Peter Fidler: Canada's Forgotten Surveyor, 1769–1822*. Toronto: McClelland and Stewart, 1966.

Masson, L. R. *Les Bourgeois de la Compagnie du Nord-Ouest*. New York: Antiquarian Press, 1960.

McCart, Joyce and Peter. *On the Road with David Thompson*. Calgary: Fifth House Press, 2000.

Moreau, William E. "To be fit for publication": The Editorial History of David Thompson's Travels, 1840–1916. Toronto: *Papers of the Bibliographical Society of Canada*. 39/2: pp. 15–44.

Morse, Eric W. *Fur Trade Canoe Routes of Canada/Then and Now*. Toronto: University of Toronto Press, 1979.

Morton, A. S. *A History of the Canadian West to 1870–71*. Toronto: University of Toronto Press, 1973.

———. "The North West Company's Columbia Enterprise and David Thompson." *Canadian Historical Review* 17 (1936): 266–88.

Newman, Peter C. *Caesars of the Wilderness*. Toronto: Penguin Books, 1987.

———. *Company of Adventurers*. Toronto: Penguin Books, 1985.

Nisbet, Jack. *Sources of the River: Tracking David Thompson Across Western North America*. Seattle, WA: Sasquatch Books, 1994.

Ross, Alexander. *Adventures of the First Settlers on the Columbia River*. Ann Arbor, MI: University Microfilms, 1966.

Ruggles, Richard I. *A Country So Interesting: The Hudson's Bay Company and Two Centuries of Mapping: 1670–1870*. Montreal and Kingston: McGill-Queen's University Press, 1991.

Smith, James K. *David Thompson: Fur Trader, Explorer, Geographer*. Toronto: Oxford University Press, 1971.

Snyder, Gerald B. *In the Footsteps of Lewis and Clark*. Washington, DC: National Geographic Society, 1970.

Thomas, Don W. *Men and Meridians: The History of Surveying and Mapping in Canada*. Ottawa: Queen's Printer, 1966.

Tyrrell, J. B., ed. *David Thompson: Narrative of His Explorations in Western North America: 1784–1812*. Toronto: The Champlain Society, 1916.

———. *Journals of Samuel Hearne and Philip Turnor*. Toronto: The Champlain Society, 1934.

Umfreville, Edward. *The present State of Hudson's Bay Containing a Full Description of That Settlement, and the Adjacent Country*. Toronto: The Ryerson Press, 1954.

Van Kirk, Sylvia. *Many Tender Ties: Women in Fur-Trade Society in Western Canada, 1670–1870*. Winnipeg: Watson & Dwyer Publishing, 1980.

Wallace, W. Stewart. *Documents Relating to the North West Company*. Toronto: The Champlain Society, 1967.

White, Catherine M., ed. *David Thompson's Journals Relating to Montana and Adjacent Regions, 1808–1812*. Missoula, MI: Montana State University Press, 1950.

PICTURE CREDITS

227: *Historical Atlas of Stormont, Dundas and Glengarry County.* Toronto, 1879. Reprinted Owen Sound, 1972.

229: Archives of Ontario

251: Archives of Ontario

254: Archives of Ontario

261: Thomas Fisher Rare Book Library, University of Toronto

267: Thomas Fisher Rare Book Library, University of Toronto

273: Thomas FisherRare Book Library, University of Toronto

279: Thomas Fisher Rare Book Library, University of Toronto

INDEX